TASK EXPERIENCE AS

A SOURCE OF ATTITUDES

THE DORSEY SERIES IN ANTHROPOLOGY AND SOCIOLOGY

EDITOR

ROBIN M. WILLIAMS, JR.
Cornell University

TASK EXPERIENCE
as a Source of Attitudes

PAUL E. BREER

and

EDWIN A. LOCKE

Both of Cornell University

1965

THE DORSEY PRESS
HOMEWOOD, ILLINOIS

First Printing, January, 1965

Library of Congress Catalog Card No. 65–12422

PRINTED IN THE UNITED STATES OF AMERICA

TO OUR PARENTS

Acknowledgments

MOST OF the research reported in this book was conducted at the School of Industrial and Labor Relations, Cornell University. In providing fully equipped laboratory facilities, a full-time Research Associate, money for recruiting subjects, unlimited computer time, a half-time secretary, and a teaching schedule which left much time for writing, the School did everything it possibly could have done to make this study possible. For all of this we are deeply grateful. Additional financial support was made available at different points along the way by the Cornell Faculty Research Grants Committee, the Social Science Research Center at Cornell, and the Foundation for Research on Human Behavior.

Robert Blain, the senior author's research assistant at the University of Wisconsin in the Spring of 1961 contributed to the initial formulation of the theory and helped to design, execute, and analyze the data from the first study reported in this book. Charles Curtis, a graduate student at Wisconsin, played an important role in the administration of that same project.

For help in carrying out the six experiments conducted at Cornell, we are indebted to Nancy Olsen (who spent a whole year analyzing data), David Sutherland (who analyzed data and played the role of accomplice in one of our experiments), Robert Gordon, Edward Tronick, and Paul Goodman (all of whom took turns filling in as experimenter), Morris Schriftman and Peter Hoffman (at least one of whom could always be depended on to round up a few subjects at the last minute), and the students in ILR 420 (who worked hard to make our first laboratory experiment a success).

The manuscript was read in its entirety by Lorne Kendall, William F. Whyte, and Robin Williams, Jr. We are grateful to each for the many comments and suggestions made. Neil Cheek, William Friedland, George Homans, and William Rothstein each read parts of the manuscript and contributed a number of useful ideas.

On more than one occasion we sought and received statistical advice from our two wise and generous colleagues, Philip McCarthy and Isadore Blumen, both of the School of Industrial and Labor Relations at Cornell.

The card punching was performed by Edith Pyle while Patricia Primer handled most of the computer operations. Each could be counted on to do her job with accuracy and dispatch.

For dependable and cooperative secretarial assistance we were fortunate enough to be able to rely on both Katherine Anderson and Evelyn Maybee. The many questionnaires used in our experiments were ably mimeographed by Russell Hovencamp.

Our greatest debt we reserve until last. Throughout the entire study, in matters of both money and motivation, we were helped and encouraged by William F. Whyte of the School of Industrial and Labor Relations. His faith in what we were doing made our task significantly easier.

PAUL E. BREER
EDWIN A. LOCKE

ITHACA, NEW YORK
May, 1964

Table of Contents

Introduction

FEW SOCIOLOGISTS would dispute the importance of studying differences in what men believe to be true, good, and desirable in the world around them. There are admittedly some who would restrict sociological inquiry to the analysis of more tangible things (e.g., the division of labor), leaving beliefs, values, attitudes and other equally mental phenomena to the social psychologists.[1] For the most part, however, the investigation of man's ideas has played a central role in the tradition of sociology.

Despite a persisting concern with both cross-cultural and historical variation in beliefs and values, we know embarrassingly little about why such ideas vary as radically as they obviously do. More often than not, we take ideas as givens, as variables to be used in explaining something else; only seldom do we consider them as problematical, as entities to be explained in and of themselves. And this we have the obligation to do. It is well within the province of sociology to study both the determinants and consequences of variation in beliefs and values.

It is commonplace in sociology and anthropology alike to preface a monograph with a discussion of value-orientations, basic assumptions, tacit premises, or some other set of abstractions, going on from there to show how these ideas are related to other elements in the social system. We are fond, for example, of pointing out how beliefs and values find their way into the economic structure, the distribution of authority, the stratification system, family relationships, and so on. Most of the time, the ideas which distinguish one culture or subculture from another are taken as givens. Once given, they are used to account for the pattern of expectations which govern behavior, and thus ultimately behavior itself.

Although the study of ideas in their capacity as prime movers of

---

[1] For one of the best statements of this position see Otis Dudly Duncan and Leo F. Schnore, "Cultural, Behavioral, and Ecological Perspectives in the Study of Social Organization," *American Journal of Sociology,* Vol. 55 (1959), pp. 132–46.

1

social action is clearly a legitimate pursuit, it can easily fall victim to the temptation of reasoning in circles. It is unfortunately too often the case that the only way to get at the major values or beliefs of a given population is to infer them from the behavior we observe. Using an approach that is at once inductive and intuitive, it is possible to locate clusters of ideas (themes) which taken collectively represent the essence of the cultural system. The fallacy lies in using these themes to "explain" the very behavior from which they were derived. It is meaningless to infer a set of abstract ideas from observations of behavior and then invoke the same ideas to account for the original behavior. It would be of little value, for example, if one were to enter a community, observe a sample of behavior, conclude that the members were generally individualistic in their relations with each other, and then point to the theme of individualism as a cause of their behavior. What is needed, of course, is a measure of ideas (in this case individualism) which is independent of the behavior to be explained.

Despite the paucity of empirically satisfying studies in this area, we agree with Parsons[2] as well as our own common sense that ideas such as beliefs and values do affect behavior. We are less concerned with the sociologist's claim that ideas play an important role in social action than we are with the sociologist's failure to explain why people have such different ideas in the first place.

We do not want to suggest that sociologists have never concerned themselves with the problem of where beliefs and values come from. The question has been raised many times before; it is the answers that are missing. Answers have been suggested but for the most part they are speculative, intuitive, and devoid of adequate empirical support. We are referring primarily to that area of study traditionally called "the sociology of knowledge." Despite, or perhaps because of, their willingness to consider all conceivable forms of "knowledge" as problematical and any kind of social experience as a potential source of variation, sociologists in this tradition have added little to our meager store of empirically verified propositions. While we enjoy the luxury of countless speculations, many of them admittedly far more imaginative than what we ordinarily find in sociology, we suffer from an acute lack of hypotheses tested and retested according to the canons of the scientific method. This shortcoming is, of course, hardly unique to the sociology of knowledge. It is endemic to sociology itself.

---

[2] For Parsons' earliest and clearest discussion of the problem see his essay, "The Role of Ideas in Social Action" in Talcott Parsons, *Essays in Sociological Theory* (Glencoe, Ill.: Free Press, 1954), pp. 19–33.

While we are made impatient by the empirical shortcomings of Marx, Scheler, Mannheim, and others who have worked in this area, we are attracted by the intellectual significance of the questions they have raised. Like those before us we want to know why men, living on different parts of the globe and in different points in time, entertain such different cognitive, evaluative, and affective orientations toward the world around them. Unlike these others, we have done our research in the small group laboratory.

These are other differences. We are less interested in those formal ideologies (political, religious, and economic) which tend to be specific to certain groups at certain points in history than we are in the broader dimensions of beliefs and values along which all cultures can be ordered at any point in time. Instead of asking, for example, why existentialism arose when and where it did, we prefer to ask why some groups of people are more individualistic, authoritarian, competitive, or achievement-conscious than others. Beliefs and values dealing with authority, competition, independence, achievement, and the like can be found in all cultures at all times. They constitute the basic ingredients of all cultural systems no matter how simple or complex.

While the questions we pose have their roots deep in the sociological tradition, the methodology we employ is of another age. Remote as the small group laboratory may seem with respect to the historical and cross-cultural phenomena we ultimately want to explain, it represents to us an appropriate place to begin. It is very difficult outside of the laboratory to collect attitudinal data which lend themselves to causal inference. Without adequate controls an empirical relationship becomes an inkblot, open to a variety of interpretations in which ideological and theoretical commitments play a prominent role. The perennial debate over Calvinism and capitalism is a case in point. In the laboratory it is possible to order the environment in such a way that, if empirical relationships are revealed, we are reasonably certain which is the independent and which is the dependent variable. With historical and cross-cultural data this is seldom feasible. As a result, we easily succumb to the comforting conclusion that "it probably works both ways."

Such is the case with beliefs and values. And, in one sense, this is the way it should be. For in all likelihood, culture acts alternately as both an independent and a dependent variable. But this is a conclusion to be established empirically. As a confession of ignorance, it is of little scientific value.

The advantages of the laboratory are widely known and accepted. Just how much is lost in studying social phenomena under highly controlled conditions is still at issue. Our own strategy calls for an initial series of laboratory experiments in which the variables most likely to be critical for a theory of culture are abstracted from their normal context and varied systematically with an eye to producing significant changes in subjects' beliefs and values. If and when we succeed in inducing and explaining cultural change in the laboratory, we shall expand our design to include field studies which lend themselves to moderately rigorous control. Whether we ever do get all the way back to the analysis of broad historical and cross-cultural differences is open to question. It is conceivable that we could develop a theory adequate to the task of explaining variation under highly controlled conditions and never reach the point of accounting for what happens in the natural setting, not because the theory is inadequate but because the appropriate measures are lacking. At present such measures *are* lacking. And this is one reason why previous attempts have contributed so little to our understanding of cultural variation.

It can hardly be demonstrated ahead of time that our laboratory strategy is a more efficient approach to the problem than that of the social historian or ethnographer. Each has its drawbacks. There are advantages to dealing with the very kind of data you want to explain, but to the extent that such evidence is impervious to measurement and control, theory tends to take the form of speculation. On the other hand, the data we gather in the laboratory are ideally suited to hypothesis testing, but to the extent that we have abstracted from reality, our generalizations become speculative. Despite its popularity, the former strategy (historical and comparative analysis) has contributed very little of scientific value to the problem we have posed. The laboratory approach is as yet untested in this regard. It is our own conviction that, given the nature of what we want to find out, we shall make more progress if we start by looking at the process of attitude formation in its simplest, most primitive form. There will be plenty of time later on to incorporate the many variables that complicate the issue in the natural setting.

The study of beliefs and values in the small group laboratory is hardly an original enterprise. Social psychologists have been doing it for years. Hovland, Janis, Kelman, Sherif, Festinger, and Scott are but a few of the many who have experimented with attitude change. For the most part, however, theirs are studies in persuasion, influence, and conformity. They are designed to locate the conditions under which an individual will alter his own attitudes in response to something said or done by someone else. The attitude, opinion, belief, value, etc., already exists in someone's mind. The problem to be solved is one of communication. Under what conditions will a person accept a communication which conflicts with what he already believes; e.g., what is the nature of the communication, who is doing the communicating, to whom is the communication being addressed, and how many other people already believe it? While studies of persuasion and influence are interesting in their own right, they contribute little to our understanding of historical or cross-cultural differences in beliefs and values. While they do help us to explain the *diffusion* of ideas within a group, they are not designed to account for the *formation* of such ideas.

Persuasion has a part to play in any theory of cultural variation. But it does not answer the question of where the ideas to be communicated come from in the first place or why they change over time. Granted that we are socialized by our parents, that we can be persuaded by lectures or movies, that we change our attitudes in response to group pressure, we still don't know how such ideas are formed or created in the first place. Why do they exist in one part of the world but not another? Why do they change from one generation to the next? It is to these questions that we address ourselves.

CHAPTER 1

A Theory of Task Experience as a Source of Attitudes

WHERE DO men get the beliefs and values by which they live? There is but one reasonable answer. They create them. Men create their own conceptions of what is true and good in the world around them. The ideas which give meaning to their lives are products of their own invention. The premises which govern their behavior are of their own making. It is men who are responsible for creating the beliefs and values which distinguish one culture from another. There is no other explanation save a religious or genetic one.

Out of what, then, are beliefs and values created? It is our contention that task experience provides much of the raw material out of which men construct their fundamental ideas about life. One reason why people in different parts of the world have such different conceptions of the true, desired, and desirable is that they have undergone radically different kinds of task experience. This is our basic proposition. The rest of the chapter is devoted to explaining what it means.

BASIC CONCEPTS

Of all the ideas people have about the world around them, we are most interested in those dealing with the very basic dimensions of human existence. In this respect our approach is similar to that of Florence Kluckhohn whose list of "human problems and their cultural solutions" has guided us in our choice of attitudinal themes to be used for experimental purposes.[1] Thus far we have done research on ideas dealing with the individual's relationship to society, the exercise of authority, the relationship between man and God, time orientation,

---

[1] Florence Rockford Kluckhohn and Fred L. Strodtbeck, *Variations in Value Orientations* (Evanston, Ill: Row, Peterson & Co., 1961).

achievement, luck, control, and man's relationship to nature. There are undoubtedly still other dimensions which are equally fundmental in that they deal with aspects of life which are universal to the "human situation." Ideas of this sort can be expressed in any one of three different *modes*: cathectic, cognitive or evaluative. A cathectic orientation implies liking or disliking for the object being referred to or, as Parsons describes it, "attachment to objects which are gratifying and rejection of those which are noxious. . . ."[2] In the language we shall be using here, a cathectic orientation represents a *preference* for one kind of behavior, activity, or relationship over another.

Cognition involves making discriminations among objects with an eye to the "location and characterization of (such) objects . . . in terms of their relevance to satisfaction of drives and their organization in motivation."[3] At the level of ideas we are concerned with, a cognitive orientation may take the form of an axiom, proposition, or empirical generalization with respect to some feature of human experience. As an existential statement about the nature of things, it involves neither liking nor disliking for the "object" referred to. In the discussion to follow we shall refer to orientations of this sort as *beliefs*.

By an "evaluative" orientation we mean something considerably more specific than what Parsons has in mind. Defined most broadly, "evaluation" refers to all the criteria the individual uses in making comparative judgments about the objects in his environment. According to Parsons, these may take the form of "cognitive standards of truthfulness, appreciative standards of appropriateness, or moral standards of rightness."[4] Given the nature of our interests, we have chosen to limit the term "evaluation" to those judgments made on moral or normative grounds. Judgments of this sort are ordinarily expressed in terms of the distinction between should and should not. An evaluative orientation to some form of human experience implies that certain modes of conduct are morally superior or more appropriate than others. When used in this sense, evaluation is clearly not the same thing as cathexis. It is quite possible, for example, to like or prefer one way of behaving without being at all convinced that this is an appropriate way to act. In this light, Kluckhohn's distinction between the desired (cathectic) and the desirable (evaluative) is very much to the point.[5]

---

[2] Talcott Parsons, Edward A. Shils, *et al.*, *Toward a General Theory of Action* (Cambridge, Mass.: Harvard University Press, 1951), p. 5.
[3] *Ibid.*
[4] *Ibid.*
[5] *Ibid.*, pp. 396–97.

In speaking of orientations of an evaluative or normative sort, we shall use the term *values*.

Individuals obviously vary in what they prefer, believe, and value. There are many reasons why. A complete explanation would presumably include references to family socialization, peer group influence, specific events in the individual's past, sources of anxiety, basic strivings, mechanisms of defense, aptitudes and skills, education, income, occupation, and the mass media. We do not propose to develop a general theory of ideas in which each of these many variables is given its proper place. We intend rather to explore the limits of one major source of cultural themes, namely task experience. It is our contention that task experience serves as an important determinant of individual and/or group differences in what men come to believe, prefer, and value. Others have previously argued in a similar vein. We shall briefly review some of their writings in the next chapter.

Webster defines task as "a piece of work to be accomplished," and offers the following as synonyms: "duty, job, chore, stint, and assignment." Thibaut and Kelley suggest a somewhat broader definition which is more in keeping with our own purposes here. For them a task is "pretty much what the common-sense definition conveys: a problem, assignment, or stimulus-complex to which the individual or group responds by performing various overt or covert operations which lead to various outcomes."[6] The breadth of the definition stems from the term "stimulus-complex" which clearly extends the meaning of "task" beyond the strictly instrumental operations implicit in the words "problem" and "assignment." We are reminded that the definition leaves room for "outcomes that follow immediately from mainly consummatory or appreciative responses, as in viewing a picture, and those that follow instrumental actions on the task, as in computing sums of numbers in an arithmetic problem."[7]

Defined in this way a task is something external to the individual; it is a "stimulus-complex" to which the organism responds. Others, however, have employed the term to refer to internal states of the organism. According to Ryan, "task" can best be thought of as "the answer to such questions as 'What are you doing?', 'What are you trying to do?', 'Where are you going?', 'What for?', and the like."[8] As

---

[6] John W. Thibaut and Harold H. Kelley, *The Social Psychology of Groups* (New York: John Wiley & Sons, Inc., 1959), p. 150.

[7] *Ibid.*

[8] T. A. Ryan, "Drives, Tasks, and the Initiation of Behavior," *American Journal of Psychology,* Vol. 71 (1958), p. 78.

more or less equivalent terms, Ryan cites "intention, desire, goal, want, wish."[9] We are reminded, however, that these are to be used in a very specific sense. By the term goal, for example, Ryan means "wanting to finish this page of typing," "getting the shopping done," "finishing the dishes" and not "inferred goals such as security or aggression, which are derived from some kind of drive-theory."[10] So defined, "task" is a way of referring to some specific feature of the individual's motivational system rather than some specific aspect of the environment in which he lives.

We prefer to use the term "task" in the latter sense. For us (as for Thibaut and Kelley) "task" refers to a complex of stimuli upon which the individual performs certain operations in order to achieve certain outcomes. To describe a task is to specify both the nature of the stimuli and the operations required. "Playing a piano," for example, is a task which can be described by specifying, first, what we mean by a piano and, second, the operations required to make it work.

Defined this way, "task" would appear to include most of the things people do in everyday life. With this in mind, the reader might wonder why we bother talking about *task* experience when the term "experience" would do just as well. The answer lies in the fact that there are dimensions of experience which are not caught up in the word "task" as we have defined it. Take, for example, listening to a lecture. Listening to a lecture is a task in that it represents a stimulus-complex to which the individual responds by performing certain operations (e.g., sitting quietly, concentrating, taking notes, etc.) in the expectation that they will lead to certain desired outcomes (e.g., increased knowledge and understanding). These are operations and outcomes common to any lecture; they say nothing about the specific content of the lecture itself. Yet the content of the lecture is an important part of the total experience. For most purposes, it may very well be the most important part of the experience. With respect to persuading the audience on some issue, this is certainly the case. Contentwise no two lectures are quite alike; taskwise they are all very similar. When we refer to listening to a lecture as a task we capture only part of its total meaning. There is more to experience than is implied by the concept task.

Although no one has ever attempted a comprehensive classification of tasks, there are some obvious distinctions that might be made. Thibaut and Kelley, for example, distinguish between conjunctive and disjunctive tasks, i.e., tasks which require the synchronized efforts of at

---

[9] *Ibid.*
[10] *Ibid.*

least two people and those which require but one individual's response.[11]
For other purposes, we might want to classify tasks according to how
hard they are (probability of success). In other cases it may be more
appropriate to distinguish between those tasks which can be completed
in the short-run and those which require longer periods of time. On
other occasions we may be more interested in whether a task requires
the individual to work with his hands or not.

It is our thesis that in working on a task an individual develops certain beliefs, values, and preferences specific to the task itself which
over time are generalized to other areas of life. The fact that an individual is engaged in a certain task we take as given. It is his ideas
about the world around him that we define as problematical. The
theory, then, constitutes an attempt to show in what way differences in
task experience can help us to account for differences in what men
believe, prefer, and value.

It is obvious that people, both within and between cultures, differ
radically in the tasks with which they are confronted from day to day.
Why this should be so we leave to others to explain. There are, however, a number of variables likely to be relevant, some social, others
personal. Ecological factors, for example, play an important role in
determining the distribution of tasks available for individual members
of society to choose from. Differences in environment (e.g., climate,
natural resources, etc.), technology, and population (size, composition,
density, etc.) are all critical in this regard. It is unlikely, however, that
ecological variables such as these will tell the whole story. Just as important, perhaps, are the experiences wrought by events unique to any
particular society at a given point in history. Contacts with other
societies, whether they take the form of conquest, assimilation, diffusion, or the like, are of this order. All conspire to shape the pattern of
tasks which individual members of society are called to work on.

It is equally clear, moreover, that culture in the form of shared
beliefs and values has a role to play in this process. Ecology, for example, is rarely so strict a master that in responding to its demands man
finds himself without choice. Given that certain problems posed by
environmental or technological considerations are amenable to a number
of solutions, the actual choice made in any specific instance may be
determined by *a priori* cultural conceptions of what is true or good.
Cultural considerations may be significant, moreover, in deciding what
problems are to be solved in the first place. In our own society, the
decision to invest billions of dollars in the exploration of space is not

[11] Thibaut and Kelley, *op. cit.*, pp. 162–64.

unrelated to the lofty position which scientific investigation holds in our hierarchy of values. Whether in solving problems or in creating them, culture helps to structure the kinds of tasks on which men work.

These three factors (ecological, historical, and cultural) are among those responsible for the distribution of tasks available at any point in time for members of society to choose from. The assignment of specific individuals to specific tasks is a function of still another whole set of variables. Among these we would include such factors as age, sex, kinship ties, class or caste affiliation, residence, education, religion, and a host of personal variables including intelligence, interests, and task-relevant skills.

A theory capable of explaining why any given individual in any society is engaged in a certain task or set of tasks is far beyond the resources of contemporary social science. In our own investigation of the relationship between task experience and preferences, beliefs, and values, we take the fact of a given individual working on a specific task as a theoretical given. No formal attempt is made to account for this fact.

THEORY

It is assumed first that in the performance of any given task certain forms of behavior will have higher instrumental reward value than others. To say that a particular form of behavior has high instrumental reward value means simply that it contributes significantly to the achievement of that goal upon which rewards are contingent.

Where two or more individuals are involved, we can speak of an interaction *pattern* as having high or low instrumental reward value. Some tasks, for example, can be performed more effectively if the several individuals involved co-operate closely than if each works independently of the other. In some cases it is to the advantage of all members concerned to delegate decision-making powers to a single individual; with other tasks it is more effective if everyone shares equally in the process. Given the nature of the task, certain patterns of behavior (social structures) are more likely to be successful (rewarded) than others. This is not to deny that some tasks lend themselves to more than one solution. We assume simply that in most cases some behaviors are more likely to be rewarded than others. Tasks obviously vary in their reinforcing properties. What is rewarded in one way may be punished in another. In any situation, the task plays an important role in determining the specific matrix of rewards and punishments to which the individual can be expected to respond.

Initially, the individual responds by cognitively discriminating among objects in his task environment, "locating and characterizing"[12] each in terms of its relevance to the satisfaction of needs which he has brought to the situation. On the basis of a whole series of such cognitions, he constructs an hypothesis with respect to the most effective way of performing the task at hand. However crudely formed, such hypotheses help to structure the individual's initial attempts at solving the task. Given the nature of the task, some forms of behavior will be rewarded and thus repeated while others get punished and undergo extinction. To the extent that these outcomes are inconsistent with the individual's original hypothesis, he can be expected to re-examine his assumptions in the light of subsequent events. Through cognitive reorientation new behavioral strategies may emerge. In this sense the process is at once deductive and inductive. As the individual proceeds from hypothesis to behavior and back again it is reasonable to assume that both cognition and behavior will take on an increasingly stable character.

Cognition, however, is but one of several orientations defining the individual's relationship to his task environment. In the process of engaging the task, it is also to be expected that the individual will develop positive attachments to those forms of behavior which have been rewarded while rejecting those for which he was punished or, better perhaps, those which failed to yield the desired result. Cathexis, once again, involves "attachment to objects which are gratifying and rejection of those which are noxious. . . ."[13] The patterns of behavior most likely to be gratifying are those which contribute most effectively to getting the task accomplished, i.e., those which are instrumental in achieving desired outcomes. Because they are gratifying or rewarding, they will be cathected, liked, and preferred to those behaviors leading to unfavorable outcomes. The cathectic orientation per se is to be distinguished from both the behavior to which it is directed and the cognitive orientation which accompanies it.

Where two or more individuals are engaged in the same task, it will be to the advantage of all concerned to legitimize those behaviors which are perceived to be instrumental to task success and in which members have some cathectic investment. To legitimize is to define as appropriate or desirable. Behavior so defined can be rightfully expected of the members involved. Rules of this sort we ordinarily refer to as "norms," statements taking the form of should and should not. A norm represents an evaluative orientation in that it involves a judgment with

---

[12] Parsons and Shils, *op. cit.*, p. 5.
[13] *Ibid.*

respect to the moral rightness or appropriateness of a given form of behavior. Evaluation, although analytically distinct from cognition and cathexis, is empirically related to both. In any given situation, the definition of a given form of behavior as appropriate or desirable assumes a cognitive awareness of the instrumental reward value of that behavior as well as a positive attachment to it in the cathectic sense. It is those forms of behavior which members perceive to be effective in solving the task and which they have come to enjoy or prefer that are most apt to be legitimized in the group setting.

Legitimization, of course, involves the use of sanctions to reinforce conformity to the norm in question, the most common sanctions being approval or disapproval on the part of other group members. This rewarding and punishing behavior on the part of members themselves constitutes a source of reinforcement supplementary to that provided by positive and negative task outcomes. The instrumental reward value of a form of behavior is thus confirmed by both task success or failure and responses from other group members.

We have spoken thus far of four response variables—behavior, cognition, cathexis, and evaluation. It is assumed that all four are relevant in any task situation and that these four in particular exhaust the meaning of the situation to the individual. Although we have treated them in sequence, it is clear that they are all interrelated parts of an ongoing process. Hypotheses are formed, tested against behavior, and subsequently confirmed, discarded, or modified to fit the facts. With rewards comes cathexis and eventually the establishment of norms. Once legitimized, behavior is subject to the sanctions of other group members. Norms, which themselves arise from the interplay of cognition, behavior, and cathexis, thus serve to stabilize behavior and, in turn, the other orientations.

Given time to act upon each other, all four variables (behavior and the three orientations) should be highly correlated in any given task situation. To the extent, for example, that a given task can be performed most effectively when the individuals present co-operate closely with each other, it is to be expected that in the course of working on the task members will (1) become cognitively aware that co-operation is instrumental to task success, (2) behave in a co-operative fashion, (3) develop a cathectic interest in co-operating with each other, and (4) establish norms defining co-operation as a legitimate and expected form of behavior.

Although we assume a tendency toward the integration of all four responses, factors beyond the task itself may have a differentiating effect. It is possible, for example, that an individual will perceive the instrumental significance of co-operation in this particular setting, and even develop a liking for it, but refuse to endorse the notion that members *should* co-operate with each other because of a prior commitment to the value that everyone should do his own work. Most likely, however, the beliefs, preferences, and values which an individual brings to the situation will themselves be highly integrated. Evidence to this effect can be found in most of the studies reported later on in this book.

It is important to note that in any situation the task itself is but one of several sources of variation in behavior and orientations. Whether a given form of behavior has high or low instrumental reward value may be influenced as well by the number of people working on the task, the similarity or dissimilarity of group members with respect to personal and social characteristics, the kind of incentive system employed, etc. It is not unreasonable to assume, for example, that the smaller the group the more rewarding will be attempts to establish a co-operative pattern of behavior. Similarly, we would expect the instrumental reward value of co-operation to be higher in those cases where a group rather than an individual incentive system was employed. There are many variables of this sort which, along with the task itself, might be thought of as making up the more general *task situation*. While task remains paramount, it is clear that these other variables can have an independent effect on behavior as well as beliefs, preferences, and values. Generally speaking, however, they are dependent on the nature of the task itself. While an employer, for example, has some flexibility in the number of people he assigns to a task, his range of alternatives is limited by the character of the task itself. The same can be said for most of the other variables entering into the task situation.

No attempt is made here to trace each of the variables in the task situation to its origins outside of the situation nor to explain how each is related to the others within a given situation. All characteristics of the task situation (including the task, group size, group composition, incentive system, etc.) are taken as given.

We have said that in any task situation some forms of behavior will be rewarded more than others. It is equally true that in any situation some individuals will be rewarded more than others. In view of the many different kinds of rewards available (both extrinsic and intrinsic), the probability that everyone will be similarly rewarded is very slight. The implication is that those who are most often or most highly rewarded for behaving in a certain way will develop the strongest cognitions, cathexes, and evaluations vis-à-vis that mode of behavior. The same principle at the group level says that the more successful a group is in dealing with its task, the more positive will be the beliefs, preferences, and values of its members toward those patterns of behavior which were instrumental to task success.

To summarize, the assumption is made that in any task situation certain patterns of behavior will have greater instrumental reward value than others. By virtue of the reinforcing quality of task outcomes, these particular forms of behavior will have a better chance of being emitted than any others. At the same time, individuals working on the task can be expected to respond cognitively (through apprehending the instrumental nature of these acts), cathectically (by developing a positive attachment for this kind of behavior), and evaluatively (by defining such behavior as legitimate and morally desirable). While we assume a tendency for all four responses to be consistent both with each other and with the demands of the task, it is to be expected that in any specific situation there will be other sources of variation beyond the task itself.

Of the four responses, behavior is of relevance here primarily because it is so intimately connected with the development of the other three. It is these three orientations (cognitive, cathectic, and evaluative) which we take to be of critical importance for the rest of the theory. Thus far we have considered them as specific responses to an isolated situation. We propose now that the orientations developed in response to a given set of task attributes will be generalized to other task situations and, through the process of induction, to the level of cultural beliefs, preferences, and values. There are two kinds of generalization involved here; the first we shall call *lateral generalization,* the second *vertical generalization.*

By lateral generalization, we mean the spilling over of orientations generated in one task situation to other situations involving tasks with more or less similar attributes. The term "lateral" is meant to signify the fact that generalization proceeds from one specific setting to another rather than from the specific to the abstract.

Lateral generalization can be illustrated in the following way. In keeping to our original example, we assume that the individual in his everyday occupational role is confronted with a series of tasks most of which can be performed successfully only if he and his fellow workers co-operate closely with one another. As previously explained, each of the members involved can be expected to develop a set of orientations to his work in which co-operation is (1) perceived as instrumental to task success, (2) cathected as intrinsically enjoyable, and (3) evaluated as normatively desirable.

If the individual in our illustration is at all typical, he will hold membership in several other groups as well. Groups are formed to get something done, whether this be raising children, organizing political activity, discussing community problems, operating a social club, or worshipping God. Assuming our individual to be involved in each, we would expect him to generalize the orientations toward co-operation developed in the formal work setting to all of them. Having perceived that co-operation is instrumental to task success at work, he is likely to bring his perception to bear on the issue of co-operation wherever this appears in his activities outside the work place, i.e., the family, community, church, social club, etc. Having found co-operation to his liking at work, he is apt to prefer it at home, in church, at his social club, and so on. Having endorsed co-operation as normatively appropriate at work, he is likely to think that people should behave the same way in these other task situations.

It is to be anticipated, however, that the original orientations will generalize more to some tasks than others. There are two major reasons for believing this to be true. Taking orientations generated in the work place to be the major source of generalization, we recognize first that some tasks are more similar to those encountered on the job than others. At first glance, the tasks that make up family life would seem quite remote from those that an individual is confronted with in the formal work setting. Assuming that our individual is some kind of manager, he will probably do more generalizing to the office-like tasks in his community organization than to the more "expressive" tasks he is likely to meet at home. A concrete prediction of this sort would, of course, involve a detailed comparison of the specific task attributes in each situation. In lieu of such information, we limit ourselves to the general rule that the more similar one task is to another, the more likely it is that orientations developed in one will generalize to the other.

The second consideration is based on the fact that individuals are more familiar with some tasks than others. The more extended the experience with a task, the more stable, certain, and unchanging will be the orientations evoked in response to it. An individual who has participated in community affairs most of his adult life will do less generalizing from his formal work experience to this task area than someone else who is newly engaged in the activity. To the extent that individuals differ in the kinds and amounts of experience they have had, generalization beyond the work place can be expected to vary from person to person. In each case generalization can be said to take the path of least resistance, where resistance is defined in terms of prior experience.

In one sense, this is an overly simple view of lateral generalization in that it fails to take into account the fact that orientations originating in each of the several task situations will generalize to all of the others —including the work place. We take orientations generated in the work place to be of predominant importance for generalization only because of the very salient role which work has in the lives of most people. While we make this assumption again later on in our discussion of cultural change, it is not essential to the theory at this point. Here we propose simply that the beliefs, preferences, and values developed in one task situation will generalize to all others (depending on similarity and familiarity), and that some experiences will play a greater role in this process than others. It is not necessary to this way of thinking that task experience in the formal work setting constitute the source from which all generalization must flow.

While lateral generalization proceeds from one specific task situation to another, vertical generalization proceeds indirectly from the specific to the abstract. There are, of course, different degrees of abstraction. From the specific task situation in which beliefs, preferences, and values are grounded, generalization can be expected to proceed vertically to levels of abstraction increasingly removed from the original source of induction. Returning once again to our example of co-operation, we start with a concrete set of orientations, all specific to a task or series of tasks to which an individual is assigned at his place of work. We assume the individual to have developed a relatively stable set of cognitive, cathectic, and evaluative orientations in which co-operation is perceived to be instrumental to favorable task outcomes, preferred to other forms of behavior, and legitimized as morally desirable.

If the individual is to generalize at all, it will be from this specific constellation of tasks to the whole class of tasks of which this series is but a member. Any given task is, of course, a member of more than one class. For this reason induction can take a variety of forms—from this task to all manual tasks, from this task to all tasks that involve two or more people, from this task to all tasks of an instrumental nature, and so on. In each case, that which gets generalized is the set of cognitive, cathectic, and evaluative orientations toward behaving co-operatively. Beyond this level, there are more abstract classes to which generalization may extend. Among other things a task is "a piece of work to be accomplished." From his specific task or series of tasks, then, the individual may generalize to all kinds of work or forms of employment. What was once a set of hypotheses with respect to the most effective way of performing a specific task now becomes an abstract belief about the importance of co-operation in any job. The preference for working closely with others in a concrete setting is here generalized to a preference for co-operation in any work setting. A willingness to endorse co-operation as appropriate in one set of tasks becomes extended to the general notion that people should co-operate in all instrumental pursuits.

To carry the induction even further, the individual may generalize his situationally specific orientations beyond the work level to all kinds of tasks, including those which are primarily expressive in nature, e.g., leisure. Eventually, the generalization process may extend all the way to those beliefs, preferences, and values which deal with the nature of existence itself. How important is co-operation in getting people what they want? Is co-operation with others to be preferred as a way of life? What is the role of co-operation in the ideal life? The answers to these questions are supplied, in part, by each individual's unique set of specific task experiences. The mechanism linking the specific to the abstract is that of induction.

In our discussion of task experience as a source of situationally specific orientations and, through lateral and vertical generalization, those beliefs, preferences, and values of a more inclusive nature, our unit of analysis has been that of the individual. It is, of course, the concrete individual who is confronted with a task, who behaves, thinks, feels, and evaluates, and who generalizes laterally to other task settings and vertically to more abstract classes of experience. Rather than speaking of a given task and a specific individual, however, we can take as our reference a *distribution* of tasks on the one hand and an *aggregate* of individuals on the other. Such is the case in the analysis of task experience as a source of culture and cultural change.

In any given society, there will be a certain distribution or profile of tasks available for members to work on. Consequently, we should find a parallel distribution of situationally specific cognitive, cathectic, and evaluative orientations from which members will generalize laterally across situations and vertically to more abstract classes of experience. It is these latter abstractions for which we reserve the term "culture."

In this sense, culture can best be thought of as a profile of abstract beliefs, preferences, and values, where profile refers to the distribution of such orientations among members of society. No one is likely to contend that all members of society believe, prefer, and value the same things to the same extent. There is no such thing as a perfectly homogeneous culture. Yet it is equally clear that, despite the inevitability of internal variation, there are significant differences between cultures taken as a whole. Not all Russians, for example, share the same beliefs, preferences, and values with respect to co-operation; but taken as a whole, Soviet culture is probably a good deal more collectivistic than that of the United States.

There are thus two kinds of variation to be explained, variation within a given society and variation between two or more societies. While there are many factors involved, we believe task experience to be of critical importance for both sets of differences. With respect to internal variation, the relevant fact is that not all members of society work on the same tasks. To the extent that abstract beliefs, preferences, and values represent inductions from situationally specific task experiences, the profile of such orientations within a given society will reflect the distribution of task experiences in the same system. With respect to variation between societies, the important thing to keep in mind is that not all societies have the same distribution of tasks. While the shape of the distribution may be roughly similar in any two societies, the position of the distribution on any given continuum may vary widely. By virtue of the inductive process, such differences in the distribution of tasks will tend to show up as cross-cultural differences in the distribution of beliefs, preferences, and values.

The implication for cultural change is clear. If the profile of beliefs, preferences, and values in any given society is a function of the distribution of tasks among its members, a change in the latter will be reflected in a change in the former. Technological innovation can be assumed to play an important role in this process through its impact on the distribution of tasks available for members of society to choose from. Tasks engaged in at the work place are apt to be of the greatest significance here, although others may be affected as well.

In a stable, unchanging system, members of society would have relatively little difficulty in finding jobs suitable to or congruent with their previously formed beliefs, preferences, and values. Where both tasks and orientations remain constant from one generation to the next, the matching process poses few problems. Children take on the beliefs and values of their parents; as they grow up, they assume work roles similar to those held by their parents. With technological innovation, however, the distribution of task opportunities undergoes change. As a result, some individuals (socialized by representatives of another generation) are compelled to take jobs which are not entirely in keeping with what they believe, prefer, or value. Others, already at work, find their tasks changed for them. In either case we can assume an asymmetry between orientations brought to the situation and the reinforcing properties of the situation itself.

Whether we talk about a specific individual vis-à-vis a specific task or a whole aggregate of people vis-à-vis a distribution of tasks, *it is this asymmetry between already formed beliefs, preferences, and values on the one hand and the nature of task demands on the other that provides the impetus to change.* The more radical the innovation, the more likely it is that *a priori* cognitions, cathexes, and evaluations will prove ill-adapted to task success. For those individuals affected, it is the situationally specific orientations that are apt to change first, with their abstract counterparts lagging considerably behind. Those beliefs, preferences, and values dealing with the most general classes of human experience, i.e., those at the end of the inductive chain, will be the least sensitive to innovation at the task level. For this reason, they can be expected to persist much longer than those orientations representing less of an abstraction from task experience. The fact that orientations vary with respect to abstractness means that some beliefs, values, and preferences will change faster than others. This may help to account for the lack of cultural homogeneity in those societies where technological innovation is frequent. Another consideration, of course, is the variety of task experiences arising from the division of labor.

The reference to cultural lag brings us to a final consideration—the circular nature of the relationship between culture and experience. It seems reasonable to assume that before man ever developed a set of abstract orientations with respect to the true, the desired, and the desirable, he was engaged in a host of everyday tasks designed to satisfy the simplest of human needs. What inductions he might have made were probably confined to classes of experience not far removed from the tasks themselves. As such they were easily influenced by changes at the task level. To the extent that abstraction rests on accumulated experience, we are safe in assuming that beliefs, preferences, and values of a general (cultural) nature did not emerge until considerable time had elapsed. Once articulated, however, they became capable of exerting an independent influence on subsequent forms of task experience.

The critical role of culture in structuring social action cannot be understood apart from the fact that the ideas which make it up are extremely abstract and hence unlikely to be affected significantly by changes in the immediate task environment. As the end products of an elaborate inductive process, such ideas are likely to persist long after the specific experiences from which they grew have given way to new and different forms. Divorced as they are from the immediate and the concrete, they take on the quality of absolutes and are transmitted to the next generaton in this form. As abstractions of an absolute, sometimes sacred character, they have an important role to play in the shaping of subsequent experience. Among other things, this includes the structuring of tasks available for members of society to engage in.

It remains true, nevertheless, that the abstractions which future generations accept as cultural givens have their roots in past experience. Despite their seemingly absolute character, they are never completely divorced from their origins. While they may appear to follow a course of their own, they are still subject to the vagaries of human experience. To the extent that they represent inductions from situationally specific task experiences, they are amenable to change. The fact that they change slowly is what gives them their autonomous appearance. Because they persist, they exert an influence all of their own. As products of human experience, however, they in turn can be changed by the course of events.

CHAPTER 2

A Discussion of Related
Theories

ALTHOUGH THE theory just presented owes a great deal to the empirical studies reported later in this book, it should be obvious that we are indebted as well to work done by others throughout the behavioral sciences. Some of our readers will think immediately of the sociology of knowledge, a discipline with a long tradition of interest in the social sources of beliefs and values. To anyone even slightly acquainted with psychology, it will be evident that we have relied heavily on basic principles of learning theory, namely those dealing with reinforcement and generalization. While we have borrowed less from social psychological theories of attitude change, it is true that our own work overlaps with some of the more recent work in that field. Strangely enough, the only branch of the behavioral sciences we have not drawn upon is anthropology.

Anthropologists, to a greater extent than any of their fellow behavioral scientists, have concerned themselves with the study of the beliefs and values men live by. Even more to the point, they have focused their attention on the fact that people *differ* in what they believe and value. Sometimes they have been content simply to describe the basic beliefs and values of a given culture; more often they have attempted to trace the impact of such ideas on the rest of the system, for example its kinship, political, and economic structure. What one rarely finds in anthropology, however, is a concern for where these basic ingredients of culture come from.

The closest one is likely to come is the study of how units of culture get *diffused* from one society to another. To explain the diffusion of a belief or value, however, is not to explain its origin. We are interested here in how beliefs and values are formed or created, not how they get moved around from one society to the next. Ask an anthropologist

22

why the Kwakiutls of Vancouver Island are so much more individualistic than our own Navajo and he will tell you that Kwakiutl culture belongs to one culture area and Navajo culture to another. This, of course, is not the answer we are looking for. To "explain" the difference between two specific cultures by placing each in some more inclusive category simply postpones the answer. We postpone the answer again when we attribute differences in beliefs to the fact that the individuals under study learned them from their parents. Either way we are led ultimately to the problem of specifying the conditions under which the belief or value was originally formulated. It is at this point that anthropology fails to enlighten us.

It is indeed strange that the discipline which is most concerned with culture should have the least to say about the origins of cultural beliefs and values. Despite the central role of ideas in most anthropological investigations, it is difficult to find cases in which the author addresses himself directly to the problem of explaining where beliefs and values come from. This should not be taken as a lack of interest in the question. We have yet to meet an anthropologist who is unwilling to sit down and talk about the problem. The reason most often given for the fact that nothing of a systematic nature has ever been done is that beliefs and values of the sort we are discussing tend to remain unchanged over very long periods of time, the implication being that the experiences on which they were based are ancient history and thus hidden from human view.

While there is some truth in this position, it seems to us that it overemphasizes the stability of culture and obscures the fact that beliefs and values are constantly being revised in the light of experience. Anthropologists have spent most of their time studying those societies which change little from one generation to the next. When observing primitive societies, one is apt to be more aware of the critical role which beliefs and values play in determining behavior than of the role which experience plays in shaping culture. The latter is much more visible in those societies undergoing rapid change, e.g., those societies in Africa, Asia, and Latin America which are just now becoming industrialized. Where new beliefs and values are being created in response to a new technological environment, the observer is more likely to think of culture as something which needs explaining, i.e., as a dependent variable. With more and more anthropologists working in settings of this very sort, we can expect a growing theoretical interest in the problem of explaining where cultural beliefs and values come from. As of this moment, however, little has been forthcoming. It is with this in mind, then, that we turn to the fields of sociology and psychology for work that is related to our own.

SOCIOLOGY OF KNOWLEDGE

Within the field of sociology, it is that area generally known as the sociology of knowledge which is most relevant to our own concern with task experience as a source of beliefs, values, and preferences. Despite a certain hesitation on the part of some of its members to speak in terms of cause and effect, the sociology of knowledge is clearly concerned with experience as a *source* of ideas.[1] In this respect, it bears a direct relationship to our own theory and research. Once we get beyond the level of abstract goals, however, it becomes increasingly obvious that there are as many differences as there are similarities.

In any attempt to assess the character of contemporary sociology of knowledge, it is essential that we first understand the distinction between what Mannheim has referred to as the particular versus the total conception of ideology. According to Mannheim, the particular conception of ideology includes "all those utterances the 'falsity' of which is due to an intentional or unintentional, conscious, semi-conscious, or unconscious, deluding of one's self or of others, taking place on a psychological level and structurally resembling lies."[2] This first conception of ideology is called *particular* because "it always refers only to specific assertions which may be regarded as concealments, falsifications, or lies without attacking the integrity of the total mental structure of the asserting subject."[3]

The total conception of ideology "takes as its problem precisely this mental structure *in its totality,* as it appears in different currents of thought and historical-social groups."[4] At this level, the individual's "whole mode of conceiving things" is held up for analysis. This is by far the more radical conception of ideology in that it takes as problematic not simply the content of an assertion but the philosophical (ontological, epistemological) assumptions which lie behind it. There is a tendency among contemporary writers to equate the sociology of knowledge with this total conception of ideology, reserving the term

---

[1] Marx left no doubt about his own view of the relationship when he said, "It is not the consciousness of men that determines their being, but, on the contrary, their social being [which] determines their consciousness." Quoted in T. B. Bottomore and Maximilien Rubel, *Karl Marx, Selected Writings in Sociology and Social Philosophy* (London: C. A. Watts & Co. Ltd., 1956), p. 51.

[2] Karl Mannheim, *Ideology and Utopia* (New York: Harcourt, Brace & World, Inc., 1936), pp. 265–66.

[3] *Ibid.,* p. 266.

[4] *Ibid.*

"ideology" itself for what was referred to above as the particular conception of ideology.

Used this way, ideology refers to any idea or system of ideas in which "some selfish or sectional interest or desire" has played a part. A set of beliefs is to be considered ideological to the extent that it is psychological in origin. Ideological thinking is thinking which has been distorted or "thrown off its course" by motivational considerations, by wishes, interests, resentments, fears, anxieties, and so on. The distortion, however, is an unwitting one; ideological thinking should never be confused with lying where the distortion of reality is deliberate. In thinking ideologically, the individual is unaware of the fact that his ideas are psychologically determined.

There is no denying the obvious fact that it is the individual who thinks, who entertains ideas, who believes, values, and chooses. What is being contended is that some of the ideas which the individual carries around with him are shaped by emotional factors residing within the individual while others are determined primarily by the social setting in which he lives. The distinction is made hazy by the fact that the object (rather than the origin) of the idea may be similar in the two cases. Ideas which have their roots in the human psyche may be just as broad and "social" as those which are social structural in origin. A good example of this is provided by Stark:

Throughout history, we find philosophies which assert that permanence is real and change a delusion—philosophies whose detail is vastly different, but whose kernel is simple and can be formulated in a very few words such as those just used. There is, near the beginning of the story, Plato with the assertion that rest is the perfection of being and movement only an impoverished form of it; there is, towards the end, Pareto with his "scientific proof" that social life is the same at all times and places since it is controlled by the unchanging "residues" while only the surface seems to show development. . . . Now both Plato and Pareto were aristocrats who lived in an age which was very unkind to aristocracy. Both saw an upsurge of egalitarianism; both disliked what they saw and turned from the real world with its changes into an unreal world of permanencies; their theories are ideological in origin and content. At their (subconscious) inception stood a practical and political preoccupation and prejudice. Underneath the threshold of consciousness there worked the anguished sentiment and desire that the world should not change; above the threshold of consciousness there formed—nourished from its subterranean root—the conviction, the delusive conviction, that the world *does* not change, does not *really* change, that change is only a ripple on the surface of the ocean which leaves the deeper layers of the water calm and unmoved.[5]

---

[5] W. Stark, *The Sociology of Knowledge* (London: Routledge & Kegan Paul, 1958), p. 51.

This is ideological thinking. Despite its social character, it is essentially psychological in origin. As such, it is to be distinguished from socially determined thought. In the latter case, the individual has nothing to "gain" from his system of ideas; they fulfill no wish, relieve no fear, express no resentment. They serve no vested interest, they harbor no delusion. What they reflect is the structure of the social situation in which the individual finds himself. By virtue of the situation in which he functions, the individual develops a *perspective* toward things in the world around him. His categories of thought, his mode of reasoning, the assumptions he makes about reality are all conditioned by the way his social life is organized. There are many different ways of looking at the world, many different ways of interpreting reality. The choice of any particular orientation will be governed by the pattern of human relationships of which the individual is a part. More generally, "every society must take up some concrete vantage point from which to survey the broad—the unbounded—acres of that which is, and every society will therefore have its own particular picture of reality because it sees reality and must see it in one particular perspective."[6]

The essence of this second approach is that ideas can be traced not only to motivational factors within the individual but to the external social situation in which that individual operates as well. Although the term "social situation" is often used to convey the idea of a whole society, it can also refer to smaller units of analysis, e.g., a social class or, smaller yet, one's place of work. With this in mind, Stark has introduced the labels "macro" and "micro" sociology of knowledge.[7] In illustrating the latter he draws on Merton's discussion of the role of the intellectual in public bureaucracy.

The professional bureaucrat has learnt to be content with a humble role. He is asked precise questions by his ministers who are politicians, and who decide on policies, and he is so conditioned as to give precise answers and not to talk out of turn. He is concerned with techniques, not with values. He will, in the ideal, and even in the typical case, work as assiduously at the implementation of a decision that goes against his valuations and private convictions as he will at the carrying-out of one that is in line with them. It is not for nothing that a civil servant is called a "servant" and his "service" will be to him a matter of pride rather than humiliation. Many academic people, accustomed as they are to relative autonomy, or at least to the absence of open controls, have found it impossible to click into that mentality. They are used to taking a more independent and comprehensive view of problems and things, to consider values as well as

---

[6] *Ibid.*, p. 49.
[7] *Ibid.*, pp. 20–21.

techniques, to pronounce on the *what* as much as on the *how*. . . . *Indeed,* they are quite likely to be doctrinaire; there is something in the professorial mode of life which tends to make professors (even English and American ones) into men of principle. Bureaucrats, on the other hand, are forced to be realistic: they are near the seat of power and must produce feasible solutions to practical problems. In a word, the thought-processes of the academic man are entirely different from those of the permanent civil servant, and they are so different *because they have gone through a different organizational mill*.[8]

Civil servants and professors have different mental habits, different modes of reasoning, different styles of thought. These differences have their roots in the organizational environment in which civil servants and professors function. Because of its concern with the relationship between social experience on the one hand and ideas on the other, this kind of analysis has an obvious place in the sociology of knowledge. It is to be considered as an exercise in the *micro*sociology of knowledge for the simple reason that the social situation involved (work place) is of relatively limited proportions. In the *macro*sociology of knowledge, a system of ideas is ordinarily traced to certain features of society taken as a whole. Stark illustrates this broader perspective with an analysis of the social sources of philosophical pragmatism:

Surely, this whole complex of ideas (pragmatism) is strikingly in line with the American way of life: the Americans are doers, not dreamers; their society has from the beginning been confronted with the supreme task of subjugating a vast continent, a task essentially technical in nature, and this all-pervading and all-determining endeavor has informed not only their economy but also their culture. This over-all direction of social life must have suggested and stimulated an all-round pragmatism. And American society was also super-individualistic. Like no other, it resembled, in the eighties of which we are speaking, a war of all against all, in which the strong could rise to the top and the weak were doomed to go under. A man had to "prove" himself in practical life if he was to become "established" in society. Is it surprising that philosophers should have developed a parallel theory concerning propositions and judgments? These too were expected to "prove themselves" in practical life before they could gain admission to the body of "established truths." It can be said, then, that pragmatism as a system of ideas rested on the contemporary social reality of the United States as its substructure.[9]

Although it is never made explicit here which features of society (economic, political, etc.) are responsible for the emergence and acceptance of pragmatism, it is quite clear that the boundaries of the

---

[8] *Ibid.*, p. 24.
[9] *Ibid.*, pp. 19–20.

"social situation" are drawn very broadly. This is macrosociology of knowledge. And macrosociology of knowledge, according to Stark, lies at the very center of the sociology of knowledge as an intellectual discipline. In this respect, both microsociology of knowledge and the study of ideology (psychologically motivated idea systems) are of but peripheral interest. The sociologist's primary obligation in this sphere is to explore the many ways in which the individual's thought processes are conditioned by the social macrocosm in which he lives.

Thus far we have pointed to two distinctions: (1) the distinction between that thought which is psychologically determined and that which is determined by the social situation, and (2) the distinction between those social situations of a relatively specific sort and those defined in very broad terms. While these distinctions do not tell us much about the substantive content of the field, they probably tell us enough to make possible an analysis of where and to what extent our own theory fits.

The most obvious feature of our own theory, in terms of the distinctions made above, is the importance which we have attached to the concept of reward. In any task situation, certain patterns of behavior will have greater instrumental reward value than others; because of their reward value, they will be perceived, cathected, and evaluated in positive terms. In this sense, it would appear that we are talking about a psychological process, the very kind of process which forms the basis for *ideological* thinking.

While a cursory glance reveals some support for this notion, a closer comparison makes it evident that the role of reward is quite different in the two cases. In the "theory" of ideology, a belief constitutes its own reward. Believing helps to reduce tension and anxiety; it fulfills wishes and expresses feeling. The conviction that the world does not really change serves to fulfill the wish that it *should* not change; for an aristocrat (like Plato or Pareto) who has little to gain from social upheaval, there is considerable comfort in the belief that the world is basically unchanging. We speak of this kind of thought as psychologically determined because it has its roots in the individual's motivational system. There is a direct link between the state of the motivational system and the content of the belief. In short, the individual believes because he finds it rewarding to believe.

In our own theory, the individual believes because he has been rewarded for behaving in a certain way. The rewards of which we speak (those contingent upon task success) may take the form of money, promotion, approval, etc. Beliefs, values, and preferences emerge and change as a function of what one gets rewarded for in the task situation. Whether these attitudes have some reward value in and of themselves is another matter altogether. In the theory of ideology, believing is rewarding in itself. The individual has some vested (psychological) interest in maintaining a particular set of ideas. In "task" theory, the individual is rewarded not for believing but for behaving. What rewards he gets, and these can be either external (money) or internal (pride), are contingent upon successful performance of the task. While we assume that everyone finds some reward value in having some sort of belief system to go by, we do not take the reward value of the belief itself as problematic in our own analysis.

When Mannheim *et al* say that an individual's beliefs are psychologically determined, they mean that the beliefs are a product of his own system of needs, wishes, fears, anxieties, and so on. The process is basically the same whether we are talking about an innocent rationalization or a full-blown ideology. In either case there is an unwitting distortion of reality in the service of some wish or interest. "Psychologically determined" beliefs are delusional in character; they represent a "turning of the mind" from the world as it really is. They may play an important function, however, in the individual's struggle to come to terms with his environment.

If this is what is meant by the psychological determination of thought, it is quite clear that our own theory deals with something else. We are interested in explaining variation in those ideas which have their roots not in the individual's motivational system but in his environment, more specifically, his task environment. When we talk about the impact of task experience on beliefs, values, and preferences, we are explicitly assigning priority to the situation rather than some set of wishes or needs internal to the individual. It remains true, however, that the *link* between the task situation on the one hand and attitude formation or change on the other is essentially a psychological one. We choose to stress the situational element only because the term "psychological" has been preempted by members of the discipline for those ideas which are essentially wish-fulfilling in nature.

It remains to say something about the distinction between microsociology of knowledge (where the situation is defined narrowly) and macrosociology (where the situation is defined broadly). The distinction is basically one of unit size. In most of Stark's examples of microsociology of knowledge, the unit tends to be some kind of organization (e.g., a university). In illustrating macrosociology of knowledge, he ordinarily speaks in terms of social classes or whole societies.

It is not altogether clear that the distinction between micro- and macrosociology of knowledge is a useful one. It may very well have the harmful effect of suggesting that two different *kinds* of theory are required, one for those situations defined narrowly and yet another where very large numbers of people are being considered. From Stark's own examples, it would appear to be more appropriate to think in terms of a continuum of situations, ranging from the microscopic (e.g., a small work group) to the macroscopic (e.g., a whole society). While we may need a more complex set of propositions to handle very large aggregates, it is quite unlikely that we shall need an altogether different kind of theory.

We have reason to believe that our own theory has relevance for social units at all points along the micro-macro continuum. The central concept in this theory is that of task, which has been defined as a stimulus-complex on which one or more persons perform certain operations in order to produce certain outcomes. One task situation may differ from another with respect to the nature of the stimulus-complex, the number of people working on it, the way in which outcomes are to be distributed, and so on. There is nothing in this particular definition of "task" which limits us to situations of any particular scope or specificity.

The same basic principles hold in all task situations, whether we are talking about a small group faced with the task of assembling a motor or a whole society faced with the task of waging a war.[10] In any task situation, certain forms of behavior will have greater instrumental reward value than others; in time, beliefs, values, and preferences will develop in which these particular forms of behavior are perceived as important for success, cathected as intrinsically enjoyable, and evaluated as morally desirable. From their original position as orientations to a specific situation, they can be expected to generalize laterally to other concrete task situations and vertically to more abstract categories of experience. The process is basically the same whether the situation is defined narrowly or whether it is defined broadly. In this sense, our theory has implications for both microsociology of knowledge and macrosociology of knowledge.

Despite the difficulties involved in fitting our own theory into the

---

[10] By virtue of its effect on the instrumental reward value of group solidarity and the centralization of control, we would expect the task of waging a war to have implications for beliefs, values, and preferences dealing with both individualism and authoritarianism.

categories typically used in the sociology of knowledge, it is clear that we are interested in the same aspect of human existence, namely the origins of ideas. It is this basic similarity which has led us to examine the field briefly with an eye to showing how and where our own theory fits in. The similarities, however, should not be allowed to obscure the very real differences.

For one thing, we are concerned with broad cultural themes rather than formal systems of thought. We are more interested, for example, in explaining why some people are more individualistic than others than we are in explaining why philosophical pragmatism arose when and where it did. Beliefs and values dealing with the individualism-collectivism theme can be found in all cultures at all points in time. Although cultures differ in the position taken vis-à-vis this theme, the theme itself is universal. It is universal, because it represents an attempt to answer a question fundamental to human existence.

To put it another way, our own "task" theory is aimed at accounting for variation in those beliefs, values, and preferences which exist in the minds of all men; the sociology of knowledge "is most directly concerned with the intellectual products of experts, whether in science or philosophy, in economic or political thought."[11] In both cases an attempt is made to trace ideas back to their roots in some sort of experience. The difference lies in *whose* ideas are to be explained. The difference, it might be added, has some very important implications for research strategy, particularly the use of quantitative techniques. So long as it remains focused on the thought processes of those few individuals whose theories and philosophies have made them famous, the sociology of knowledge will continue to be qualitative, intuitive, and unsystematic. It is doubtful that this approach will take us very far toward the development of an empirically based theory of ideas.

Although there seems to be a pretty obvious difference between the kind of ideas we are interested in (basic cultural themes) and the sorts of things usually studied by sociologists of knowledge (political and economic theories, philosophical systems, etc.), we have reason to believe that the two are not entirely unrelated. There are at least two ways in which broad cultural themes are related to specific systems of thought. In the first place, the themes make up the attitudinal base from which more formal belief systems are elaborated. Beyond this, the

---

[11] Robert K. Merton, *Social Theory and Social Structure* (Glencoe, Ill.: Free Press, 1957), p. 441.

presence or absence of a given theme in the culture may have a lot to do with whether or not a particular ideology or theory is accepted.

With respect to the first point, Stark (in an example quoted on p. 27) traces the emergence of philosophical pragmatism to the highly individualistic and competitive nature of life in America during the late nineteenth century. It was, he says, a "war of all against all, in which the strong could rise to the top and the weak were doomed to go under."[12] He proceeds to show how the notion that everyone should stand on his own two feet found its way into the philosophical concept of the pragmatic criterion. The point is that individualism, as a cultural theme, provided an appropriate context for the articulation of a specifically pragmatic philosophy.

A similar argument could be made for the role of cultural values in the development of ideologies rationalizing the position of employers-managers vis-à-vis their workers. In introducing a detailed comparison of entrepreneurial ideologies in England and Russia, Bendix has the following to say: "All economic enterprises have in common a basic social relation between the employers who exercise authority and the workers who obey. And all ideologies of management have in common the effort to interpret the exercise of authority in a favorable light. . . . To do this, the exercise of authority is either denied altogether on the ground that the few merely order what the many want; or it is justified with the assertion that the few have qualities of excellence which enable them to realize the interests of the many."[13] The former is more typical of Russia and the East; the latter more typical of England and the West.

The prominent role of collectivistic values in Russian culture is reflected in the fact that industrial leadership is justified on the grounds that the leaders are only taking orders from the representatives of the people (i.e., the Party). In the more individualistic West, "authority in industry is justified explicitly on the ground that the man who already enjoys the good things in life has earned them and is entitled to the privileges they confer. Hence the employer's authority as well as his earnings and privileges are the rewards of past and present exertions."[14] This would suggest that the content of an ideology may be determined in part by the beliefs and values making up the general culture. Broad cultural themes like individualism and collectivism constitute the basic

---

[12] Stark, *op. cit.*
[13] Reinhard Bendix, *Work and Authority in Industry* (New York: John Wiley & Sons, Inc., 1956), p. 13.
[14] *Ibid.,* p. 11.

ingredients out of which more specific and formal systems of thought are created. There are, of course, other ingredients which may be just as important. In analyzing entrepreneurial ideologies of the sort described by Bendix, we would have to consider certain facts about the structure of the economy, the role of the government in industrial administration, certain historical events and figures, and so on. Knowing that Russian culture is and has been for many generations more collectivistic than American culture is not sufficient to explain the specific ideologies that emerged in the two societies. Without some awareness of the important differences between the two cultures, however, it is unlikely that we should get very far in understanding why the two ideologies appeared when and where they did.

The presence or absence of a cultural theme may have a lot to do with the emergence of a particular system of beliefs; it may also have a lot to do with whether or not that system of beliefs, once stated, gets widely accepted. The ability of a group (e.g., of managers) to get a specific set of beliefs (e.g., about authority) accepted by the population at large depends very much on the kinds of general beliefs and values which make up the culture of that population. Knowing what we do about the prominent role of collectivistic values in Russian culture, it seems quite unlikely that the ideological justifications for authority generally accepted in our own society would have much appeal in the Soviet Union. It is equally improbable that the attempt to justify authority on the grounds that "the few merely order what the many want" would be sympathetically received in the more individualistic West. The point hardly needs belaboring. The likelihood that a specific set of beliefs will be widely accepted in a population depends on the more basic beliefs and values which members of that population already endorse. These basic beliefs and values have their own roots in, among other things, present and past task experiences.

We have suggested two rather obvious ways in which the study of cultural beliefs and values (which is what we are interested in) is related to the study of specific systems of thought (the province of the sociology of knowledge). In the first place, the presence of certain beliefs and values in the general culture make it more or less likely that a specific system of ideas will emerge; in the second place, they make it more or less likely that those ideas, once articulated, will be widely accepted. To the extent that this is true, any successful attempt to account for variation in cultural beliefs and values constitutes a contribution (of an indirect sort) to the sociology of knowledge. It is less obvious that the sociology of knowledge (at least in its present state) has anything to contribute to the study of cultural beliefs and values. Until such time as it develops some sort of theoretical structure and an acceptable methodology, the sociology of knowledge is unlikely to have much of an impact on the mainstream of sociological thought. Paradigms are no substitutes for propositions; nor are insights, however imaginative, equivalent to empirical generalizations. At this point in time, the sociology of knowledge remains at the periphery of social science.

LEARNING THEORY

While the questions to which we have addressed ourselves have their origins in the sociology of knowledge, the theory we have presented owes much more to psychological learning theory. Our debt to learning theory is twofold. On the one hand, we have leaned heavily on the principle of reinforcement. On the other, we have assigned a prominent role to the concept of generalization.

We have assumed, to begin with, that behavior is some function of its consequences. Those acts or patterns of acts which get rewarded are most likely to be emitted again. Whether or not a pattern of behavior gets rewarded depends on the environmental conditions under which it is emitted. It is clear that the same piece of behavior may be rewarded in some settings and punished in others. We have made the assumption that the task involved has important implications for what kinds of behavior will be rewarded and punished. Those patterns of behavior which are instrumental to task success are most likely to be rewarded; once rewarded, they are likely to be repeated. Those forms of behavior which end in task failure have a low probability of being emitted again.

This much we have borrowed from reinforcement theory. What we have attempted to add is the notion that task behavior is the object of cognitive, cathectic, and evaluative orientations which, by virtue of their relationship to behavior, can be traced ultimately to the task situation. These beliefs, preferences, and values may be thought of as responses to the situation, but responses of a nonbehavioral sort. Because they are "mental" or covert responses, they are not conditionable in the same manner as the behavior which they take as their object. This is not to deny, of course, that beliefs, preferences, and values can be expressed verbally and that, in this form, they are subject to conditioning just like any other kind of behavior. Be that as it may, our theory deals not with the conditioning of verbalized beliefs, preferences, and values, but with the induction of these orientations from behavior.

The emergence of a set of orientations consistent with but distinct from overt behavior cannot be explained in traditional reinforcement terms. Just what mechanisms are involved we cannot say. In this regard, we have done little beyond pointing to the fact that these orientations do emerge in the process of operating on a task and that they tend to get generalized to other situations.

We have found the concept of generalization as developed in learning theory highly congenial to our own interests in analyzing the role of task experience in the formation of cultural beliefs, preferences, and values. Again, however, there is a difference in emphasis. The learning theorist is interested in the generalization of behavioral responses from one stimulus to another; we are interested in the generalization of beliefs, preferences, and values from one task situation to another. The underlying principle is nevertheless the same. In behavioral terms, it is said that the greater the similarity of a new stimulus to the one that was the occasion for the original reinforcement, the greater is the likelihood that the same response will be emitted. In terms of our own theory, we have suggested that the greater the similarity between two task situations, the more likely it is that orientations developed in one situation will generalize to the other. This is what we have called "lateral generalization," i.e., generalization from one specific stimulus-complex to another. We have hypothesized that generalization also proceeds vertically, i.e., along an inductive chain from the specific to the increasingly abstract. Here, too, it is clear that we owe much to the psychologists.

With respect to two principles, those of reinforcement and generalization, it can be said that our own theory constitutes an extension of learning theory into the realm of ideas. It is, however, an extension and not simply an application. If we can allow Skinner to speak for the learning theorists, we find little concern with ideas (e.g., beliefs and values) as phenomena distinct from behavior and interesting in their own right. The concept of value, for example, is reduced to "a way of describing what is either immediately or in the long run reinforcing to man." Skinner continues, "It is no accident that we use the same word 'good' for the coffee and crullers we had this morning and for the life we want to lead. Values are values because of certain properties of organisms. What has value for a horse does not necessarily have value for me. I do not relish uncooked oats and hay."[15]

Value, here, is employed as an independent rather than a dependent

---

[15] A comment by B. F. Skinner in the discussion, "Cultural Evolution as Viewed by Psychologists," *Daedalus*, Vol. 90 (1961), p. 576.

variable. Variation in values (we would substitute the term "prefer-ences") is to be used in explaining variation in behavior. Values (the things you want) reside in the organism. Horses like hay; people prefer ice cream. Nowhere do we find any concern with why people (let alone horses) differ in what they value. And this, of course, is the nub of the matter as far as we are concerned. Our own theory is designed to contribute to an explanation of why people differ in what they believe, value, and prefer in the world around them. Learning theory is relevant to this pursuit in that it can help us to explain behavior which is in-timately related to the development of beliefs, values, and preferences. Learning theory, however, has little to say directly about the develop-ment of such beliefs, values, and preferences. It is in this sense that we think of our own efforts as an extension of basic learning theory principles into an area (the area of ideas and attitudes) traditionally reserved for other disciplines.

It would be inaccurate, however, to think of this as a novel enterprise. Only recently, Alex Inkeles, a sociologist, has attempted to show how simple reinforcement principles can be used to explain cross-cultural similarities and differences in "perceptions, attitudes, and values."[16] His comparisons of attitude data taken from surveys carried out in several highly industrialized societies indicate that members of the different social classes stand in very much the same relationship to each other in all industrial societies, although societies as a whole differ significantly from one another. The explanation the author gives sounds very much like our own. He says, "It is assumed that people have ex-periences, develop attitudes, and form values in response to the forces or pressures which their environment creates. By 'environment' we mean, particularly, networks of interpersonal relations and the pat-terns of reward and punishment one normally experiences in them."[17]

A lower class American presumably faces pretty much the same kind of environment as his counterpart in Russia, Germany, Japan, or any other highly industrialized society. On the basis of this similarity in environment, it is to be expected that lower class members from all in-dustrial societies will endorse many of the same attitudes. Compared to members of the middle class, they prove to be less satisfied with their jobs, less concerned with getting ahead, more concerned with obedience in their children, less optimistic about the future, and so on. Just why all of this should be so, however, is never explained in systematic

---

[16] Alex Inkeles, "Industrial Man: The Relation of Status to Experience, Perception, and Value," *American Journal of Sociology*, Vol. 66 (1960), pp.1–31.

[17] *Ibid.*, p. 2.

terms. It is contended simply that "within broad limits, the same situational pressures, the same framework for living, will be experienced as similar and will *generate* the same or similar response by people from different countries."[18] Or, as Inkeles puts it later on, "men's environment, as expressed in the institutionalized patterns they adopt or have introduced to them, *shapes* their experience, and through this their perceptions, attitudes and values, in standardized ways which are manifest from country to country, despite the countervailing randomizing influence of traditional cultural patterns."[19] The latter phrase refers to the fact that the impact of environment on attitudes may be "muted" by long-standing, cultural ways of thinking.

While the Inkeles approach leaves much to be desired in its explanation of *how* environment acts upon attitudes, it does represent one of the few attempts to apply psychological principles to the understanding of broad, cultural and subcultural differences in what men believe, value, and prefer.

ATTITUDE THEORY

Where learning theory principles do find their way into the study of ideas, it tends to be at the level of specific opinions and preferences. This is the field of attitude research, a field ordinarily associated with social as opposed to experimental psychology. The term "attitude" is most often used to refer to what we have called "cathectic orientations" (preferences); it is employed somewhat less often to refer to orientations of a cognitive nature (beliefs), and only rarely to orientations involving a moral judgment (values). Despite this tendency to associate "attitudes" with preferences and/or beliefs, we shall use the term to refer to all three kinds of orientations: cathectic, cognitive, and evaluative. We do this for convenience of exposition. It is considerably easier to say "attitudes" than "beliefs, values and preferences." "Attitude," as we shall use it then, is simply a generic term for an individual's cognitive, cathectic, and evaluative orientations toward objects in his environment.

It is possible to distinguish three relatively independent approaches to the study of attitudes in contemporary social psychology. Only one of these (what might be called "instrumentality" theory) overlaps significantly with our own. The other two (communication-persuasion theory and balance theory) are not specifically designed (as is our own

---

[18] *Ibid.*, italics added.
[19] *Ibid.*, italics added.

theory) to explain where attitudes come from. A brief look at each of the three will help to make the differences clear.

Instrumentality Theory

By "instrumentality theories" we mean theories which view attitudes as dependent on the degree to which the object of the attitude is seen as instrumental in achieving some valued state or goal. Whether or not an object (person, thing, idea, etc.) is liked depends on whether or not it is perceived as having instrumental value in helping the individual to reach one or more of his goals. This implies, of course, that it is possible to change an individual's attitudes toward something by making that something appear either more or less instrumental to the achievement of some other goal.

One of the first models of this sort was proposed by Woodruff and DiVesta.[20] They found a correlation between attitude toward fraternities and degree to which subjects felt fraternities would help them achieve "their most cherished values." They also found that attitude toward (liking for) fraternities could be changed by presenting subjects with information designed to change the perceived instrumentality of fraternity life to the achievement of their own personal goals.

A study by Smith revealed that attitudes toward Russia were systematically related to the manner in which Russia was seen as affecting or engaging personal values (e.g., liberty).[21] The object here was to show how deep-seated, general values (e.g., liberty) were related to more specific preferences (i.e., liking for Russia).

Peak has also adopted an instrumentality theory of attitudes.[22] In one of her experiments, she successfully changed students' attitudes toward various academic policies (e.g., giving unannounced quizzes) by arousing (to various degrees) the perception of an instrumental relationship between the stated academic policy and the goal of getting good grades. She also found a relationship between *initial* instrumentality ratings and initial attitudes; that is, policies perceived as having good consequences were liked and vice versa.

Related studies by DiVesta and Merwin[23] and another by Carlson[24]

---

[20] A. D. Woodruff and F. J. DiVesta, "The Relationship Between Values, Concepts, and Attitudes," *Educational and Psychological Measurement*, Vol. 8 (1948), pp. 645–59.

[21] M. B. Smith, "Personal Values as Determinants of a Political Attitude," *Journal of Psychology*, Vol. 28 (1949), pp. 477–86.

[22] Helen Peak, "The Effect of Aroused Motivation on Attitudes," *Journal of Abnormal and Social Psychology*, Vol. 61 (1960), pp.463–68.

[23] F. J. DiVesta and J. C. Merwin, "The Effects of Need-Oriented Communications on Attitude Change," *Journal of Abnormal and Social Psychology*, Vol. 60 (1960), pp. 80–85.

[24] E. R. Carlson, "Attitude Change Through Modification of Attitude Structure," *Journal of Abnormal and Social Psychology*, Vol. 52 (1956), pp. 256–61.

have yielded similar results. DiVesta and Merwin found that attitudes toward teaching as a career could be changed by altering the perceived instrumentality of teaching in fulfilling individual needs of the subjects. Carlson found that attitudes toward integrated housing could be changed by altering the perceived relationship between integration and other values of the subjects.

There are others that might be cited. Those already mentioned should be sufficient to impart the general flavor of the instrumentality approach. The approach is especially relevant here because, in some ways, it sounds a lot like our own. In our own theory we start with the assumption that in any task situation some forms of behavior will have greater instrumental reward value than others. In general, those with the greatest instrumental reward value have the greatest probability of being emitted. These are the same forms of behavior which tend to be perceived as instrumental for task success (cognitive orientation). Because they are rewarded, they also become more intrinsically enjoyable. In time, they become defined as appropriate or morally desirable. Stated a bit differently, we hold attitudes (the three orientations) to be some function of the relationship between the object of the attitude and some valued state or goal. If co-operation is instrumental to achieving task success (and the things that are attendant upon success, e.g., money, promotion, pride, etc.), it will be perceived as important for solving the task, cathected as intrinsically enjoyable, and evaluated as legitimate and appropriate. Attitudes toward co-operation can thus be explained in terms of the object of the attitude (co-operation) and the individual goals (success) to which it is instrumentally related.

There are nevertheless important differences between instrumentality theory and our own. We are primarily interested in the origins of attitudes; more specifically, we want to find out to what extent attitude differences (between individuals or between whole societies) can be traced to variation in task experience. It is specifically the task and other elements in the task situation that we take as the most immediate determinants of the instrumental reward value of a given form of behavior. Our theory is thus tied to one kind of experience, namely task experience.

Researchers who have used the instrumentality approach have made no attempt to specify the variables that determine *what* will be perceived as instrumental to individual goals. In the studies cited, subjects were exposed to some kind of persuasive communication designed to change their perceptions of the relationship between some object (e.g., unannounced quizzes) and their personal goals (e.g., high grades). Subjects were simply *told*, in other words, that unannounced quizzes were helpful in getting good grades. The researchers were interested in finding out whether or not this would lead subjects to change their attitudes toward (liking for) unannounced quizzes. There is no attempt here, as in our own task theory, to specify the conditions under which an individual will come to perceive one way of doing things as any more instrumental than another. This theory, at least in its present state, is not designed to explain how attitudes originate but how they change as a result of exposure to some sort of communication. In this sense, instrumentality theory (and practice) can be seen as part of that more inclusive body of thought which we have earlier referred to as communications-persuasion theory.

Communications-Persuasion Theory

While there clearly exists a body of thought dealing with communication and persuasion, it is perhaps premature to speak of it as a theory. What we have can best be described as a collection of empirical generalizations loosely organized around a very simple learning model. Most studies in this area, despite their very real differences, are designed to specify the conditions under which persuasive communications are successful. In their efforts to isolate all relevant conditions, researchers have brought their experimental tools to bear upon such variables as personality, credibility of the communicator, order of presentation, complexity of issue, intensity of arousal, original position, and a host of others.[25]

Whatever the specific condition involved, it is assumed that subjects can be induced to change their attitudes by presenting them with new information which is then "averaged in" with attitudes already held. The process has been described by Brehm and Cohen as a "judgmental" one,[26] meaning that the individual attempts to assess new information in terms of existing cognitions and come up with some sort of compromise solution. This makes communications-persuasion theory similar to ours in one sense and very different in another.

The two theories (communications-persuasion and our own) are similar in that they both view the process of attitude change as a learning process. The main difference lies in the kind of learning involved. In persuasion theory, the individual learns by assimilating a communication expressly designed to change his attitudes. In our own

---

[25] For an early summary of work in this field see C. I. Hovland, I. L. Janis, and H. H. Kelley, *Communication and Persuasion* (New Haven: Yale University Press, 1953).

[26] Jack W. Brehm and Arthur R. Cohen, *Explorations in Cognitive Dissonance* (New York: John Wiley & Sons, Inc., 1962), pp. 105 ff.

theory, the individual learns by doing, i.e., by working on a task. In the former, overt reference is made to the attitude involved; the object is to persuade through communication. In the latter, there is no need for any verbal reference to the attitude involved; it is held that attitudes have their roots in task experience.

What we are suggesting is that there are at least two different sources of attitude formation and change, persuasive communications and task experience. Of all the differences between the two, one stands out above all the rest. Communication theory is concerned with the *diffusion* of ideas; we are interested in their *origin*. In persuasion studies, it is taken as given that someone has a set of attitudes which he is trying to communicate to someone else. It might be a parent trying to socialize his child, a political figure trying to indoctrinate his audience, or, more frequently, an experimenter attempting to change the opinions of his subjects. In any event, there already exists a set of attitudes which is to be communicated. The communications researcher is not interested in where the original attitudes came from; his job is to find out under what conditions the communication will have its optimal effect. He is primarily interested in the diffusion of attitudes, from one generation to the next, from one person to another.

While we recognize that any general theory of attitudes will have to deal with both the origin and diffusion of ideas, our present interests are confined to the former. The theory we have developed represents an attempt to explain where beliefs, values, and preferences come from; it takes for granted the fact that attitudes, once formed out of task experience, will be transmitted to other people. Our theory is directed to the process by which attitudes are created; we leave to others the study of how attitudes, once articulated, get diffused throughout the social system.

This distinction between origins and diffusion, however clear it might be to us, is sometimes obscured (and here we are thinking of our students) by the fact that our own studies, like those of the communications researchers, are actually studies in attitude *change*. It might be contended that if we were really interested in the origins rather than the diffusion of attitudes, we should not be studying attitude change but rather the creation of attitudes where none previously existed. The contention is analytically sound but methodologically naïve. To study the creation of attitudes directly, we should have to find subjects who had no attitudes (e.g., no thoughts on individualism) to begin with. This is next to impossible. The only reasonable solution is to take subjects with already formed attitudes, expose them to a certain kind of task experience, and see if their attitudes change. The experiments to be reported later all follow this pattern. While such a design does not deal directly with the origins of attitudes, it does allow us to make reasonable inferences to this effect. The point to be made is that the superficial similarity between persuasion research and our own (both involving the study of attitude change) should not be allowed to obscure the fact that two radically different questions are involved, one concerning the conditions under which an attitude is originally formed, the other the conditions under which an attitude is successfully communicated from one person to another.

Balance Theory

Most of the balance theories are descended in some way from Heider's original formulation.[27] What they have in common is the notion that beliefs, values, and preferences are all part of an attitude *system,* with the implication that a change in one element of the system will precipitate predictable changes in other parts of the system. It is assumed that incongruence between two or more elements in the system will lead to an attempt to restore equilibrium or balance through the modification of existing elements or the incorporation of new elements into the system.

It should be noted that the methodology used in testing theories of this sort overlaps considerably with that ordinarily employed in the communication-persuasion experiments. Incongruence is often created by exposing the subject to new information which contradicts his previously held attitudes. The subject is then observed to see what changes he makes in other beliefs, values, and preferences as he goes about trying to accommodate the new information to an ongoing system of attitudes. This is not to say that all studies in this area utilize the same technique. Rosenberg, for example, presents evidence showing that *hypnotically* induced changes in the liking for an object lead to a change in beliefs about the object.[28]

The fact remains, however, that the method most often used to create incongruence or imbalance involves making an overt, verbal reference to one or more of the attitudes in the system. In other words, the sub-

---

[27] F. Heider, "Attitudes and Cognitive Organization," *Journal of Psychology,* Vol. 21 (1946), pp. 107–12. See also: C. E. Osgood and P. H. Tannenbaum, "The Principle of Congruity in the Prediction of Attitude Change," *Psychological Review,* Vol. 62, (1955), pp. 42–55; Leon Festinger, *A Theory of Cognitive Dissonance* (Evanston, Ill.: Row, Peterson & Co., 1957); Milton J. Rosenberg *et al., Attitude Organization and Change* (New Haven: Yale University Press, 1960).

[28] Milton J. Rosenberg, "An Analysis of Affective-Cognitive Consistency," in Rosenberg *et al., op. cit.,* pp. 15–64.

ject is *told* something by the experimenter, just as in the communi-cations-persuasion experiment discussed earlier. The two approaches differ in that persuasion theory is interested in the impact of the stim-ulus on the attitude to which it actually refers whereas balance theory is more concerned with the indirect effect of the communication on other elements in the attitude system. Both differ from our own ap-proach, once again, in that no attempt is made to explain how attitudes are created.

There is one version of balance theory, however, which is different enough from the others to warrant a closer look, namely "cognitive dissonance" theory. According to Brehm and Cohen, dissonance theory is uniquely qualified to explain those cases of "imbalance" involving a definite behavioral commitment. To commit oneself is to choose one alternative over another. Having chosen, one is often faced with cognitions (e.g., facts) that are incongruent or dissonant with the choice made. Sometimes it is possible to relieve the dissonance by re-versing the decision, i.e., by "uncommitting" oneself. Where this is too difficult, dissonance can be reduced by changing the cognitions which are at odds with the commitment. This may involve convincing oneself for example, that a given pattern of behavior, idea, object, or person is really not so bad after all.

As Brehm and Cohen put it, "dissonance processes have the flavor of an either-or phenomenon."[29] A decision is made and the individual has to live with it. There is no going back. Any cognitions that are dissonant with this commitment have to be "readjusted." It should be clear that our own theory has quite a different flavor. Commitment plays a very minor role. The idea that one is "stuck" with an imperfect choice and has to make the best of it is missing altogether. The process by which attitudes are formed out of experience on a task has more the flavor of a rational, problem-solving exercise. The emphasis is not on dissonance reduction but on learning, more specifically learning by do-ing. Basically, what this involves is the processing of task feedback and the assimilation of findings into an a priori attitude system.

Brehm and Cohen refer to this as a "judgmental process" which they distinguish from those processes involving dissonance reduction. In the judgmental process, "any incoming bit of information is given its due, and the individual makes some compromise judgment between the in-formation and his existing cognitions or between bits of information in-consistent with each other and with his existing cognitions. The analogy here is to some estimate he makes of all the various cognitions, to some

---

[29] Brehm and Cohen, *op. cit.*, p. 106.

arithmetic average of his cognitions."[30] The dissonance process, on the other hand, hinges on a clear-cut commitment. Once the individual has committed himself, he "cannot process information and make some compromise judgment; he must accommodate his cognitions to his commitment."[31]

Although this description of the "judgmental process" was written with communications-persuasion theory in mind, it applies to our own theory as well. Like the persuasion studies in which subjects are given a lecture, shown a movie, etc., the experiments described later in this book are basically exercises in learning, with the important difference that it is learning from task experience rather than learning from the written or spoken word. In either case, cognitive dissonance theory has little to contribute.

There are two other considerations which should be mentioned, both of which emphasize the fact that cognitive dissonance theory and our own task theory are designed to explain two different kinds of phenomena. According to dissonance theory, an individual will suffer dissonance and reduce it through attitude change if he simply *commits* himself to doing something disagreeable; it is not necessary that he act upon his decision. Brehm and Cohen report evidence indicating that this is in fact the case.[32] Our own theory would predict (1) that no attitude change will take place until the individual has become actively engaged in performing his task and (2) that the longer he works at it (up to a point) the greater will be its effect on his attitudes.

The other difference concerns rewards. One of the most nonobvious features of dissonance theory is that it predicts (and successfully so) that an individual who is highly rewarded for committing himself to a disagreeable chore (e.g., writing an essay against his private view on some issue) will change less (toward that view) than a person who is given a paltry reward for doing the same thing.[33] Any reward given will be consonant with the decision to write the essay. The greater the reward given, the less dissonance there will be to reduce. The less dissonance there is, the less need there will be for a change in attitudes. Our own theory predicts just the opposite, namely that the more highly a person is rewarded for performing a task in a certain way, the *more* his attitudes will change in the direction of favoring the rewarded behavior.

---

[30] *Ibid.*
[31] *Ibid.*
[32] *Ibid.*, pp. 115–16.
[33] *Ibid.*, pp. 73–78.

These are both important differences. Taken together they leave little doubt that cognitive dissonance theory and our own theory are directed to two very different kinds of events. Put simply, one is a decision theory, the other a modified learning theory. The fact that they appear to lead to contrary predictions implies no conflict; they are not intended to explain the same phenomena.

CONCLUSIONS

Our theory of attitude formation and change emerges directly from reinforcement theory. It is our contention that the principles of reinforcement and generalization which are ordinarily invoked to explain the shaping of behavior can be extended to account for the formation of beliefs, values, and preferences. The application of learning principles to the study of attitudes is not entirely new. In our brief review of attitude theories we came across one approach (instrumentality theory) which has fairly obvious ties to learning theory and another (communications-persuasion) where the ties exist but are less clearly articulated. In neither case, however, nor in the third set of theories discussed (balance theories) did we find any real interest in accounting for the nonverbal origins of an individual's beliefs, values, and preferences.

The only people who have demonstrated a continuing, theoretical interest in the origins of ideas are those sociologists, social philosophers, and historians who work in the area traditionally known as the sociology of knowledge. The problem here, however, is the almost total lack of any systematic theory or body of principles which might be used to generate specific, testable propositions. It is unlikely, however, that this state of affairs will last forever. In addition to theories of their own making, sociologists have much to gain from the borrowing of principles employed in other branches of the behavioral sciences. Certain elements in learning theory, duly elaborated to fit the social setting, may provide an appropriate foothold in some cases.[34] Our own efforts have been directed to this end. While it is impossible to overlook the difficulties involved in applying a rather simple set of psychological principles to the study of very abstract ideas, we are convinced that this is at least a strategic place to begin.

---

[34] For one of the best examples of what can be done, see George C. Homans, *Social Behavior: Its Elementary Forms* (New York: Harcourt, Brace & World, Inc., 1961).

CHAPTER 3

The Wisconsin Experiment

THE STUDY to be reported here (Wisconsin, 1961) was the first, the most complex, and the least successful of the seven we conducted. Like the others to follow, it represents an attempt to change beliefs, values, and preferences through systematic variation in task experience. Unlike our subsequent experiments, it was not originally designed with this purpose in mind. In the beginning, we were primarily interested in learning more about the major determinants of social structure in small groups. Our interest in attitudes did not develop until later.

In its original conception, the study was designed to test a number of propositions relating situational variables on the one hand to social structural variables on the other. With one eye to the literature and another to the facilities at hand, we settled on four situational variables (task, incentive system, homogeneity, and group size) and two dimensions of social structure (leadership and solidarity). The assumption was made that each of the situational variables would have implications for both dimensions of group structure.

It was not until the basic design of the experiment had been worked out that we became interested in the possibility (1) that subjects' attitudes would change as a result of exposure to experimental conditions and (2) that those changes could be predicted from the four situational variables referred to above. Although in the beginning this interest in attitude change was little more than an appendage to the main body of the study, it very soon became our primary concern.

THEORY

Social Structure

Bales' early work was especially useful in helping us to decide which dimensions of group structure to isolate for experimental purposes. His own efforts at specifying "the most general or universal kinds of differentiations which exist or develop between persons as concrete units in small groups" resulted in a set of four dimensions: (1) access to resources, (2) control, (3) prestige, and (4) solidarity.[1] Access to resources refers primarily to the distribution of property and as such has only limited applicability in the small group setting. Stratification in terms of importance or prestige, while obviously relevant to the analysis of group structure, is a more complex variable resting in part on the first two. To some extent, for example, differences in the distribution of prestige reflect differences in the distribution of control.

Control and solidarity would seem to be more fundamental, more easily conceptualized than either of the other two. That many others feel the same way is evidenced by the growing number of research papers on what most authors tend to call "leadership" and "cohesiveness." In many studies, leadership (control) and cohesiveness (solidarity) are treated as independent variables, to be used in accounting for variation in subsequent measures of productivity, satisfaction, and the like. In other settings, however, they have been taken as problematical, as variables to be explained in their own right. It is these latter studies which are most relevant to our own interests.

Social structure can be defined in either normative or behavioral terms. *Solidarity,* at the normative or institutional level, consists of an obligation and a right: "the obligation to identify one's self cognitively, affectively, and conatively with the other, to perceive one's self as a part of a larger whole, to feel the other's concerns as one's own, to cooperate with the other, to share the other's fate; and the right to expect these attitudes and actions from the others."[2] In behavioral terms, solidarity takes the form of acts of affection, encouragement, and cooperation as well as verbal expressions of identification with other group members.

Control refers to one person's ability or right to influence the activities of another person or set of persons. In some groups, members are highly differentiated with respect to the degree of control which they exercise over each other; in other groups, members share equally in the process, i.e., no one exerts any more influence than any one else. In general, groups can be thought of as making up a continuum based on the degree to which control is *centralized.* It is the centralization of control rather than control itself which represents the social structural analogue of our first dimension, solidarity.

---

[1] Robert F. Bales, *Interaction Process Analysis* (Cambridge, Mass.: Addison-Wesley Press, Inc., 1950), p. 73.

[2] *Ibid.,* p. 79.

Whether or not there is any systematic relationship between solidarity and centralization of control is unclear. Groups high on solidarity can apparently be either centralized (e.g., a squad in combat) or equalitarian (e.g., an adolescent clique), but is it possible for a group with a highly centralized control structure to be low on solidarity? Common sense would suggest that some degree of institutionalized co-operation is necessary before an authority structure could develop. It is also likely, as Bales argues, that "if status differences increase for any reason, such as an increase of differences between persons in degree of property or authority, these differentials between persons will tend to conflict with their basic solidarity."[3] In lieu of systematic data, perhaps the most reasonable assumption we can make is that low solidarity inhibits the emergence of centralization and that an elaborate control system inhibits the growth of solidarity. Otherwise the relationship is indeterminate.

Groups differ markedly in how closely knit (solidary) and authoritarian (centralized) they are. There are many reasons why this should be so. In this particular study, we decided to work with four variables, each of which was thought to have implications for both dimensions of social structure. The choice of these four in particular was dictated by several considerations: (1) relevance for both solidarity and centralization, (2) perceived importance in the amount of variance they would account for, (3) operational feasibility.

Task. In their own discussion of tasks and group structure, Thibaut and Kelley speak of *conjunctive* tasks (synchronized efforts of several individuals required for success) and *disjunctive* tasks (can be solved as long as one individual makes the right response).[4] There is good reason to believe that this distinction has implications for both solidarity and the centralization of control. With respect to the former, we can assume that where the co-ordination of several individual efforts has high instrumental reward value, it will be "to the ultimate advantage of every person in the group to have the obligation to co-operate and to subordinate individualized interests made explicit and a matter of legitimate expectations."[5] Other things being equal, groups which are confronted with conjunctive tasks are more apt to develop a solidary social structure than those engaged in disjunctive tasks.

With respect to our second dimension of social structure, it is clear

[2] *Ibid.*, p. 79.
[4] John W. Thibaut and Harold H. Kelley, *The Social Psychology of Groups* (New York: John Wiley & Sons, Inc., 1959) p. 162–64.
[5] Bales, *op. cit.*, p. 79.

that conjunctive tasks favor the centralization of control. To the extent that success requires the synchronization of several different activities, it will be to the advantage of all concerned to co-ordinate these activities "by coming to an agreement that some person or persons shall be given the right to control the activities of those persons who are addressing their efforts directly to the task."[6] A highly centralized control structure is most likely where co-ordination has high instrumental reward value. Whether or not co-ordination is necessary for success will depend, in turn, on the nature of the task.

Incentive System. Operations on a task can be expected to lead to certain outcomes. In the language adopted by Thibaut and Kelley, outcomes are *correspondent* when "the task requirements they must meet in order to achieve A's best outcomes are identical with the requirements to be met for B's best outcomes."[7] Conversely, noncorrespondence of outcomes exists when the operations necessary for one member to maximize his outcomes interfere with another member's chances of maximizing his own. Where outcomes are correspondent, as in a group incentive, there is good reason for group members to help each other, since everyone succeeds or fails together. On the other hand, there is little instrumental reward value in co-operation for those who face a situation in which success for one member means failure for another. Holding other things constant, then, we would expect to find greater solidarity among individuals facing correspondent outcomes than among those whose outcomes are noncorrespondent.

There is some reason to believe, although the evidence is not entirely convincing, that the incentive system has implications for the centralization of control as well. Deutsch, for example, has argued that under conditions of co-operation (correspondence of outcomes) individual group members will be more willing to let the most able members lead since, unlike the competitive situation, all share equally in whatever rewards are attained regardless of differences in individual contribution.[8] Under competitive conditions, no one will be allowed to assume a position of dominance over the others.

Group Size. Small groups are apt to be more closely knit (solidary) than large ones.[9] The explanation lies not so much in the greater re-

[6] *Ibid.,* p. 76.

[7] Thibaut and Kelley, *op. cit.,* p. 165.

[8] Morton Deutsch, "The Effects of Cooperation and Competition upon Group Process," in Dorwin Cartwright and Alvin Zander, *Group Dynamics* (Evanston, Ill.: Row, Peterson & Co., 1960), pp. 414–48.

[9] See, for example, Stanley Seashore, *Group Cohesiveness in the Industrial Work Group* (Ann Arbor: Survey Research Center, Institute for Social Research, University of Michigan, 1954).

ward value of co-operation in the small group setting as in the greater opportunity for interaction. Members of small groups are in a better position to get to know each other well. Assuming, with Homans,[10] that an increase in interaction generally leads to an increase in liking, it is reasonable to expect that small groups will be more cohesive in their sentiments while showing greater solidarity in their behavior.

The relationship between group size and centralization of control is relatively straightforward. We already have evidence from several sources to the effect that large groups are more centralized than small ones.[11] This makes good sense if we can assume, as most would, that the instrumental reward value of co-ordination increases with an expansion in the number of group members.

Homogeneity. Although the evidence is sketchy, there is some reason to believe that the more similar group members are with respect to the attributes they bring into the situation, the more likely it is that they will develop a closely knit group structure.[12] In part, this is due to the fact that, being similar, they have something to gain from co-operating with each other. However, the proposition need not be explained in terms of rewards or gains. Whyte suggests, as did Bales in an earlier quote (page 47), that people with similar personal and social characteristics "will tend to view the world around them in similar terms, and this will facilitate cohesive group action."[13] Whether we see the relationship in instrumental or perceptual terms, there is good reason to believe that, other things being equal, homogeneity leads to solidarity.

Homogeneity may also have implications for the centralization of control. We refer here to homogeneity in those skills and traits which are relevant to the achievement of group goals. A clear-cut differentiation of group members with respect to control is most likely, holding other things equal, where the individuals involved differ radically in their task-related abilities. The assumption is, of course, that the member or members with the most ability will end up wielding the greatest amount of influence. Conversely, we can expect to find the least cen-

---

[10] George C. Homans, *The Human Group* (New York: Harcourt, Brace & Co., 1950), pp. 110–13. For supporting evidence, see Muzafer Sherif *et al., Intergroup Conflict and Cooperation* (Norman, Okla.: Institute of Group Relations, University of Oklahoma, 1961).

[11] R. F. Bales, F. L. Strodtbeck, T. M. Mills, and Mary Roseborough, "Channels of Communication in Small Groups," *American Sociological Review,* Vol. 16 (1951), pp. 461–68. See also J. K. Hemphill, "Relations Between the Size of the Group and the Behavior of 'Superior' Leaders," *Journal of Social Psychology,* Vol. 32 (1950), pp. 11–22.

[12] Some of the evidence we do have is summarized by William F. Whyte in *Men at Work* (Homewood, Ill.: Dorsey Press, Inc., 1961), pp. 540–42. For another brief review see David Krech, Richard S. Crutchfield, and Egerton L. Ballachey, *Individual in Society* (New York: McGraw-Hill, 1962), pp. 463–64.

[13] Whyte, *op. cit.,* p. 543.

tralization of control in those groups whose members are most similar in those traits directly relevant to task success.

Attitudes

Task, incentive system, group size, and homogeneity are all features of the task situation; solidarity and centralization of control are patterns of behavior representing responses to that situation. Although behavior is the most obvious response to any situation, there are other ways of responding that are just as important from our own point of view.

A person confronted with a situation in which a particular form of behavior has very obvious instrumental reward value can be expected to develop a set of beliefs, preferences, and values vis-à-vis the situation in which that pattern of behavior is seen in a very favorable light. Over time, orientations developed in response to a specific task setting will be generalized to a much broader range of phenomena. Behavior which is seen as effective, enjoyable, and morally desirable in one specific situation will tend, over time, to be seen the same way *generally*.

With respect to our first dimension (solidarity), it seems likely that persons who adapt to the demands of the task situation by developing a network of highly solidary relationships will over time come to share a more positive orientation to the general idea of working together, co-operating with others, and identifying with other group members. Having found it in their immediate interests to co-operate, they will come to think of this way of behaving as effective, enjoyable, and normatively desirable—not simply with respect to the task at hand, but in general.

A similar case can be made for the control dimension. Under those conditions (task, incentive system, etc.) where a highly centralized control system is necessary for success, individuals will not only learn to organize themselves in a hierarchical manner, but beyond this to "appreciate" more fully the value of an authoritarian form of social organization. Having been rewarded for adopting a centralized leadership structure in one situation, they will come to share a more favorable set of attitudes toward authority in general.

In experimental terms, this kind of analysis implies that if you confront a group of subjects with a combination of situational variables (task, incentive system, group size, and homogeneity) favorable to a particular pattern of behavior, they will *change* their general beliefs, preferences, and values in a way which reflects the form of behavior adopted. Subjects, for example, who are exposed to a situation involving a *conjunctive task,* a *group incentive system,* a *small group membership,* and a *high degree of similarity* among members should not only develop a highly solidary social structure but should also become more favorable in their attitudes toward co-operation, whatever the situation. With respect to the second dimension, subjects who are asked to work on a *conjunctive task,* under a *group incentive,* where the *group is large,* and *heterogeneous in membership* can be expected to develop a relatively well-centralized control system *and* become more positive in their beliefs, preferences, and values toward the notion of centralization of control defined broadly.

The model employed here is a modified reinforcement one. Whether or not a pattern of behavior is adopted depends on the extent to which it is rewarded. Other things being equal, the more highly a person is rewarded for behaving in a certain way, the more positive will be his beliefs, preferences, and values with respect to that pattern of behavior. In dynamic terms, the more he is rewarded, the more positive his attitudes will *become.* If, on the contrary, he is actually *punished* for behaving in a certain way, he will change his attitudes in the opposite direction. For example, in a classroom situation which "calls" for close co-operation, a student who is highly rewarded will become more positive in his attitudes toward co-operation, whereas the student who is punished (i.e., receives a failing grade) can be expected to change in the other direction.

Religion

In the process of making predictions for the two kinds of attitude change referred to above, the thought occurred to us that religious beliefs might be affected by the systematic variation of situational conditions. We started with the assumption that the individual's relationship with God is an *interpersonal* relationship. As such it has much in common with the relationships we often study in sociology, those between one individual and another. While our theory concerns the latter, we propose that it can be generalized to the former. We propose, more specifically, that the same combination of situational variables which favors the centralization of control will also favor belief in a personal God.

God is an authority figure. He is the perfect leader, all-knowing, all-powerful, merciful, and just. Yet not everyone is convinced that he exists. In any attempt to account for this variation, there are a number of factors that would have to be considered: indoctrination by parents, persuasion on the part of teachers and peers, personality differences, and the like. It is possible as well that those who believe in God are those to whom God has revealed himself. Beyond all of these explanations we would suggest that the idea of a transcendental, omnipotent God is favored by the experience of being reinforced, in the secular world, for accepting or participating in a highly centralized leadership structure. We have already argued that certain situational conditions (conjunctive task, large group, etc.) will lead to the centralization of control at the social structural level and to a change in attitudes favoring authority at the cultural level. What we are proposing here is that the predicted change in attitudes toward authority will generalize ultimately to the belief in God's existence.

In some sense, a person who believes in God is more authoritarian than one who doesn't. For the atheist, man is capable of, or should, or has to solve his problems on his own. There is no omnipotent, omniscient Supreme Being to whom he can look for support, guidance, or direction. Such a belief is more likely to develop, other things being equal, in a setting where an equalitarian, leaderless structure has proven to be the most efficient way of organizing interpersonal relations. It is here that people will be rewarded for getting along without a strong, powerful figure on whom they can rely for support and direction. Holding a host of other factors constant, we would contend that by virtue of this secular experience such people are less likely to accept or invent the idea of a divine, Supreme Being whose will is absolute and inscrutable.

ATTITUDE QUESTIONNAIRE

Although it seems more appropriate to talk about the propositions and their rationale before discussing the actual measures employed, it does not, in this case, do justice to the role which our attitude measures played in formulating the propositions in the first place. At the time we were designing the original part of the experiment (that dealing solely with behavior) we had in front of us a copy of the Bales and Couch "Value Profile," a Likert-type questionnaire made up of over 200 items dealing with a wide variety of topics.[14] Of special interest was the factor analysis of this questionnaire which revealed the following factors: (1) *acceptance of authority* (best item: "Obedience and respect for authority are the most important virtues children should learn."); (2) *need-determined expression versus value-determined restraint* ("Since there are no values that can be eternal, the only real values

[14] Robert F. Bales and Arthur S. Couch, "The Value Profile: A Factor Analytic Study of Value Statements," unpublished paper, 1959.

are those which meet the needs of the given moment."); (3) *equalitarianism* ("Everyone should have an equal chance and an equal say.") ; (4) *individualism* ("It is the man who stands alone who excites our admiration.").

The possibility of getting attitude change along with differences in behavior was first suggested by the resemblance between two of the dimensions in the Value Profile (individualism and equalitarianism) and our own two behavioral variables (solidarity and centralization of control.) From a careful reading of the item content of the two value factors, we concluded that these were the *cultural* equivalents of solidarity and centralization of control, which are *social structure* variables. Individualism, for example, can be thought of as a very abstract set of ideas about solidarity. Most of the items highly loaded on this dimension suggest the common theme of "going it alone" in life, being independent, standing on one's own two feet, etc. Solidarity, it will be recalled from an earlier discussion, involves the related notions of identification with the group, co-operation, and the subordination of individual interests to the welfare of fellow group members. The fact that, so defined, individualism and solidarity appear to be opposites is due simply to Bales' choice of one end of the continuum for labeling purposes and our own previous choice of the other end. It is clear that we are tapping the same dimension at two different levels—the levels of culture and social structure.

A similar cultural analogue can be found for our second social structural variable, centralization of control. At first glance it appeared that either factor I (acceptance of authority) or factor III (equalitarianism) might be appropriate. A more careful reading of the items, however, convinced us that factor I, despite the presence of the word "authority" in the label, was only peripherally related to our own concept of centralization. Bales' factor I contains a wide variety of statements dealing with tolerance, conventionality, aggression, patriotism, sexuality—in fact most of the subareas measured by the California F scale.[15] It is not surprising, then, that the F scale (included as a marker variable) has a loading of .90 on factor I.[16]

While it was conceivable that we could get change on factor I, it seemed much more likely that, if we were fortunate enough to get any change at all, it would be on items similar to those in Bales' third factor (equalitarianism). There are items in this factor as well, however,

---

[15] T. W. Adorno, *et al., The Authoritarian Personality* (New York: Harper & Bros., 1950).

[16] Bales and Couch, *op. cit.,* p. 11.

which bear little or no resemblance to the problem of centralization of control (e.g., "It is the duty of every good citizen to correct anti-minority remarks made in his presence."). There are others, on the other hand, which are very clearly relevant (e.g., "A group of equals will work a lot better than a group with a rigid hierarchy."). What we did was to select all those statements that had something to say about the distribution of control and then fill in the rest of the scale with items of our own.

In adding items of our own invention to both factor I and factor III in the Value Profile, we were guided by Parsons' analysis of culture in terms of its cognitive, cathectic, and evaluative components.[17] It wasn't so much that we felt bound to use any particular classification of cultural elements, but simply that the system helped us to systematize the oftentimes chaotic process of operationalizing an ideological concept. Our motives were twofold. We wanted, on the one hand, to cover the two dimensions of individualism and equalitarianism as exhaustively as possible. Thinking in terms of three kinds of items (cognitive, cathectic, and evaluative) made this considerably easier. Beyond this, we were attracted by the possibility that certain kinds of items would reveal more change than others in the experiment (we might, for example, get very significant change on our cognitive items and none at all on the evaluative ones). At the time, this seemed like a potentially significant bit of exploration that might have implications for later theory building.

A cathectic (or affective) orientation to something involves the notion of liking versus disliking. Thus our cathectic items were usually prefaced with phrases such as "I like groups where . . .," "I would prefer . . .," or "I would find it frustrating to . . .," etc. The object of the orientation in each case is a way of behaving, or relating to other people—a way of organizing interpersonal relationships. On one dimension the statements dealt with the choice between independence and interdependence while on the other they involved questions of leadership and participation. In either case the respondent was asked to tell us how much he liked or disliked the relationship involved.

Approximately a third of the items in the original questionnaire were written in the form of beliefs, i.e., existential statements about the nature of things, in this case the relative efficiency of organizing groups one way rather than another. These were our cognitive items. They dealt not so much with liking or disliking but with truth. They took the form of axioms, propositions, and empirical generalizations. As

[17] See Chapter I for fuller discussion of these terms.

such, they differed as well from our third class of statements, the evaluative or normative ones. Items in this third category referred to the moral desirability of a given form of behavior. Each statement involved the question of whether one should or should not behave in a certain way.

In its final form, the questionnaire contained 70 items, 30 devoted to individualism, another 30 to equalitarianism, and ten to religion. Within each of the two sets of 30, ten were written in the cathectic mode, ten in the cognitive mode, and ten in the evaluative mode. With-in each set of ten half were worded positively (e.g., in favor of individualism), the other five negatively. The response form for each statement was made up of six categories: Strongly Disagree, Disagree, Slightly Disagree, Slightly Agree, Agree, Strongly Agree. Each category was assigned a numerical value ranging from one to seven. The value of four was assigned when no response was given.

The questionnaire was administered twice to the same population, once at the beginning of the term and again at the end. A factor analysis was performed using the raw scores of all subjects for both administrations of the questionnaire. Since the computer program available at that time could take only 40 variables, it was decided to treat the religious items separately and to drop the 20 items with the lowest interitem correlations. Five factors were extracted (centroid method) and rotated (quartimax). Factors I and III (both dealing with individualism) were reduced to a single dimension through further rotation; the same was done for the two equalitarianism factors (II and IV). The last factor was dropped altogether. Internal consistencies for the two remaining factor scales were estimated at .85 (individualism) and .79 (equalitarianism).[18]

A similar estimate for the ten-item theism scale yielded a consistency of .87. The items making up each of the three scales are shown in Exhibit A at the end of this chapter.

To get a measure of change on each of the two dimensions, the following procedure was adopted: First, raw scores on the *before* questionnaire were converted to scores standardized separately for each in-

---

[18] In computing a measure of internal consistency for each of the two scales, we included all items with a factor loading of .30 or better. The formula used was:

$$r_{aa} = \frac{a r_{11}}{1 + (a-1)\, r_{11}} \qquad \text{where } r_{aa}$$

is the internal consistency of a composite, r_{11} is the average intercorrelation of the separate items in the composite and a is the number of items in the composite. Taken from C. C. Peters and W. R. Van Voorhis, *Statistical Procedures and their Mathematical Bases* (New York: McGraw-Hill, 1940), p. 194.

dividual. This was done in order to control for the well-known fact that individuals vary widely in their use of the response form provided. For a person whose responses range all the way from Strongly Disagree to Strongly Agree, a shift from Slightly Agree to Agree may be inconsequential. For a person, however, whose responses are compressed between Slightly Disagree and Agree, the same shift would be a highly significant one. By standardizing each individual's scores on his *own* distribution of responses, such differences can be taken into account.

Our second step consisted of doing the same thing for the *after* questionnaire. It is possible, although perhaps not too likely, that an individual will distribute his responses differently on the second administration from the way he did the first time he took the questionnaire. In such an event, the same response (e.g., Slightly Agree) would have two different meanings. If, for example, his whole distribution shifted from the disagree side to the agree side, the meaning of Slightly Agree would have changed from a highly positive response to a relatively neutral one. For such a person we would conclude that even though he answered Slightly Agree on both the before and after questionnaires, his attitude had indeed changed.

Once we had computed standard scores for each item on both the before and after questionnaires, it was easy enough to subtract one from the other to get a measure of change. To get a scale score (e.g., for individualism), we simply multiplied the difference between the two standard scores by the factor loading of the item and then summed across items. This had the obvious effect of giving greatest weight to the "purest" items.

While some might argue that the technique employed for computing scale scores is more refined than the data would warrant, there were good reasons for getting as sensitive a measure of change as possible. Among them we would mention the abstract nature of the items involved, the absence of any verbal persuasion, and the very brief duration of the experiment. To speak from our own point of view, we were frankly skeptical about the possibility of producing significant attitude change under such seemingly unfavorable conditions. To our way of thinking, the best we could hope for would be relatively slight changes of a systematic sort. The methodology employed was conceived with this in mind.

PROCEDURE

The experiment was carried out with students enrolled in the senior author's Sociology of the Family course at the University of Wisconsin in the spring of 1961. On the first day of class (in lecture) the instructor explained that he would like to try an educational experiment in which weekly discussion sections were to be varied according to task, grading system, size, and composition in the hopes of learning something that would help us to improve upon teaching procedures now employed. No mention was made of our interest in attitude change. After the design had been described in some detail, students were asked to indicate on a slip of paper whether or not they wanted to take part in the experiment.

The instructor made it clear that participation was to be strictly voluntary. Students were told that sections organized along traditional lines would be made available for those who did not care to participate. They were further reminded that if they did decide to take part, they would *not* be given the opportunity to choose the kind of section they wanted to be in. Assignments were to be made by the instructor and, within the limits imposed by students' schedules, these assignments were to be random. Of the 120 students at that first lecture, not a single individual declined the invitation to participate in the experiment.

The course itself was organized along the usual lines with two lectures and a weekly discussion section. Less traditional perhaps were the sections themselves. Before the experiment was even conceived, it had been decided to let the students assume primary responsibility for running the discussions themselves. Each section was to have an instructor who would "lead" only to the extent of raising questions designed to bring out some of the more important issues touched upon in the lectures and reading. Although based on educational considerations, the decision to set up the sections in this way proved highly congenial to our interest in studying group differences in the centralization of control. With the instructor abdicating his traditional leadership role, each section was free to develop its own influence structure.

Sixteen weekly sections were set up in such a way as to permit the simultaneous testing of propositions relating task, grading system, group size, and homogeneity of membership on the one hand to social structure (solidarity and the centralization of control) and attitude change (individualism and equalitarianism) on the other. The four-variable design is shown in Figure 3–1. Blue Book and Discussion refer to the nature of the task, Curve and Single Grade to the grading system, Large and Small to group size, and Heterogeneous and Homogeneous to group composition.

The four situational variables were established in the following manner:

Task. All sections opened with a broad discussion question posed by the instructor. Half of the groups were given the task of writing a single 20–30 minute essay on the question posed. Each week the instructor, after reading the question, would place a blue book (exam booklet) in the middle of the table. One essay for the whole group was

FIGURE 3–1
Design of the Experiment

| | | CURVE | | SINGLE GRADE | |
		LARGE	SMALL	LARGE	SMALL
BLUE BOOK	HET	1	2	3	4
	HOM	5	6	7	8
DISCUSSION	HET	9	10	11	12
	HOM	13	14	15	16

required. It was suggested to the students that they take 20–30 minutes to discuss the problem before writing the essay. Just how the essay was to be written (each person writing a paragraph, appointing a secretary, etc.) was left up to the group. The blue book was to he handed in to the instructor at the end of the 50-minute period.

The other eight groups were given the same question at the beginning of each meeting, but instead of requiring a single blue-book essay the instructor simply asked them to discuss it. In this sense these sections were very much like others the students had previously been in with the exception of the fact that the instructor did very little talking. Compared to the blue-book groups, the task here was more disjunctive in that considerably less synchronization of member efforts was required to achieve satisfactory outcomes.

Incentive System. Noncorrespondence of outcomes was established for half the groups by grading on the curve. In these eight groups students were told that in the weekly grading a rigid curve was to be employed, with so many individuals getting A's, so many B's, and so on.

Only in unusual circumstances (exceptionally good or poor perform-ances) was the instructor allowed to deviate from the formal curve. Correspondence of outcomes was established for the remaining eight sections by giving all students in the same section the same grade, de-pending on how well the group did as a whole.

It should be kept in mind that of the eight groups being graded on a curve, four were writing a blue-book essay while four others simply discussed the question posed by the instructor. The same task break-down holds for the sections in which students all received the same grade. Although the two variables (nature of the task and grading sys-tem) are defined independently of one another, certain adjustments in the grading procedure were called for by virtue of the task differ-ences involved.

In the single-grade sections writing an essay, the instructor based his weekly grade exclusively on his reading of the essay. In the curve sec-tions writing an essay, it was impossible to tell from a reading of the essay who had contributed what, so that grades were based instead on each student's verbal contribution to the essay, regardless of what actually got written down. This is, of course, the way grades were determined in those sections which were also marked on a curve but which simply discussed the question instead of writing an essay on it.

In the single-grade sections discussing the question instead of writing an essay on it, grades were determined in the following manner: at the end of the hour the instructor wrote down a grade for each student in the section, depending on the quality of his or her contribution to the discussion. He would then average the grades, throw away the in-dividual marks and record the average for everyone in the section.

From the viewpoint of the experiment we could just as easily have assigned a single grade to the group depending on the quality of the discussion as a whole, regardless of who contributed what. This is the way it was done in Deutsch's study.[19] In light of the educational goals of the course, however, it seemed an inappropriate way to go about it. If the group's grade were to be a function of the quality of the dis-cussion, regardless of individual contributions, the rational thing for group members to do would be to let their most intelligent, articulate members do all the talking. Only by assigning each individual a grade and then taking the average as the grade to be entered could we be sure that everyone would participate in the discussion. Students who said nothing were automatically given an F.

Having decided upon this particular way of grading, we were forced

_____
[19] Deutsch, op. cit.

to go back and reconsider one of our original hypotheses, namely that single grade groups would be more centralized than those graded on a curve. This is what Deutsch found and explained in terms of the greater substitutability of functions under a group incentive system.[20] In the light of our decision to base the group grade on the average of *all* individual grades, however, it was clear that we had set up conditions favoring a highly equalitarian social structure. Under the circumstances, no group could afford to let one or two individuals do most of the talking; unless everyone was given the opportunity to comment now and then, no one would get a good grade.

This reasoning, of course, applies only to those single-grade groups which were asked to discuss the instructor's question rather than writing an essay on it. In the latter, there was no averaging of individual grades; the instructor simply graded the essay and gave everyone that grade. In line with Deutsch's principle of substitutability, we would expect such groups to become quite centralized. Assuming this to be the case, what we have is an interaction between grading system and task in which single-grade groups are predicted to be more centralized than curve groups when the task involves writing a blue-book essay but less so when the task consists solely of verbal discussion. While we have posed the prediction in terms of behavior (centralization of control), it should be clear that it applies equally well to attitude change. Because of the relevance of centralization for both, this includes equalitarianism on the one hand and theism on the other.

Size. Given an enrollment of 120 students and 16 sections to put them in, we decided to assign ten to each of our eight "large" groups and five to each of our eight "small" groups. With the initial shifting around necessitated by changes in students' schedules, some of the sections ended up with eleven members, others with nine, some with four and one with only three students in it. By the time things settled down, our large groups ranged from eight to eleven members, our small sections from three to five.

Homogeneity. Eight "homogeneous" sections were created by putting together students with fairly similar academic records, namely those with grade-point averages ranging form 2.2 to 2.8. The choice of this particular range was dictated by the fact that there were more of these students than any other kind. The eight "heterogeneous" groups were composed of students whose averages ranged all the way from 1.9 to 3.9. Thus, half the sections were made up of people quite similar in ability (to the extent that this is measured by previous grades)

---

[20] *Ibid.*

while the other half were composed of students highly dissimilar in this respect.

Measuring Behavior

An attempt was made to tape record each weekly meeting of each of the 16 sections. Each section met 13 times over the course of the term, the first and last meetings being devoted to filling out questionnaires. A sample of five tapes (representing weeks six through ten) was drawn for purposes of content analysis. The first step in analyzing the tapes involved training an assistant in the use of Bales' 12-category system for scoring interaction.[21] This is not a difficult system to master, as long as the scorer is observing a live group from behind a one-way mirror. When the scoring is to be done from tapes, however, there is a real problem in identifying voices. To facilitate the learning of voices, two of the three instructors prepared written protocols in which students' names appeared opposite their recorded comments. This was done for several of the early section meetings. The third instructor (Breer) sat down with the assistant, played a sample of tapes and identified the voices in his sections verbally. It took approximately 15 hours of practice before the assistant and Breer achieved susbtantial consensus on the assignment of acts to both *individuals* and *categories.*

In addition to the 12 categories of the Interaction Process Analysis System, scores were made for self-references (I, my, mine) and group references (we, us, our). From these 14 categories two alternative indices of solidarity were computed. For the first, following Bales, the percentage of each individual's scores in categories 10 (shows disagreement) and 12 (shows antagonism) were subtracted from the corresponding percentages in categories 1 (shows solidarity) and 3 (shows agreement).[22] This was done for each individual using all the relevant acts he or she initiated throughout the five-week period included in the sample.

For the second measure of solidarity, following White and Lippitt, a ratio was computed for each individual by dividing the total number of group references made by the number of self-references made.[23] It was thought desirable to include both measures since neither really exhausts

---

[21] Bales, *op. cit.,* chap. 3 and appendix.

[22] The reason behind omitting categories 2 (jokes and laughs) and 11 (shows tension) is that (in percentage form) they are unrelated to the four categories already mentioned. For a factor analysis of all 12 Bales' categories, see Arthur S. Couch, "Psychological Determinants of Interpersonal Behavior," unpublished doctoral dissertation (Harvard University, 1960).

[23] Ralph White and Ronald Lippitt, "Leader Behavior and Member Reaction in Three 'Social Climates,' " in Cartwright and Zander, *op. cit.,* pp. 527–53.

the meaning of solidarity as we have used it. While the Bales index focuses on the warm, agreeable, co-operative component in solidarity, the group/self ratio was designed to pick up the element of group identification which many, including Bales, have associated with the term "solidarity."

The second dimension of social structure, centralization of control, can be approached by looking at the *distribution* of acts among group members. Not all acts, of course, are designed to control the behavior of others in the group. In Bales' set of 12 categories, numbers 4 (gives suggestion) and 5 (gives opinion) represent the most appropriate vehicles for attempts of a controlling nature. The measure of centralization actually decided upon was the standard deviation of acts in the two categories combined. A standard deviation, based on individual totals in categories four and five, was computed for each group for each of the five weeks making up the sample. The proposed association between group conditions and centralization of control was tested with these data.

Summary of Predictions

Task. Blue-book essay groups will be more solidary and more centralized than the discussion groups. Students in the blue-book groups will, over the course of the term, become less individualistic and less equalitarian in their attitudes while those in the discussion groups will become more individualistic and more equalitarian. Members of blue-book groups will become more theistic, members of discussion groups less so. All these changes will be most pronounced among students who are rewarded with good grades; among those who do very poorly, attitudes will change in the opposite direction. This latter expectation is common to all four situational variables.

Incentive System. Single-grade groups will be more solidary than curve groups. Students in the single-grade groups will become less individualistic (than they were at the beginning of the term) while those in the curve groups become more individualistic. With respect to centralization, equalitarianism, and theism, we expect incentive system to interact with task.

Group Size. Small groups will be more solidary and less centralized than the large ones. Members of the small sections will become less individualistic and more equalitarian, while those assigned to large sections will become more individualistic and less equalitarian. Students in the small groups will become less theistic, students in the large groups more theistic.

Homogeneity. Homogeneous groups will be more solidary and less centralized than the heterogeneous ones. Students assigned to homogeneous groups will go down on individualism and up on equalitarianism, while those assigned to the heterogeneous groups will do just the opposite. Members of homogeneous sections will become less theistic, members of heterogeneous sections more theistic.

RESULTS

Solidarity

Table 3–1 shows the results of an analysis of variance on the first of our two solidarity measures.[24] The index, it will be recalled, was computed by adding (for each individual) all acts in Bales' categories one and three, subtracting those in categories ten and twelve, and dividing by the total number of acts initiated.

TABLE 3–1
Solidarity (Bales' Index) as a Function of
Four Experimental Conditions

Source	SS	df	MS	F	p
Task	235.62	1	235.62	17.32	.001
Incentive	216.09	1	216.09	15.88	.001
Size	723.61	1	723.61	53.21	.001
Homogeneity	12.96	1	12.96	0.95	ns
Task × incentive	13.69	1	13.69	1.01	ns
Task × size	56.25	1	56.25	4.13	.05
Task × homogeneity	404.00	1	404.00	29.71	.001
Incentive × size	44.22	1	44.22	3.25	.10
Incentive × homogeneity...	105.06	1	105.06	7.73	.01
Size × homogeneity	0.00	1	0.00	0.00	ns
Residual	439.50	5	87.90	6.47	.001
	2,251.08	15			

Three of the four main effects are highly significant, all in the predicted direction.[25] Measuring solidarity in this way, blue-book groups were more solidary than discussion groups, single-grade more solidary than curve and small more solidary than large. Homogeneity (of cumulative averages) appears to have had no effect at all.

There are four significant interaction effects, only one of which (incentive × homogeneity) we think we understand. Among those sections receiving a single grade, the homogeneous ones were more

[24] Because of unequal cell entries, an approximation method was used in which computations were actually done on cell means: B. J. Winer, *Statistical Principles in Experimental Design* (New York: McGraw-Hill, 1962), pp. 241–44.

[25] All of the tests of significance reported in this book are two-tailed.

solidary than those made up of students of mixed ability. Among the sections graded on a curve, however, it worked the other way around. The homogeneous groups, it will be recalled, were composed of students whose all-course averages were in the C+ to B— range. Very few of these students had ever received an A before. Yet in the curve sections they were told that each week so many people had to receive A's, so many B's, and so on. The fact that they were so similar in ability to begin with probably had the effect of making a moderately competitive situation an intensely competitive one. In the heteogeneous groups, it was obvious after a few weeks that certain individuals were going to get the A's, certain others the B's, and so on down the line. Given the rather fixed nature of the status hierarchy, there was relatively little to compete over. The result was that in the curve sections those groups made up of students with varied abilities evidenced greater solidarity than those composed of students very similar in ability.

The very significant interaction between homogeneity and task is surprising. It would appear, at least in this setting, that homogeneity in ability leads to solidarity when the task is a conjunctive one (writing a joint essay) but not so when the task is relatively disjunctive (discussion) Why this should be so is not at all obvious. The same could be said for the two lesser interaction effects (task with size and incentive with size).

A similar analysis of variance was performed on our alternative measure of solidarity, a ratio (computed for each individual) of group references (we, us, our) to self-references (I, my, mine). The results are shown in Table 3–2. The two measures of solidarity (the Bales and

TABLE 3–2

Solidarity (Group/Self References) as a Function of
Four Experimental Conditions

Source	SS	df	MS	F	p
Task	193.84	1	193.84	11.90	.001
Incentive	176.82	1	176.82	10.85	.01
Size	3.46	1	3.46	0.21	ns
Homogeneity	170.76	1	170.76	10.48	.01
Task × incentive	135.21	1	135.21	8.30	.01
Task × size	18.63	1	18.63	1.14	ns
Task × homogeneity	137.06	1	137.06	8.41	.01
Incentive × size	57.95	1	57.95	3.56	ns
Incentive × homogeneity	126.18	1	126.18	7.75	.01
Size × homogeneity	2.02	1	2.02	0.12	ns
Residual	356.20	5	71.24	4.37	.01
	1,378.13	15			

group/self) are only correlated +.15 (with $N = 110$, $p < .10$). Despite the low correlation, the two sets of findings are quite similar, the major difference being that size is no longer significant while homogeneity is. There is some shifting in the interaction effects, although the two largest ones from Table 3–1 remain (homogeneity with task and homogeneity with incentive).

Important differences notwithstanding, the two tables suggest that our four antecedent conditions were responsible for a good deal of the variation in observed behavior, sometimes directly, sometimes in interaction with each other. This is what we originally set out to demonstrate.

TABLE 3–3

Attitude Change (Individualism) as a Function of
Four Experimental Conditions

Source	SS	df	MS	F	p
Task	13.97	1	13.97	0.16	ns
Incentive	421.17	1	421.17	4.72	.05
Size	430.04	1	430.04	4.82	.05
Homogeneity	57.04	1	57.04	0.64	ns
Task × incentive	118.22	1	118.22	1.32	ns
Task × size	83.04	1	83.04	0.93	ns
Task × homogeneity	141.09	1	141.09	1.58	ns
Incentive × size	50.10	1	50.10	0.56	ns
Incentive × homogeneity	183.94	1	183.94	2.06	ns
Size × homogeneity	11.25	1	11.25	0.13	ns
Residual	581.23	5	116.25	1.30	ns
	2,024.23	15			

Attitude Change—Individualism

Few readers will be surprised to find that it is more difficult to change attitudes (without persuasion) than to produce differences in behavior. Despite its rather anemic appearance, however, Table 3–3 does give evidence of a measure of success. Two of the predicted main effects are significant at the .05 level. The single-grade sections went down on individualism while the curved groups went up. Also, as anticipated, students in the large sections became more individualistic while those in the smaller groups became less so. If we can believe Table 3–1(rather than Table 3–2), these changes in attitude can be thought to reflect (in direction if not in intensity) the very significant differences found at the behavioral level. Something of the same sort can be found among the interaction effects. Although none of them even approaches significance, it is of some interest to note that the two which come closest (task with homogeneity and incentive with homogeneity) also have the highest F values in Table 3–1.

There is still no getting around the confusing fact that the task variable (blue book versus discussion) which proved so important for behavior. Despite its rather anemic appearance, however, Table 3–3 does attitude change. The failure of homogeneity to account for any significant change is less bothersome, perhaps, because of its weak showing in Table 3–1. Before we start offering post hoc excuses, however, it might be wise to recall that only two of the predictions tested proved to be significant, and these two but slightly beyond the .05 level. In this light, it might be more meaningful to ask why incentive and size *did* work, rather than why the others did not.

Attitude Change and Individual Success

A partial answer to that question is suggested by the data in Table 3–4. At an earlier point in this chapter we argued that the grade a student received in his section would affect the way in which his attitudes changed. The precise nature of that effect would depend, it was suggested, on the kind of section he was assigned to. Under conditions favoring solidarity, students who were rewarded with good grades were expected to become less individualistic in their values, beliefs, and preferences, while students in the same group who did poorly (were "punished") were predicted to become more individualistic. Just the opposite was predicted for students working under conditions *un*favorable to the development of solidarity.

Whether or not a specific grade is perceived to be rewarding obviously depends on what one is accustomed to receiving. In classifying students according to success or failure, we compared each individual's section grade with his university course average. Students placed in either of the top two cells (success) are those who received section grades which exceeded their all-course averages. We considered these students to have been rewarded. Those who received grades equal to or lower than their cumulative averages were considered to have "failed" and were placed in the bottom row. This is not a median split. There are approximately twice as many students who "succeeded" as "failed." Students are more evenly divided with respect to the second variable (attitude change), with 61 going up on individualism and 49 going down. Chi-squares were computed separately for both conditions on each of the four independent variables.

From the four tables on the *left,* it is clear that succeeding versus failing had a rather substantial impact on attitude change. And the

TABLE 3–4

Attitude Change (Individualism) as a Function of Experimental Conditions and Grades

Blue Book	Up	Down
Success	13	19
Failure	17	2

$$\chi^2 = 9.73$$
$$p < .01$$

Discussion	Up	Down
Success	21	21
Failure	10	7

$$\chi^2 = 0.11$$
$$\text{ns}$$

Single Grade	Up	Down
Success	15	27
Failure	8	3

$$\chi^2 = 3.48$$
$$p < .10$$

Curve	Up	Down
Success	19	13
Failure	19	6

$$\chi^2 = 1.03$$
$$\text{ns}$$

Small	Up	Down
Success	9	18
Failure	5	4

$$\chi^2 = 0.62$$
$$\text{ns}$$

Large	Up	Down
Success	25	22
Failure	22	5

$$\chi^2 = 4.87$$
$$p < .05$$

Homogeneous	Up	Down
Success	16	24
Failure	14	2

$$\chi^2 = 8.44$$
$$p < .01$$

Heterogeneous	Up	Down
Success	18	6
Failure	13	7

$$\chi^2 = 0.33$$
$$\text{ns}$$

impact, in all four cases, is in keeping with our reinforcement-generalization model. These are the four conditions which were thought to favor solidarity. We reasoned that students who were rewarded in their efforts to succeed under these conditions would become less individualistic in their preferences, values, and beliefs. Evidence of a confirming if not overwhelming sort is given in the top rows of the four tables on the left. The bottom rows of the same tables indicate how attitudes changed among those who received poor grades. As expected, students who were "punished" with grades lower than what they were accustomed to became more individualistic. It is important to note that the association between success and attitude change is strongest in the blue-book and the homogeneous sections. Task and homogeneity, it will be recalled from Table 3–3, were the two variables which failed to show any over-all effect on attitude change.

If all had gone as expected, the four tables on the *right* would show results opposite to those on the left. On the right are the conditions (discussion, curve, large, and heterogeneous) thought to inhibit the development of group solidarity. Success in a task setting where independence has high instrumental reward value should make one more individualistic in his attitudes toward life, while failure could be expected to produce the opposite effect.

According to that data, it doesn't really matter what grade you get; there is no consistent association between success or failure on the one hand and attitude change on the other. Among the successes there is some very slight hint of change in the individualistic direction. Among those who failed, there is more than a slight hint that they changed in a direction opposite to the one predicted; they became *more* individualistic when they were expected to become less individualistic. In this sense they resemble the failures over on the left-hand side under the high solidarity conditions. In both cases the students who received poor grades became more individualistic.

To varying degrees, all of our groups acted like solidary groups. Sections predicted to be high on solidarity yielded results very much in line with what we expected in the way of attitude change. In the other groups we find not the opposite but, to a limted extent, more of the same. The answer could very well lie in the fact that, compared to typical classroom sections, our own groups were *all* higher on solidarity. To be sure some were considerably more solidary than others and this is perhaps why the results varied as they did. But compared to the typical section in other courses, even the least solidary of our own groups was probably more closely knit.

Assuming that this is indeed the case, we can think of two reasons why it should be so. In the first place, all of our sections (even the "large" ones) were significantly smaller than the typical 25-member sections common throughout the University of Wisconsin. Very few of our students had ever participated in a discussion section made up of only ten students and an instructor. No one had ever been in a group as small as five (the size of half of our own groups). This may have been enough to produce a fairly high degree of solidarity even in those groups which, on other grounds, we had predicted would develop a loosely knit, fragmented social structure. Aside from the size factor, our "low solidarity" groups were quite similar to the sections in other courses. In our own groups, just as in the others, discussion was the major form of activity, grades were curved, and students of mixed ability were included.

TABLE 3–5
Attitude Change (Individualism) as a Function
of Grades

All Groups	Up	Down
Success	34	40
Failure	27	9

$$\chi^2 = 7.06$$
$$p < .01$$

In the second place, all of our students knew that they were taking part in a special experiment. It would have been difficult to forget this fact in view of the many questionnaires they were asked to fill out, the tape recording made of their discussion each week, the special rooms in which sessions were held, the size of the groups, and the role of the instructor. Although there is no way of knowing for certain, there is good reason to believe that this "special treatment" led students to identify somewhat with each other and with the groups to which they had been assigned.

While this interpretation does make the attitude changes among unsuccessful students more intelligible, it leaves unexplained the failure of the successful ones to change even slightly in the opposite direction. To be consistent with this explanation those students who were most successful in the least solidary groups should have become slightly less individualistic in their attitudes. The evidence indicates at best no change, at worst a slight change in the other direction.

Disregarding group differences for the moment, it is quite clear that, taking the sample as a whole, grades did have an independent effect on attitude change. As Table 3–5 indicates, this is most evident among the students who received section grades lower than what they were accustomed to getting. These students were in the minority. In line with what was said above, it is likely that they came to associate doing poorly with membership in a small, relatively intimate group. Whether they were competing or co-operating with others, they were faced with a situation in which their grades were very closely linked up with how well others in the group were doing. Having done poorly under such circumstances, it is understandable that they should have become more individualistic in their beliefs, values, and preferences.

Centralization of Control

Going back to behavior once again, we start by examining the relationship between each of our four experimental conditions on the one hand and our measure of centralization on the other. Centralization of control, it will be recalled, was operationally defined as the standard deviation of acts in Bales' categories four and five (suggestions and opinions) in a sample of five consecutive weekly meetings.

From casual inspection it was clear that the standard deviations calculated in this way varied little from one group to the next. Given the rather elaborate calculations required for the analysis we had planned, it was decided to run a test for homogeneity of variances before going any further. The results confirmed our original impression, indicating insufficient variation to make further tests of main and interaction effects meaningful.

In the hope of finding related measures of centralization more heterogeneous than the first, standard deviations were again computed for (1) acts in categories four, five, and six combined (category six, gives orientation, representing a somewhat less obvious attempt at influencing others), and (2) *all* acts initiated (all 12 categories combined). Substantially the same results were found in both cases. As with the original measure, there was no significant variation between groups.

The Bales scores did suggest, however, that certain categories of behavior were used more frequently in some groups than in others. As might be expected, for example, students in the blue-book groups were more likely to *make suggestions* than those in the discussion sections. With a single, joint blue-book essay due at the end of the hour, someone had to suggest how to go about it—what material was to be covered, in what order, conclusions to come to, etc. It is hardly surprising, given the nature of the task, that attempts to guide and direct were more frequent here than in those groups where no essay was called for. The relevant question, however, is not so much what acts were initiated but how these acts were distributed among group members. Despite the higher frequency of influence attempts in the blue-book groups, there is no evidence to indicate that such acts were any more centralized here than in those sections which simply discussed the problem.

There is no getting around the fact that our four antecedent conditions failed to produce the expected variation in centralization of control. This is somewhat strange in the light of previous work done in the area. It is conceivable, of course, that the fault lay not with the propositions but with the means used to test them. In this regard it is appropriate to recall the manner in which the behavioral scores were arrived at.

The Bales interaction scoring was done not on the meetings themselves but on tape recordings of those meetings. It was done, moreover, by someone who had never seen the students who took part in the discussions. This procedure obviously made difficult the problem of associating names with voices. To facilitate the identification of students from their voices, two of the instructors in the course provided the scorer with written protocols (as in a play) for two sessions in each one of their groups. (In the third case, the instructor listened to several tapes with the scorer and identified the voices verbally.) By reading a protocol as he listened to the same meeting on tape, the scorer learned to identify students from their voices. When he felt secure in his identifications, he went on to score the other three meetings (the sample was made up of five consecutive meetings) from the tapes alone.

Even with the protocols there were times, not altogether infrequent we suspect, when the voices were unclear and, as a consequence, an act was assigned to the wrong person. In comparing group *means* (as in the case of our solidarity measure), this kind of error may be of minor importance, as long as acts are assigned to the right *category*. When the researcher's intent, however, is to get a measure of the *distribution* of acts among group members, the scorer's failure to assign each act to the right person is of critical importance. The lack of any significant differences between groups in the distribution of acts (centralization) could very well be traced to an accumulation of random scoring errors of this sort.

We find some confirmation of this interpretation in the fact that significant between group differences in centralization are evident in an alternative measure developed for use in another part of the study. In the last section meeting of the course, students were asked to fill out a brief questionnaire "designed to get at your perception of how people in your section ordinarily relate to each other." The following four items were included in that measure, students being asked to respond to each on a six-point scale running from Strongly Disagree to Strongly Agree:

1. There are no leaders in this group.
2. In most of our meetings one or two people end up leading the discussion.
3. In this section everyone contributes equally to the discussion.
4. In this section one or two people ordinarily take the initiative in guiding and directing the discussion.

Each individual was given a score computed by subtracting his responses to items one and three from those given to statements two and four. Using the same technique employed with the solidarity and individualism data, a four-way analysis of variance was then performed on the 16-group means. Recalling our earlier discussion, it was predicted that blue-book groups would be more centralized than the discussion groups, the large groups more centralized than small, and the heterogeneous groups more centralized than homogeneous groups; it was also predicted that grading system would interact with task (i.e., single-grade more centralized than curve in the blue-book groups and less so in the discussion groups).

TABLE 3–6
Centralization (Perceived) as a Function of Four Experimental Conditions

Source	SS	df	MS	F	p
Task	0.02	1	0.02	0.01	ns
Incentive	9.40	1	9.40	6.03	.05
Size	4.54	1	4.54	2.91	ns
Homogeneity	7.48	1	7.48	4.80	.05
Task × incentive	3.05	1	3.05	1.96	ns
Task × size	26.01	1	26.01	16.67	.001
Task × homogeneity	8.79	1	8.79	5.64	.05
Incentive × size	2.36	1	2.36	1.51	ns
Incentive × homogeneity	27.52	1	27.52	17.64	.001
Size × homogeneity	37.70	1	37.70	24.17	.001
Residual	21.53	5	4.31	2.76	ns
	148.40	15			

The results reported in Table 3–6 lend modest support to these predictions. There are two significant main effects indicating that curve

groups were more centralized than single-grade groups, and heterogeneous groups more centralized than the homogeneous ones. The predicted interaction between grading system and task failed to materialize,
although several others did. By themselves, these findings (specifically
the two main effects) are of limited importance. In conjunction with
what follows on attitude change, however, they are of considerable
interest.

Attitude Change—Equalitarianism

It is probably not altogether coincidental that the two highest F
ratios in Table 3–7 are the same two which reached significance in

TABLE 3–7

Attitude Change (Equalitarianism) as a Function
of Four Experimental Conditions

Source	SS	df	MS	F	p
Task	1.61	1	1.61	0.01	ns
Incentive	470.78	1	470.78	3.63	.10
Size	101.85	1	101.85	0.78	ns
Homogeneity	400.13	1	400.13	3.08	.10
Task × incentive	280.47	1	280.47	2.16	ns
Task × size	30.17	1	30.17	0.23	ns
Task × homogeneity	114.83	1	114.83	0.88	ns
Incentive × size	64.45	1	64.45	0.50	ns
Incentive × homogeneity	21.29	1	21.29	0.16	ns
Size × homogeneity	5.39	1	5.39	0.04	ns
Residual	298.42	5	59.68	0.46	ns
	1,789.39	15			

Table 3–6. At the behavioral level (as measured by students' perception of group structure), single-grade groups were less centralized than
curve groups. With respect to attitudes, students in the single-grade
sections went up on equalitarianism while those in the competitive groups
went down. At the same time, homogeneous groups proved to be less
centralized than the heterogeneous ones and students in the former
went up on equalitarianism while those in the latter went down.

While the results with respect to behavioral differences and attitude
change are consistent with one another, the relationship may be an
artifact of our behavioral measure. It is possible, having measured "behavior" by asking students for their *perceptions* of group structure,
that attitude change came first and was responsible for the perceptual
differences. Students who, for one reason or another, became more
equalitarian in their attitudes may have been led to perceive their groups

as equalitarian even when they were highly centralized. It is in light of this possibility that we have tried elsewhere to avoid asking subjects to tell us how they *think* they and others in their group behaved, relying instead on the observations of a scorer who did not participate in the group meetings.

Attitude Change and Individual Success

There is little to report in this regard. Only one of the eight tables (in Table 3–8) shows a significant association between grades and attitude change. Among students in the curve groups, those who received high grades became less equalitarian while those who "failed" became more equalitarian. In view of the fact that curve groups were significantly more centralized (Table 3–6) than the single-grade groups, this finding, isolated though it may be, is in keeping with the theoretical model advanced earlier. It is interesting to note, moreover, that in the single-grade groups success and attitude change are related in exactly the opposite fashion. While the association here is nonsignificant, it, too, is consistent with our expectations. Single-grade groups were less centralized than curve groups. Students who did well in the single-grade groups should have become more equalitarian in their beliefs, values, and preferences. Those who did poorly should have become less equalitarian. In a very limited way, this is precisely what did happen.

There is a simple way of finding out whether the relationship between grades and attitude change is significantly different in the two settings (single grade versus curve).[26] In Table 3–9 the two smaller tables are combined to form one big table. Diagonals in the small tables are added to form a single cell in the large table. Thus, $26 + 7$ $(a + c$ for Single Grade) equals 33 $(a$ in Table 3–9). Table 3–9 indicates that the relationship between grades and attitude change is very much a function of the kind of grading system used.

It is not at all clear why this finding appears here and not in the other three conditions (task, size, and homogeneity). Possibly it appears here because it was precisely here that we found the most significant over-all difference on attitude change (Table 3–7). Yet in our earlier analysis of changes on individualism, we found that grades and attitude change were most closely associated under those conditions where there was *no* significant over-all difference on attitude change (Tables 3–3 and 3–4). Grading system and group size both made a

---

[26] This technique was suggested to us by Robert McGinnis of the Department of Sociology at Cornell.

TABLE 3-8
Attitude Change (Equalitarianism) as a Function
of Experimental Conditions and Grades

Blue Book	Up	Down
Success	17	15
Failure	9	10

$$\chi^2 = 0.01$$
ns

Discussion	Up	Down
Success	18	24
Failure	10	7

$$\chi^2 = 0.74$$
ns

Single Grade	Up	Down
Success	26	16
Failure	4	7

$$\chi^2 = 1.35$$
ns

Curve	Up	Down
Success	9	23
Failure	15	10

$$\chi^2 = 4.67$$
$$p < .05$$

Small	Up	Down
Success	10	17
Failure	6	3

$$\chi^2 = 1.35$$
ns

Large	Up	Down
Success	25	22
Failure	13	14

$$\chi^2 = 0.04$$
ns

Homogeneous	Up	Down
Success	20	20
Failure	11	5

$$\chi^2 = 0.92$$
ns

Heterogeneous	Up	Down
Success	15	19
Failure	8	13

$$\chi^2 = 0.03$$
ns

difference in which way students changed their attitude, but it was only when groups were divided by task and homogeneity that success had any predictive value.

TABLE 3–9
Attitude Change (Equalitarianism) as a Function of
Incentive System and Success/Failure
(*Based on Data from Table 3–8*)

	$a + d$	$b + c$
Single Grade	33	20
Curve	19	38

$$\chi^2 = 8.05$$
$$p < .01$$

Religion

On the grounds that the relationship between man and God abstractly resembles the relationship between leader and follower in a small group, it was predicted that students in sections favoring the centralization of control would become more theistic while those in sections favoring an equalitarian distribution of power would become less theistic. An analysis of variance of the changes (Table 3–10) reveals one main effect just significant at the .05 level and another which approaches significance. Students in the blue-book sections did not change their religious beliefs, while those in the discussion sections became con-

TABLE 3–10
Attitude Change (Religion) as a Function of
Four Experimental Conditions

Source	SS	df	MS	F	p
Task	248.28	1	248.28	3.95	.05
Incentive	228.30	1	228.30	3.63	.10
Size	4.86	1	4.86	0.08	ns
Homogeneity	70.68	1	70.68	1.13	ns
Task × incentive	6.91	1	6.91	0.11	ns
Task × size	59.83	1	59.83	0.95	ns
Task × homogeneity	54.46	1	54.46	0.87	ns
Incentive × size	35.41	1	35.41	0.56	ns
Incentive × homogeneity ..	27.91	1	27.91	0.44	ns
Size × homogeneity	4.21	1	4.21	0.06	ns
Residual	616.65	5	123.33	1.95	ns
	1,357.50	15			

siderably less theistic. Students in the single-grade sections maintained their religious beliefs while those who competed with each other in the curve sections became less theistic.

A clear majority (72 out of 110) of the students had lower scores on religion at the end of the course than at the beginning. Part of this change could be attributed to a lecture on the role of family relations in religious symbolism in which the instructor endeavored to make a case for Freud's point of view as this is summarized in *Future of an Illusion.*[27]   More likely, the change in scores was part of the general attrition in religious beliefs (at least those of a conventional sort) ordinarily found at the college level.

The fact remains, however, that not all students went down on theism. Students in the blue-book and single-grade groups held on to their religious beliefs. The difference between blue-book and discussion groups is consistent with our prediction based on the abstract parallel between divine and secular authority. Students who were asked to discuss a question each week had less of a need for centralized control than those who were required to write a joint essay. On the assumption that God is, in part, a generalization from secular authority, the former should have become less theistic, the latter more theistic. Taking into account the shift of the whole population in the atheistic direction, this is pretty much what did happen. There is still no evidence, however, to indicate that the discussion sections were any more equalitarian than the blue-book groups. The predicted changes in religious beliefs were based on the expectation that task differences would lead to behavioral differences in the centralization of control. Given the fact that the blue-book sections were no more or less centralized than the discussion sections, the difference in attitude change between the two conditions cannot be explained as proposed.

It is doubtful that change in religious beliefs had anything at all to do with the centralization of control. Confirming these doubts is the fact that single-grade groups showed no loss of belief in God while the curve groups evidenced considerable change in the atheistic direction. Our finding from Table 3–6 indicates that the single-grade sections were less centralized than the curve sections. In other words, the least centralized groups (single grade), instead of becoming less theistic stayed the same, while the more centralized groups (curved grades), instead of becoming more theistic became significantly less so. Taken jointly, the findings suggest strongly that whatever *is* happening here,

---

[27] Sigmund Freud, *The Future of an Illusion* (New York: Liveright Publishing Corp., 1953).

it has little to do with leadership or authority. Looked at from another point of view, however, the findings become quite reasonable.

According to Table 3–10, task and incentive system both had a slight effect on religious beliefs. The students most likely to give up their religious beliefs were those in the *discussion* sections being graded on a *curve*. Students who wrote joint blue-book essays and received a single group grade were least likely to relinquish such beliefs. In looking for clues to explain this set of events, it is instructive to glance again at Tables 3–1 and 3–2 which summarize the findings for group differences in solidarity. Regardless of which measure of behavioral solidarity is employed, the blue-book groups were clearly more solidary than the discussion groups and single-grade more solidary than curve groups. In this light, it is possible that changes in religious beliefs were mediated by group differences in solidarity rather than the centralization of control.

In a setting where most students were becoming less theistic, we find that those in the most solidary sections tended to resist such change while those in the least solidary sections changed more than anyone else. Although unpredicted, the relationship between solidarity and theism can be explained in terms of extant theory, liberally interpreted to fit the small-group setting.

Miller and Swanson,[28] following Durkheim,[29] have argued that religion (in its teleological form) reflects "experiences of transcendent purpose encountered in the course of relations with other people." Before a person can impute purpose and design to the physical world in which he lives, he must experience collective purpose in his relations with other people. Those individuals most likely to believe that the world has purpose, that it was designed, that it is governed (presumably by God), are those who have experienced collective purpose in their everyday lives. "Transcendent" is taken, in this case, to refer to something exterior to the individual and exercising constraint over him. According to the authors, "it is likely that only experiences provided by the organization of a unit as large and pervasive as a total society are adequate to provide these 'transcendent' social conditions."[30]

If we were to take this last statement literally, there would be little point in continuing with the explanation since our own 5–10 man

---

[28] Daniel R. Miller and Guy E. Swanson, *The Changing American Parent* (New York: John Wiley & Sons, Inc., 1958), p. 277.
[29] Émile Durkheim, *The Elementary Forms of the Religious Life* (Glencoe, Ill.: Free Press, 1954).
[30] Miller and Swanson, *op. cit.*, p. 278.

groups fall considerably short of being as large and pervasive as total societies. In a very limited way, however, our groups did involve the individual student in a sense of collective purpose. At least some of them did. In some, the competitive groups for example, it was pretty much every man for himself. Goals may have been similar among individual members, but they were not shared, they were not "transcendent." In the blue-book and single-grade groups, however, the feeling of joint purpose was quite salient. If any one were to develop a sense of transcendent purpose, it would have been the students in these sections. These were the groups that scored the highest on solidarity. More than the rest, they tended to promote co-operation, orderliness, and the perception of one's self as a part of a larger whole.

Theism is, among other things, a statement of transcendent purpose, God's design for mankind. Assuming that such a belief reflects the feeling of collective purpose as this is experienced in the everyday secular world, we could legitimately expect individuals to differ in their religious beliefs according to the nature of their social environment. It is with this in mind that Miller and Swanson attempt to relate parental differences in occupational role (bureaucratic versus entrepreneurial) to student variation in religious beliefs and activities. It is in keeping with this rationale that we can interpret changes in religious beliefs among our subjects as a function of differences in group solidarity.

This is at best a tenuous explanation. It is difficult to believe that writing a joint essay versus talking made a difference in our subjects' religious beliefs. Equally implausible is the fact that receiving a group grade had one effect while being graded on a curve had another. Yet, to a limited extent, this is what did happen. Whether these changes have anything to do with solidarity and collective purpose is, however, another matter altogether. Research conducted subsequent to this study and reported in Chapter 7 would suggest that the relationship between solidarity and theism is considerably more complex.

When changes on individualism were broken down by success and failure, a number of consistent findings emerged, indicating that the best prediction is one which takes into consideration both external conditions (task, incentives, etc.) and degree of success or failure. When changes on equalitarianism were analyzed in the same fashion, only two of the eight chi-square tables reached or approached significance. In keeping with our earlier reasoning with respect to the effects of success and failure on attitude change, the same procedure was followed in the case of religion. The results are presented in Table 3–11.

Not one of the eight tables reveals any significant association between success and attitude change. It is worth noting, however, that what little there is makes sense in terms of our theory. In both the discussion sec-

TABLE 3–11
Attitude Change (Religion) as a Function of Experimental Condition and Grade

Blue Book	Up	Down
Success	15	17
Failure	7	12

$$\chi^2 = 0.18$$
ns

Discussion	Up	Down
Success	9	33
Failure	7	10

$$\chi^2 = 1.70$$
ns

Single Grade	Up	Down
Success	17	25
Failure	4	7

$$\chi^2 = 0.00$$
ns

Curve	Up	Down
Success	7	25
Failure	10	15

$$\chi^2 = 1.28$$
ns

Small	Up	Down
Success	9	18
Failure	3	7

$$\chi^2 = 0.14$$
ns

Large	Up	Down
Success	15	32
Failure	11	16

$$\chi^2 = 0.00$$
ns

Homogeneous	Up	Down
Success	11	29
Failure	6	10

$$\chi^2 = 0.00$$
ns

Heterogeneous	Up	Down
Success	13	21
Failure	8	12

$$\chi^2 = 0.25$$
ns

tions and those marked on a curve (both low on solidarity), students who were successful were more likely to go down on theism than those who failed. When the discussion sections are compared with the blue-book groups (according to the procedure described on page 75), we get a chi-square of 4.06 (p <.05) indicating that the relationship between success and religious change is itself a function of the nature of the task. In the discussion sections, students who did well were more likely to give up their religious beliefs than those who failed, while in the blue-book groups it worked very slightly in the opposite fashion. Something of the same sort, though less significant, can be seen in comparing curve groups with those in which everyone received the same grade.

These are fragile results, suggestive at best. They are of interest primarily in that they lend modest confirmation to the themes central to this study. We have proposed that subjects' attitudes can be changed, without persuasion, simply by subjecting them to conditions in which they will be rewarded for certain kinds of behavior. We have suggested, further, that the direction and intensity of change will vary with the degree to which the subject is actually rewarded. A number of findings reported earlier in this chapter give us reason to believe that we are not completely off the mark. The religious changes, however slight, can be interpreted as lending further support to these ideas. They are perhaps the most interesting of all in that they indicate how far-reaching the effects of a very limited social experience can be with respect to what an individual believes to be true and good in the world around him.

DISCUSSION

The results here can best be described as inconclusive. The only findings of indisputable significance were those relating situational variables to measures of behavior. At the attitude level the differences were considerably smaller, although those which did emerge tended to be consistent with the theory presented in Chapter 1. Among other things we found that incentive system and group size both had a significant effect on attitudes concerning individualism. The predicted relationship between success and attitude change emerged for some groups, but not all.

On the second dimension there was too little variation in our behavioral measure of centralization of control to make further testing worthwhile. When we switched to a perceptual measure of centralization, however, we found significant relationships with both incentive system and homogeneity, in the predicted direction. This finding took on new meaning when the same two variables reappeared in the next table as the only two showing a moderately significant association with change on the equalitarianism scale, again in the predicted direction.

Religion was strictly an afterthought in this study. On the assumption that belief in God had something in common with acceptance of secular control, all the predictions made for equalitarianism were repeated for religious beliefs. Of the four situational variables involved, two (task and incentive system) had a modest effect on religion. Neither relationship could be explained in a manner consistent with what we already knew about centralization of control at the behavioral level. More reasonable, we believed, was an alternative interpretation relating changes in theism to group differences in solidarity. The rationale here (borrowed from Miller and Swanson) was that the concept of transcendent purpose in the nonempirical world has its roots in the perception of collective purpose in the empirical world.

Although the few results that did reach statistical significance are generally consistent with our theory, they can hardly be said to constitute a clear-cut validation of that theory. While the fault may very well lie with the theory, it is quite plausible that something was wrong with our methodology. There are a number of features of the experimental design as well as the specific operations employed that come to mind.

For one thing, the 16 sections were led by three different instructors. Despite our efforts to standardize the instructors' behavior, it is clear from the tape recordings that they differed widely in how much they talked, what they talked about, etc. The instructors' behavior is an additional variable which could only serve to attenuate the impact of those variables which were formally built into the study. Of the many methodological shortcomings in this experiment, our failure to standardize the instructor's role was probably the most serious.

We have already spoken of the problems involved in taking interaction scores from a tape recording. Although we have no way of knowing for sure, it is our hunch that the difficulties involved in identifying voices with names had something to do with our failure to find any between group variation in the centralization of control.

There was one weakness in the design of the experiment over which we had little control. We refer to the fact that subjects met for only 50 minutes a week. This meant that the 12 hours of task experience intervening between the first and second administrations of the attitude questionnaire were spread out over a period of four months. It is not unreasonable to assume that the 12 hours of class time were over-shadowed by the many other experiences that each subject must have undergone during that time. It occurred to us at the end of the experiment that the same 12 hours compressed into a single week might have had a much more striking effect on subjects' attitudes. This hunch was subsequently borne out in the laboratory experiments described later in this book.

There are other problems that might be mentioned. In devising the attitude questionnaire, for example, we probably should have used a more sensitive response format. The six-category format employed very likely missed some of the minor changes that would have been picked up with nine or ten categories. Given the borderline nature of many of our results, this could have been an important factor.

Finally, with respect to the design of the experiment, it is clear that some of the independent variables were more difficult to establish than others. We are thinking specifically of the trouble we had in making the blue-book task meaningful to those groups operating under a curved grading system. Since it was impossible to tell who had contributed what just by looking at the single blue-book handed in to the instructor at the end of the hour, we ended up grading students according to their *verbal* contribution to the blue-book essay. As a result, the students paid less and less attention to what actually got written down in the blue-book. In the process, they became increasingly similar to those groups which were supposed to discuss the question posed by the instructor without writing an essay on it. As a consequence, the task variable lost most of its importance for those subjects in the curve groups. This was unfortunate in view of the fact that we were more interested in this situational variable than any of the others.[31]

CONCLUSIONS

Perhaps the safest conclusion we can draw from this particular study is that more research is required before accepting or rejecting the reasoning on which it is based. There is good reason, we feel, for believing that such an effort would be fruitful. Although the results reported here can hardly be called impressive, they would seem to indicate that the theory has some predictive value. At the very least, they suggest that it might be worthwhile to explore the matter a bit further. The results of such an exploration are described in the next chapter.

[31] Thanks to Deutsch's MIT study (*op. cit.*) we anticipated some difficulty, but, given the limits of the classroom situation, could think of no way of getting around the problem.

EXHIBIT A

	I*	II	
1.	.73	—.03	The independent spirit—spurning all aid, needing no one, self-reliant and free—this is man at his best.
2.	.69	.07	In life, an individual should for the most part "go it alone," assuring himself of privacy, having much time to himself, attempting to control his own life.
3.	.66	.14	For the most part, I get along quite well on my own—I don't need other people.
4.	—.59	.06	Life would be pretty empty without some kind of group to identify with, belong to, feel a part of.
5.	.56	—.01	One must avoid dependence upon persons or things—the center of life should be found within oneself.
6.	.52	—.12	Man's state is one of isolation—there is no possibility of genuine communication with others.
7.	.51	.06	My privacy means more to me than almost anything else.
8.	—.50	.02	When there is a choice between working by myself and working together with some friends, I ordinarily choose to work with my friends.
9.	.48	.06	I am probably too much of an individualist to be a good team member.
10.	—.48	.04	In any definition of the good life, companionship, friendship, and fellowship should all receive high priority.
11.	.46	.01	People should solve their problems by themselves.
12.	—.46	.21	The group spirit—working together, sharing each other's goals, co-operating as a team—this is something worth striving for.
13.	.44	—.14	The best way to avoid trouble is to be as completely self-sufficient as possible.
14.	—.42	.25	I like the feeling of being part of a group where people work together, trust each other, and devote themselves to the welfare of the group as a whole.
15.	.41	—.09	Whenever I do take part in group activities, I am something of a nonconformist.
16.	.39	.01	My freedom and autonomy mean more to me than almost anything else.
17.	—.33	.13	I like groups in which there is a real spirit of cohesiveness.
18.	—.30	—.04	It is very important to me to know that there is a group, clique, neighborhood, or community to which I can "belong."
19.	.25	—.22	Most human relationships reduce in the last analysis to a question of who is going to be boss and who is going to obey.

---

* Factor I is individualism, factor II, equalitarianism. The two columns of numbers indicate the loading of each item on each of the two factors.

	I	II	
20.	.23	—.06	I usually have trouble adjusting to those groups in which everyone is expected to play down his own individual interests and needs and work for the greater good of the group as a whole.
21.	.17	.29	The ideal society is one in which no one is in a position to exercise power or authority over anyone else.
22.	.14	.18	Obedience and respect for authority are the most important virtues children should learn.
23.	.13	.55	I would prefer an equalitarian group to one with a well-defined leadership structure.
24.	.13	—.46	In most groups it is better to choose somebody to take charge and run things and then hold him responsible, even if he does some things the members don't like.
25.	.11	—.43	I often get impatient with groups that require that all decisions be unanimous.
26.	.09	—.50	I would find it frustrating to take part in a group in which everyone insisted on having an equal voice in the decisions that had to be made.
27.	—.09	.61	I like groups in which the members talk things over and decide what should be done unanimously.
28.	—.08	—.26	There should be a definite hierarchy in an organization, with definite duties for everyone.
29.	.07	.50	In a small group there should be no leaders—everyone should have an equal say.
30.	—.07	—.27	It is a rare group that can survive for very long without some kind of leadership.
31.	—.06	.48	A group of people who treat each other as equals will work a lot better together than a group with a rigid hierarchy.
32.	—.06	—.28	There is no such thing as a perfectly democratic group.
33.	—.06	.48	In general, a person in authority can get better results from his subordinates if he treats them in an equalitarian rather than an authoritarian fashion.
34.	—.06	.08	You have to respect authority, and when you stop respecting authority your situation isn't worth much.
35.	—.06	.35	The leaderless group is often the most spontaneous, creative, and productive.
36.	—.05	—.26	People need someone strong to lean on.
37.	.03	.37	No man should ever be given the right to order someone else to do something against his will.
38.	.02	—.36	I find it very upsetting to participate in groups in which no one has the responsibility for making decisions.
39.	.01	—.44	I prefer groups in which someone is appointed leader and given clear-cut responsibility for making decisions.
40.	.01	.55	A good group is democratic—the members should talk things over and decide what should be done unanimously.

RELIGION†

1. Heaven and Hell are products of man's imagination, and do not actually exist. (—)
2. Every explanation of man and the world is incomplete unless it takes into account God's will. (+)
3. Christianity and all other religions are, at best, partly true. (—)
4. In addition to faith, we need help from God in order to resist temptation. (+)
5. There is no supernatural world and no supernatural rewards and punishments. (—)
6. Man can solve all his important problems without help from a Supreme Being. (—)
7. Every person should have complete faith in some supernatural power, whose decisions he obeys without question. (+)
8. There is a higher power above man. (+)
9. All the evidence goes to show that the universe has evolved in accordance with natural principles, so there is no necessity to assume a God behind it. (—)
10. Many events in human history took place only because a Supreme Being stepped in to make them happen. (+)

† No factor analysis was performed on the religion items (see text). In computing scale scores, each of the ten items was given the same weight. A (+) indicates that the item was weighted in the theistic direction, a (—) that the item was weighted in the atheistic direction.

CHAPTER 4

Individualism—Collectivism (1)

THE WISCONSIN STUDY was originally designed to explore some of the major determinants of group structure. In formulating an experiment suitable to this intent, we became interested in the possibility that our subjects, in responding behaviorally to the situational conditions we had posed, would alter some of their cultural beliefs, values, and preferences in such a way as to reflect the experience they had just undergone. Taken collectively, the results of the Wisconsin study indicated that this possibility was real enough to warrant further exploration.

It was the senior author's original intention to replicate the Wisconsin experiment (with a few minor changes) with one of his classes at Cornell. This proved to be impossible, however, when a sizable minority of the class voted against participating in the experiment.

Of the two major possibilities remaining, laboratory experiment and field study, we decided to start with the former. Given the borderline nature of many of our findings at Wisconsin where students met 12 or 13 times over the course of a term, it seemed unlikely that we could get significant attitude change in a contrived setting lasting but a few hours unless the experience could be made a very intense one. This possibility we felt was worth exploring. In searching for ways to make the experience as unequivocal as possible, we came up with what we believed to be three critical conditions.

The first step was to formalize the trial and error process which was implicit in the operations of our Wisconsin groups. In that setting, for example, a group faced with the problem of writing a joint essay in 50 minutes might start out in a very egalitarian fashion with everyone sharing equally in the decision-making process. Hypothetically, we would expect that, after several weeks of negative feedback (low grades), the members involved would agree to allow some one or two individuals to take major responsibility for guiding the actions of the group as a whole. Such a group, it seemed to us, would be more likely to undergo significant attitude change than one in which "errors" had never been made at the outset. The learning effect here is twofold, with members being rewarded for certain forms of organization while being "punished" for alternative patterns of behavior. We would argue (some evidence will be presented in a later chapter) that the sharper the contrast between the two, the more likely it is that attitude change will take place.

We can assume that most groups, given an extended period of time, eventually get around to experimenting with a variety of forms of social organization. In the time-bound laboratory setting, however, it is possible that some, if not most, groups never get around to adopting more than a single strategy. Assuming that contrast between differentially rewarding structures is critical for attitude change, it thus becomes necessary in the laboratory to formalize the trial-and-error process. It was with this in mind that we decided to confront our subjects with an experience in which they would be asked to work on a task in two different ways (together versus alone), while seeing to it that they would be rewarded for doing it one way and punished (rewarded less) for doing it the other.

The first of our three innovations, then, was to make the instrumental value of a certain form of organization more salient by deliberately contrasting it with an alternative, less efficient form of organization. The second innovation involved taking precautions to guarantee that the subjects would see one kind of organization as consistently superior to the other. Rather than waiting for the "natural" superiority of one form of organization to assert itself, we deliberately controlled performance feedback throughout the experiment. This procedure we felt to be dictated by the very limited amount of time at our disposal.

Thirdly, we asked our subjects to participate in three different sessions of the experiment, arranged in such a way that no two individuals would ever be together more than once. We wanted to avoid the possibility that our subjects would attribute their success or failure to being in a group made up of especially able or inept students, instead of attributing it to the superiority of one form of organization over another. By systematically rotating group composition, we hoped to minimize the effects of personality differences while maximizing the salience of social organization.

ATTITUDE QUESTIONNAIRE

There were innovations as well in our measure of beliefs, preferences, and values. In the Wisconsin study we limited our items to those of a relatively general or abstract character, using as our model the Bales-

Couch Value Profile.[1] In the process of making up a new questionnaire, the thought occurred to us that attitudes which were tied to more specific situations (e.g., the family or community) would be affected by task experience as well. In Chapter 1 we referred to this process as one of "lateral generalization." By this we meant the generalization of orientations from one concrete task situation to another. To this we contrasted the generalization of situationally specific beliefs, preferences, and values (vertically) to more abstract, inclusive categories of experience in which many different tasks are represented. In the Wisconsin study we confined ourselves to generalization of the vertical variety. In the interests of testing for lateral generalization in the present study, we expanded our measure to include items dealing with a number of task situations ranging from school work to the practice of religion.

Regardless of the specific task situation to which the items were addressed, they were all intended to be expressions of a single, common dimension—individualism versus collectivism. With this theme in mind, we wrote items to cover the following areas: (1) homework, (2) family, (3) neighborhood, (4) church, and (5) man's relationship to God. In addition we included items (many taken from the Wisconsin questionnaire) dealing with individualism in general. With regards to the first five scales, there were essentially two considerations which governed our choice. First of all, we found the theme of individualism-collectivism to be more salient in some settings than others. Homework, family, neighborhood, and church seemed especially appropriate for items dealing with the issue of "going it alone" versus doing things together with other people.

A second consideration in our decision to use these particular task areas was variety. We wanted to test (more accurately, explore) the proposition that attitudes developed in one situation (the laboratory) would generalize laterally to other situations along a gradient of similarity. Given the experimental situation as the starting point, we picked five different task situations (areas) which seemed to vary along a continuum of similarity. Homework, for example, we felt to be more similar to the experimental task than any of the others, primarily because of the common emphasis on rational problem-solving behavior. The church scale, dealing with private versus public worship, was included precisely because it seemed so remote from the highly instrumental operations of the laboratory. Family and neighborhood seemed to fall somewhere in between, no attempt being made to differentiate

---

[1] Robert F. Bales and Arthur S. Couch, "The Value Profile: A Factor Analytic Study of Value Statements," unpublished paper, 1959.

between the two. Given the difficulty of determining just how similar any two task situations were, we decided to sit back and wait for the results before engaging in any further speculations.

The items dealing with the relationship between man and God were frankly included as a lark. In trying to carry the theme of alone versus together as far as we could, we thought we detected something of this sort in the theological or metaphysical realm—more specifically the philosophy of mysticism. Several of our items were designed to capture what some writers feel to be the essence of the mystical experience; i.e., the loss of identity in a pervasive, transcendental sense of oneness.

The questionnaire which was to be given before and after the experiment included 160 items. Thirty of these were designed to measure attitudes toward individualism in general. Of the remaining 130 items, thirty each were assigned to homework, family, neighborhood, and church, with the last ten being devoted to the man-God relationship. In all cases but the last, items were distributed evenly among our three modes of orientation (cathectic, cognitive, and evaluative). Within each subset, approximately half of the items were phrased in an individualistic direction and half in a collectivistic direction.

The response format was a 10-point scale anchored at each end with the words Strongly Agree and Strongly Disagree.[2] Subjects were asked to indicate their degree of agreement or disagreement by placing an X over one of the ten dashes provided. We felt that such a format would best satisfy the somewhat contradictory criteria of reliability and sensitivity. To insure adequate reliability, a narrow enough response range was needed so that responses to similar items would not be too variable or unstable; to insure adequate sensitivity, a broad enough response range was needed so that when they were given the after questionnaire, subjects could not recall exactly how they had answered each item at the time of the first administration.

Since the computer facilities at Cornell could not at this time handle a correlation matrix of 160 items, we decided to analyze each area separately (using the *before* questionnaires of 73 subjects). For each area we intercorrelated all items, factor analyzed the matrix by the centroid method, and rotated the factors using the quartimax method. Factor scores for both before and after questionnaires were computed by summing the responses to all items in a given factor satisfying the following four criteria: (1) a mean between 3.0 and 8.0, (2) a standard deviation equal to or greater than 2.0, (3) a factor loading equal

---

[2] In the Wisconsin study the questionnaire had only six possible response categories. This was probably too few categories even for that study and thus definitely too few for this study in which subjects were to meet for a total of only six hours.

to or greater than .30, and (4) no higher loading on any other factor (with one exception).[3] The actual items making up each factor can be seen in Exhibit B at the end of this chapter.

Once the item content of each factor had been decided upon, a measure of internal consistency was computed from the average inter-correlation of the items corrected by the Spearman-Brown formula.[4] All factors with internal consistencies less than .60 (ordinarily the last factors to be extracted in each area) were excluded from further analysis. For each of the remaining 13 scales we also computed a correlation between scores on the first administration of the questionnaire and scores on the second administration. These test-retest reliabilities are shown in Table 4–1 along with the internal consistencies already

TABLE 4–1

Internal Consistencies and Reliabilities for Factor Scales

Area	Factor	Number of Items	Internal Consistency	Test-Retest Reliability	
				CL	ID
Homework	I	9	.86	.35	.78
Homework	II	6	.64	.50	.63
Homework	III	7	.66	.64	.73
Family	I	5	.60	.64	.54
Family	II	5	.62	.67	.78
Family	III	9	.73	.68	.72
Neighborhood	I	7	.77	.97	.91
Neighborhood	II	5	.65	.54	.65
Neighborhood	III	6	.78	.76	.64
Church	I	20	.94	.96	.95
Man-God	I	7	.70	.70	.88
General	I	9	.74	.77	.73
General	II	6	.63	.49	.79

mentioned. Although we haven't discussed the experimental design yet, it should be noted here that subjects were divided into two groups, one receiving the "individualistic" treatment (ID's), the other the "collectivistic" treatment (CL's). Since the two groups of subjects were expected to change their attitudes in opposite directions, the test-retest correlations were computed separately for each group.[5]

---

[3] All items were given an equal weight regardless of factor loading. A reanalysis of the Wisconsin data had indicated that it made little difference whether unit weights or factor weights were used.

[4] See Chapter 3, footnote 18.

[5] Given the fact that subjects (for a number of reasons) varied widely in how much their attitudes changed, these before-after correlations should be viewed as very conservative estimates of the true test-retest reliabilities.

The questionnaire just described was administered before and after the experiment. In a further attempt to improve upon the Wisconsin study, another brief questionnaire was given at the end of the experiment. The justification for this additional measure (given only *after* the experiment) follows directly from the theory as described in Chapter 1. We have postulated that when an individual is confronted with a new experience, the first attitudes to be affected are those directly related to the experience itself. Once formed, they can be expected to generalize to other situations. The attitude questionnaire described above deals with a variety of settings to which attitudes developed in the experiment might conceivably generalize. What we needed in addition was a set of items designed to measure the more specific orientations developed vis-à-vis the experimental situation itself. Unless significant differences emerged here, we could not expect generalization to more remote areas.

In keeping with our threefold conception of the attitudinal universe, we also included cathectic, cognitive, and evaluative items in this questionnaire. All items were written in such a way as to be specific to the experimental situation itself. Since the experiment involved performing a task alternately together and alone, the questionnaire was constructed around this theme. Nine items in all were written, three in each mode. Subjects were asked, in a variety of ways, which of the two ways of performing the task they *preferred* and which they felt to be the more *efficient*. They were also asked to indicate what they felt to be *appropriate* behavior in that part of the experiment where subjects were working together. The three sets of items (cathectic, cognitive, and evaluative) proved to be highly interrelated. In this case the corrected average interitem correlation was .92.

Finally, one behavioral measure was taken during the experiment whenever the subjects worked in groups. As in the Wisconsin study, a record was made of the number of group- and self-references, the prediction being that group solidarity (ratio of group- to self-references) would correlate positively with success. The prediction, while of interest in its own right, is peripheral to our main concern with attitude change. This will become clear once we have described the actual experimental procedure.

PROCEDURE

The subjects for this experiment were recruited from an introductory psychology course at Cornell about one to two weeks before the experiment began. Students were administered the 160-item questionnaire during the last half hour of a weekly section meeting. It should be noted here that, under these conditions, not all students were motivated to do a careful job as evidenced by the fact that many finished and left after only 15 or 20 minutes. This is important because of the contrast with post-test conditions which will be described below. On the face sheet of the questionnaire students were asked if they would like to be subjects in a small group experiment. They were told they could earn anywhere from five to ten dollars, depending on their performance.

Out of a total of approximately 150 students in the course, 93 males indicated a desire to participate in the experiment. Twenty had to be excluded because of failure to complete the questionnaire. In 15 cases this was because they could not answer the religious items, most of which assumed some minimal belief in God (students were instructed to leave them blank if they did not endorse even this minimal belief). Of the 73 remaining, 48 were chosen at random and contacted for specific appointments by phone. All were males, most of them in their first year of college.

Each subject was asked to attend three two-hour sessions within a period of approximately one week (e.g., Monday, Wednesday, and Friday). Of the 48 originally signed up, 45 came all three times. Subjects were invited to come in groups of five. With very few exceptions, each subject was placed with a different group of people for each of the three sessions.

The experiment was introduced in the first session as a study of the relative efficiency of working alone versus working together in solving logical problems. It was emphasized that the research was of an exploratory nature, that the experimenter had no idea as to how the results would actually turn out. The task was explained in the following manner.

I have here a questionnaire which was filled out last year by a student at Cornell. This questionnaire is unrelated to the one you filled out in Psychology 101 a week or two ago. On the copies to be handed out we have indicated with circles how this student actually answered the first four items. What we want you to do is to predict, starting with item number five, how this person actually filled out the rest of the questionnaire. Read over the first four statements and answers so that you have some idea of what this person is like. When you have decided on a prediction for item number five, tell me and I will check my master sheet to see what the right answer is. [Hand out copies of questionnaire.] As you can see, there are six possible answers to each statement, ranging from Strongly Disagree to Strongly Agree. If you guess the answer right on the nose, you will get a blue chip worth ten cents. If you are one off in either direction (e.g., if the answer is Slightly Agree and you say Agree or Slightly Disagree) you will receive a red chip worth five cents. If you are two off in either direction, I will give you a white chip worth one cent. If you are more than two off, you won't receive anything. One thing that makes this task difficult is that when you are one or two off, you will not be told in which *direction* you have erred. This you must try to figure out for yourselves.

It was then explained that the experimental session would be divided into four phases (approximately 30 minutes each). The task would be the same in each case although there would be different questionnaires and different Cornell students to be predicted in each period. The first half hour was to be spent working on the task together, the second period alone, the third together, and the fourth alone.[6] In the "together" periods, students were told that they must come to a unanimous decision for each item being predicted. When all five members of the group agreed on a single answer, they were to relay this answer to the experimenter who would give them the appropriate chip. It was explained that each individual in the group would receive in cash an amount equivalent to the value of the chips on the table at the end of the period. In the two "alone" conditions, subjects were moved to individual tables, facing the walls, where they were asked to go through the same operation of predicting responses to a questionnaire, only this time independently of the others. When an individual was ready to make a prediction, he would raise his hand, on which signal the experimenter would come over, look at the prediction circled, check his master sheet, and drop the appropriate chip on the table.

The prediction task as described above was developed by Bales at Harvard. We considered it to be ideal in terms of meeting several important criteria: (1) it was realistic, yet completely new to all of our subjects; (2) it was an ego-involving task whether done alone or together; (3) the rewards were frequent (since they were given for every item), (4) the criteria for judging degrees of success were clear-cut (compared, for example, to those involved in grading an essay exam), and (5) the task was difficult enough so that the experimenter could manipulate the rewards without arousing any suspicion on the part of the subjects.

Given our interest in simulating a trial and error experience in which

---

[6] Actually, the order depended on the treatment. For CL's, it was alone-together-alone-together; for ID's it was together-alone-together-alone. This procedure was dictated by the assumption that treatment effects would be more salient if subjects always ended up with a "rewarded" session.

one mode of organization very clearly emerges as superior to another, complete control over task results was assumed to be of critical importance. With subjects having only four answers to go on and a limited amount of time to predict responses to a variety of statements which were only slightly correlated, it proved relatively easy to achieve the desired control.

Subjects were randomly assigned to either the "individualistic" or the "collectivistic" treatment before arriving for the first session. While groups were arranged so that, with few exceptions, no two individuals were in the same group more than once, once an individual had been assigned to one of the two treatments, he remained in such throughout the three sessions of the experiment. Those who were assigned to the individualistic treatment (the ID's) were consistently rewarded more for doing the task alone than together. Those in the other half of the sample (the CL's) always did better at the task when performing it together in a group with four other subjects. While the experimenter always took pains to look up the "correct" answers on what appeared to be a master sheet, the approximate amount to be earned in any half hour period was always determined in advance. The same procedure (same task, same reinforcement schedule) was followed in all three sessions of the experiment.

During the "rewarded" half hours, subjects earned (due to the manipulation of the experimenter) between 80 cents and one dollar, with an average of approximately 90 cents. During the "nonrewarded" half hours, they made from 35 to 55 cents, with an average of close to 45 cents. Thus a subject assigned to the individualistic treatment might start by making 35 cents in the first period (together), 85 cents in the second period (alone), 50 cents in the third (together) and 95 cents in the final half hour (alone). Subjects assigned to the collectivistic treatment were reinforced in just the opposite fashion. The amounts earned in each period were deliberately varied so as to avoid arousing subjects' suspicions. The effect, however, was consistent within each two hour session as well as across the three different sessions. The 22 subjects in the individualistic treatment always did better alone than together, the opposite being true for the 23 subjects in the collectivistic treatment. Subjects were not paid until after the third session, although they were always aware of how much they had won since they were asked to count up their chips at the end of each half hour period. All subjects ended up making approximately $8.00 for their six hours' work.

Summary of Predictions

Now that both the attitude questionnaire and the procedure have been described, it might be helpful to review our predictions. The first prediction involved the nine-item postexperimental questionnaire in which subjects were asked to respond to a set of statements dealing specifically with the experiment itself. In comparing the 22 subjects in the individualistic treatment (the ID's) with the 23 in the collectivistic treatment (the CL's), we expected to find a significant difference in: (1) preferences for doing the task alone or together, (2) beliefs with respect to the relative efficiency of performing the task alone versus together, and (3) norms specifying how co-operative the individual should be while in the group setting.

On the assumption that we would be successful in developing situationally specific attitudes of this sort, we made the further prediction that the orientations developed here would generalize laterally to other situations more or less similar in nature and vertically to the theme of individualism-collectivism stated at a very abstract level. More specifically, we predicted that the ID's would become more individualistic and the CL's more collectivistic on each of the 13 factors listed in Table 4-1. With respect to "lateral" generalization, we predicted that homework would show the most change and religion the least, with the family and neighborhood factors falling somewhere in between. No prediction was made for where the two "general" factors (vertical generalization) would fall relative to the others.

Finally, we predicted that the subjects who were rewarded more for performing the task together would be more solidary in their behavior than those who were rewarded more for working alone. The measure employed (group/self references) refers, of course, only to the behavior in the group setting, since no talking was allowed when subjects were working alone.

RESULTS

Behavior

Subjects who were rewarded more for performing the task together than alone proved to be significantly more solidary in their behavior than those who received greater rewards for doing it alone. The group/-self reference means for the two subsamples were .2683 and .1549 respectively, the difference being significant at the .01 level ($t = 3.17$). This means simply that, at least with this kind of task, the more successful a group is, the more solidary will be the behavior of its members.

Postmeeting Reactions

To the extent that our experimental manipulations were successful we would expect to find differences in subjects' cathectic, cognitive, and evaluative orientations to the experimental situation itself. This is very clearly what did happen. When the nine items measuring these reactions were summed to form a single postmeeting reaction index, the mean scores for ID and CL subjects proved to be significantly different beyond the .001 level ($t = 18.78$). Subjects who were rewarded more for performing the task together were more likely to say that they preferred to do it together, that it could be done more efficiently together, and that when working in a group the individual should do his best to make the group as cohesive as possible.

When the over-all index is broken down into its three component parts, we find very sharp differences (between CL's and ID's) on both cathectic and cognitive items, but only a modest (.05) difference on the evaluative or normative items. While this is in keeping with our earlier speculation (cf. Chapter 1) that norms emerge only after cathexis and cognition are highly developed, the finding can better be attributed to the wording of the items. Like our behavior measure (and for the same reasons) the three normative items in the postmeeting questionnaire were oriented exclusively to the "together" parts of the together-alone-together-alone sequence. While the cathectic and cognitive items dealt with the difference between doing the task together versus doing it alone, the normative set was confined to what happened in the together condition. Given this asymmetry, it would be unwise to attribute the relatively poor showing of the normative items simply to the fact that they were normative rather than cathectic or cognitive.

Attitude Change

Changes by Item. Our greatest concern in this study was, of course, the degree to which attitudes developed in the experimental situation were generalized to settings beyond the laboratory. Before looking to see how subjects changed on each of the 13 factors, it might be helpful to examine the questionnaire as a whole. For each of the 160 items in the questionnaire we can compute mean changes for ID's and CL's, substract one from the other, and see if the difference between the changes is in the predicted direction. An analysis of this sort reveals that 93 items changed in the expected direction, 61 in the "wrong" direction, with the remaining 6 showing no change at all. Excluding the latter, this yields a chi-square value of 6.24 ($p < .05$), indicating that the experiment had a significant effect on subjects' attitudes taken as a whole.

Changes by Factor.   There were 19 factors for which before and after scores were computed. Six of these 19 were so grossly unreliable that they were excluded from formal analysis. We did, however, actually compute the t ratios for mean change differences between CL's and ID's on these factors and found none of them to be significant.

For the 13 factors that were retained, Table 4–2 shows the mean change scores separately for the ID and CL groups, the difference between the two changes, the t ratios for the differences, and the appropriate p values.[7] All factors are presented in such a way that a positive change means that the subjects became more collectivistic, a minus sign indicating change in the individualistic direction. If everything had worked as predicted, all the scores in column one (ID's) would be negative, and those in column two (CL's) positive. Since the scores in column three were computed by subtracting the second column from the first, these too should be all positive. The same, of course, applies to the t ratios in column four.

Of the 13 factors for which predictions were made, Table 4–3 shows four to be significant at the .05 level and a fifth (neighborhood III) that just missed. All five of these differences were in the expected direction. In four cases (homework II and III, family III, and neighborhood III) the CL's (those rewarded more for performing the task together) became more collectivistic while the ID's (those rewarded more for doing it alone) became more individualistic. In the fifth case (church I), the ID's failed to change at all ($\bar{x} = .18$), but the CL's moved far enough in the collectivistic direction to yield a significant difference between the two subsamples, in the predicted direction. Although there were no striking reversals, it should be noted that on neighborhood II, ID's and CL's both moved in the wrong direction, yielding a t of -1.88, which is significant at the .10 level. At the same level ($p = .10$) we also find a difference between CL's and ID's on those items dealing with

---

[7] In this experiment as in each of those that follows, we shall be performing a number of different tests of significance. It has been aptly pointed out by Ryan [T. A. Ryan, "Multiple Comparisons in Psychological Research," *Psychological Bulletin,* Vol. 56 (1959), pp. 26–47] that the probability of obtaining results significant at the .05 level is greater than .05 if more than a single significance test is made in a given experiment. Thus the results of any particular test should be interpreted with due caution. To see whether the over-all results of each experiment were significant or not, we have constantly taken the precaution of making an over-all test using *items* as our unit of analysis.

TABLE 4–2

Attitude Change by Factor

Area	Factor	Mean Change		Diff.	t	p
		ID	CL	(CL — ID)		
Homework	I	0.32	3.17	2.85	0.97	ns
Homework	II	−2.59	1.61	4.20	2.11	.05
Homework	III	−1.00	6.22	7.22	2.98	.01
Family	I	1.64	−0.04	−1.68	−0.94	ns
Family	II	−0.09	−0.30	−0.21	−0.15	ns
Family	III	−2.23	3.22	5.45	2.16	.05
Neighborhood	I	−0.91	−0.30	0.61	0.42	ns
Neighborhood	II	2.00	−1.69	−3.69	−1.88	.10
Neighborhood	III	−1.73	2.00	3.73	2.00	.10
Church	I	0.18	9.82	9.64	2.56	.05
Man-God	I	−3.59	−2.50	1.09	1.70	.10
General	I	−4.09	−4.13	−0.04	−0.14	ns
General	II	0.27	−2.13	−2.40	−1.07	ns

the relationship between man and God, this time in the expected direction.

The question arises at this point as to why these particular factors changed and not the others.[8] We made the prediction that the homework factors would change the most and religion the least, with the others somewhere in between. While Table 4–2 shows that we were more successful with the homework factors than with the family or neighborhood factors, it also shows that we were just as successful on the religious items as we were on homework. This is difficult to explain in terms of relative similarity to the experimental situation. While we might be tempted to explain the very significant change on homework III in terms of the fact that most of the items in that factor involve working on group projects (papers, labs, etc.) and in this sense are similar to what happened in the experiment, it is absurd to extend this interpretation to our church items. Just what the issue of worshipping in private versus worshipping in church has in common with predicting responses to a questionnaire is not at all clear.

There is another explanation for the findings. More important than similarity, perhaps, is the certainty with which the individual holds his original attitudes. The more fixed (although not necessarily extreme)

---

[8] One possible explanation for the results is that the CL's and ID's were very different to begin with and, by virtue of *differential regression,* changed in the predicted direction. To test this possibility, *t*-tests were performed on the *before* factor scores. ID's and CL's proved to be significantly different right from the beginning on two factors: family I and neighborhood II. However, since we found no significant experimental effect on either of these two factors, differential regression must be ruled out as an explanation for our results.

an individual is in the attitudes he brings to the experimental situation, the less likely he will be to change his attitudes as a result of the experience he is confronted with when he gets there. With respect to our findings here, it is possible that college freshmen are less certain about their responses to items dealing with homework and religion than those which involve family and neighborhood activities. Having grown up in families and interacted with neighbors, they know what they believe, value, and prefer when it comes to these areas of life. While these freshmen have done homework before, it is unlikely that they have very

TABLE 4–3
Number of Subjects Changing, by Factor and Condition

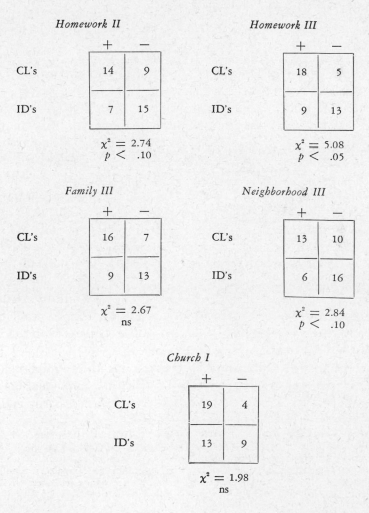

Homework II

	+	−
CL's	14	9
ID's	7	15

$$\chi^2 = 2.74$$
$$p < .10$$

Homework III

	+	−
CL's	18	5
ID's	9	13

$$\chi^2 = 5.08$$
$$p < .05$$

Family III

	+	−
CL's	16	7
ID's	9	13

$$\chi^2 = 2.67$$
ns

Neighborhood III

	+	−
CL's	13	10
ID's	6	16

$$\chi^2 = 2.84$$
$$p < .10$$

Church I

	+	−
CL's	19	4
ID's	13	9

$$\chi^2 = 1.98$$
ns

fixed attitudes about doing homework together versus doing it alone. The same is probably true for religion. Although religion is a favorite topic for dormitory bullsessions, we doubt that many students have given systematic thought to the issue of worshipping alone versus worshipping together.

Changes by Subjects. There is also another way of looking at the same data. Beyond testing for the *magnitude* of factor changes, we would like to know *how many* of the subjects changed in the predicted direction. We would expect that, for those factors on which the mean change scores were significantly different, the majority of subjects changed in the predicted direction. This need not be the case, however. It is possible, for example, for half of the subjects in each treatment to change very slightly in the wrong direction while the rest change sharply in the predicted direction. This might yield a significant *mean* difference between the two groups even though the number of *subjects* in each group changing as predicted is no better than chance.

Table 4–3 shows the number of subjects changing in each direction on each of the five factors with *t* ratios (Table 4–2) significant at the .06 level or better. Again, all factors are positioned such that a positive score (+) indicates change in the *collectivistic* direction. It can be seen that only one of the five chi-square values reaches significance at the .05 level, although all are in the predicted direction. It appears that, on the average, somewhat over 60 per cent of the subjects changed in the expected direction.

Beliefs, Values, and Preferences

A careful inspection of the data revealed no systematic differences in changes of items phrased in the cathectic, cognitive, or evaluative mode. This complements the findings of the factor analysis which showed no tendency for items to cluster by mode. It also confirms the results of the Wisconsin study where no significant differences of this sort were found. It would appear that the cathectic, cognitive, and evaluative items represent little more than different ways of asking the same basic question and that differentiating among modes has no empirical relevance as far as this study is concerned.

Initial Position and Amount of Change

Results from recent *persuasion* studies suggest that the relationship between initial position and amount of change is a rather complicated one. Several investigators have reported a positive relationship between amount of attitude change obtained and the amount of change advocated in the communication.[9] In other words, the greater the discrepancy between the stand of the communicator and the initial position of the subject, the greater the change that will take place. We also have evidence, however, to indicate that people whose initial attitudes are extreme in either direction change less than those whose initial attitudes are more moderate.[10] It would appear that when the discrepancy between communicator and subject is very large, the subject will not only resist the communication but may even move further in the opposite direction. When, on the other hand, the subject holds an extreme attitude which is similar to that of the communicator, he will not change because there is no more room on the continuum ("ceiling effect").

The positive correlation between discrepancy and amount of change must therefore be qualified to read "except where the initial attitudes are extreme." According to Hovland and Pritzker, the finding should be further qualified to read "except on issues where the individual is deeply involved."[11] In the latter case, the very opposite is to be expected, namely that the people most likely to change are those whose opinions are already somewhat similar to those of the communicator. Hovland, Harvey, and Sherif offer some evidence to indicate that on issues in which the individual is deeply involved, subjects who initially disagree with the communicator will not change at all.[12]

In our own study, no attempt was made to predict what kind of relationship we would find between original position and amount of change. We did, however, compute correlations between initial position and amount of change for each of the 13 factor scales. This was not as simple as it might sound, since our subject population was divided into two subsamples which were exposed to two very different kinds of treatment (in persuasion studies the analogue to treatment would be communication). In order to include both ID's and CL's in the same analysis, it was necessary to transfer the two sets of attitude scores to a common scale. To do this for the initial position scores we took the

[9] C. I. Hovland and H. A. Pritzker, "Extent of Opinion Change as a Function of Amount of Change Advocated," *Journal of Abnormal and Social Psychology*, Vol. 54 (1957), pp. 257–61; W. Weiss, "The Relationship between Judgments of a Communicator's Position and Extent of Opinion Change," *Journal of Abnormal and Social Psychology*, Vol. 56 (1958), pp. 380–84.

[10] P. H. Tannenbaum, "Initial Attitude Toward Source and Concept as Factors in Attitude Change Through Communication," *Public Opinion Quarterly*, Vol. 20 (1956), pp. 413–25; C. I. Hovland, O. J. Harvey, and M. Sherif, "Assimilation and Contrast Effects in Reactions to Communication and Attitude Change," *Journal of Abnormal and Social Psychology*, Vol. 55 (1957), pp. 244–52.

[11] Hovland and Pritzker, *op. cit.*

[12] Hovland, Harvey, and Sherif, *op. cit.*

mean of all subjects on a given factor as the zero point and computed initial position scores as deviations from this mean. Only after we had adjusted the signs on both the initial position scores and the change scores to take into consideration the fact that ID's were supposed to change one way and CL's another, were we ready to compute a single correlation between original position and change for both groups at the same time.

The correlations are shown for each factor in Table 4–4. A negative correlation indicates that the closer a subject is in his original attitudes

TABLE 4–4

Correlation between Initial Position and
Amount of Attitude Change Induced

N = 45

Area	Factor	r
Homework	I	−.58†
	II	−.43†
	III	−.50†
Family	I	−.27
	II	−.53†
	III	−.38*
Neighborhood	I	−.35*
	II	−.50†
	III	−.40†
Church	I	−.36*
Man–God	I	−.35*
General	I	−.45†
	II	−.51†

* $p < .05$.
† $p < .01$.

to what he can be expected to "learn" from the experiment, the less likely it is that his attitudes will change. It can be seen that all the correlations are, in fact, negative and all but one are significant at the .05 level or better. The strong, linear relationship between initial position and amount of change can be seen even more clearly in Figure 4–1. Change scores were computed separately for each fifth of the subject population, from that fifth with the highest discrepancy between original position and treatment to the fifth with attitudes most similar to the treatment received. In computing original position and change alike, only scores from the five factors showing significant t ratios were used. These five scores were then combined. Means were computed separately for ID's and CL's and then averaged. Thus, the first point on the graph (Figure 4–1) represents the average change score for that

20 per cent of the ID population with the most collectivistic initial attitudes *and* that 20 per cent of the CL population with most individualistic initial attitudes.

FIGURE 4–1

Amount of Change in Predicted Direction as a Function of
Amount of Discrepancy between Original Attitude and
Type of Treatment for ID's and CL's Combined on
Five Factors

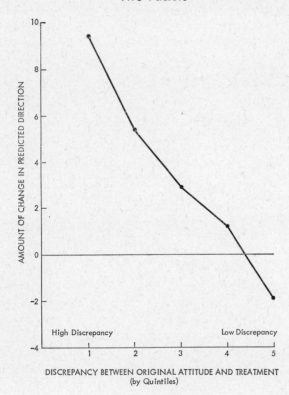

DISCREPANCY BETWEEN ORIGINAL ATTITUDE AND TREATMENT
(by Quintiles)

DISCUSSION

A number of contaminating factors need to be taken into consideration in evaluating the results of this study. In the first place, the pre-test and post-test were administered under radically different conditions. Many of our subjects told us after the experiment that they did not take the questionnaire as seriously the first time when it was given as part of a discussion section in an introductory psychology course. During the second administration subjects were paid two cents a minute for filling out the questionnaire, in addition to what they had made in the experiment per se. A comparison of before and after scores indicated a very significant regression effect. Subjects who had rushed through the questionnaire during the first administration (checking many extreme responses) were more likely to qualify their answers in the more serious second administration. This had the obvious effect of introducing a great deal of variation into the change scores which could not be accounted for by treatment differences.

Secondly, a period of two to three weeks elapsed between pre- and post-tests, thus allowing considerable opportunity for other experiences unrelated to the experiment to affect attitudes. For example, one student, during an interview at the end of the experiment, indicated that she had recently tried studying together with several classmates and found it rewarding. The fact that this affected her responses to our post-test is exactly what we would expect given our theory; the trouble is, she was in the ID sample and hence should have become more individualistic on the second administration. While it is true that outside experiences of this sort probably cancel each other out, the fact remains that this represents additional variation which is uncontrolled in the experiment itself. The effect, of course, is to make less salient that variation due to conditions imposed by the experimenter.

This is related to a third consideration, namely that the experimental experience was spread out over so long a period (roughly six hours in one week) that there was ample opportunity for the laboratory experience to get "lost" in a host of competing events. Although there was no way of knowing at this point, the thought occurred to us that it might have been more effective to compress the six hours into one session or, at the most, two sessions on successive afternoons.

Finally, and there can be little doubt about this, some of our factors left a great deal to be desired with respect to internal consistency and test-re-test reliability. Out of the 13 factors on which change scores were computed only two had internal consistencies higher than .80, and only two had test-re-test reliabilities over .80 for both ID and CL groups, leaving considerable room for measurement error which could only work to attenuate any treatment effects that might have emerged.

CONCLUSIONS

In spite of these several uncontrolled sources of variation, it does appear that we were moderately successful in inducing the desired effects. The major question this study was designed to answer was whether or not significant attitude change could be induced in the laboratory setting. Although the results obtained were far from overwhelming, they clearly represent something beyond chance variation. In this sense we felt that we had taken an important step beyond the Wisconsin study. The possibility of studying attitude induction in the laboratory offers many advantages in theory development. One of these is time. While it took close to six months to run and analyze the Wisconsin experiment, the study reported here was executed and analyzed in less than six weeks. Another consideration is the difficulty of finding settings of the Wisconsin type. This was made clear by our own unsuccessful attempts at trying to replicate that study at Cornell. Most important of all, the laboratory lends itself to an infinite number of designs, a luxury denied to the investigator who does his research in the field.

There were several questions that remained unanswered in this study. Most prominent among them was the question of why attitudes induced in one setting generalized to some areas but not to others. While similarity of experience was probably one of the factors involved, it was clearly not the only one. Certainty of original positions seemed to be another. Given the instruments used, it was impossible to draw any definite conclusions about the relative importance of each.

Also left unanswered by this experiment was the question of generality across attitude dimensions. Given the fact that most of our significant results in the Wisconsin study came with the individualism scale (with next to nothing on the equalitarianism factor), the possibility remained that our theory was applicable to this dimension and no others. The next experiment was designed to explore this very possibility.

EXHIBIT B

HOMEWORK: FACTOR I*

1. When preparing for an exam, I would rather work by myself than together with other people taking the same course. (—)
2. I need to be alone when I am preparing for an exam. (—)
3. I can't study with anyone else around. (—)
4. I like the idea of getting together with other people before an exam and going over the lecture and reading notes as a group. (+)
5. I find group studying a very frustrating and generally unpleasant experience. (—)
6. When it comes to getting good grades in college, it's every man for himself. (—)

---

* A (—) indicates item was weighted in the "individualistic" direction.
  A (+) indicates item was weighted in the "collectivistic" direction.
  This applies to all subsequent factors as well.

7. In preparing for an exam, each student in a course should work strictly on his own. (—)
8. The most efficient way to review for an exam is to go someplace where no one can bother you. (—)
9. Studying with others before an exam usually leads to "goofing off" and a lack of concrete accomplishment. (—)

HOMEWORK: FACTOR II

1. Whenever possible, students in the same course should help each other prepare for examinations. (+)
2. If the subject matter is at all appropriate, the instructor should assign some group reports and papers. (+)
3. Wherever possible students with high marks should try to help those with low marks. (+)
4. Students taking the same course should periodically get together outside of class for informal discussions of ideas brought out in lectures and the reading. (+)
5. It is easier to get a comprehensive picture of a course through group discussion than through individual study. (+)
6. It has been found that science students do better lab work when they work in pairs than when they work alone. (+)

HOMEWORK: FACTOR III

1. I would feel stifled if I had to work with others on a lab or a class project. (—)
2. Studying can be fun if done in groups. (+)
3. I would rather do a group paper or lab than do one alone. (+)
4. The assigning of group grades for co-operative work would be a good thing. (+)
5. It has been found that science students do better lab work when they work in pairs than when they work alone. (+)
6. It is probably true that when students work on term papers together they do a better job than when they work all by themselves. (+)
7. I would suspect that few group reports or papers can match the quality of those turned in by individuals. (—)

FAMILY: FACTOR I

1. In the ideal marriage, husband and wife are so completely and intimately a part of each other that it is only in the most literal sense that we continue to speak of the tie as a relationship between two individuals. (+)
2. A tightly knit, cohesive family is necessary to guarantee a child's emotional security. (+)
3. Neurosis in children is most frequent in families where both the father and mother have jobs which prevent them from spending more than a minimal amount of time with their children. (+)

4. Family solidarity is one of society's most effective safeguards against mental illness. (+)
5. A man is lost in this world if he doesn't have a family to stick by him in time of need. (—)

FAMILY: FACTOR II

1. The kind of marital relationship I look forward to is one in which each person feels free to pursue his or her own private interests independently of the other. (—)
2. The kind of marital relationship that appeals most to me is the one that allows for the maximum autonomy, independence, and freedom of movement. (—)
3. In the ideal family, each member should feel completely free to pursue his own interests even though this means that the family rarely does anything as a group. (—)
4. An individual's first obligations are to himself, and only secondarily to other members of his family. (—)
5. Most men would prefer to spend less time with their families than they actually do. (—)

FAMILY: FACTOR III

1. To me, one of the most attractive features of family life is the very deep sense of belonging it provides. (+)
2. I want my children to be each other's best friend. (+)
3. When my children grow up, I hope they can live close enough to me so that we can go on doing things together. (+)
4. I like the feeling of being a part of a family where everyone enjoys going places and doing things together. (+)
5. There are few satisfactions more meaningful than being part of a closely knit family. (+)
6. I don't especially like doing things together with other members of my family. (—)
7. Family members should always stick up for each other regardless of what any one of them does. (+)
8. Parents should be careful not to infringe on the privacy and autonomy of their children. (—)
9. Parents should encourage their children to spend as much of their free time as possible in joint activities involving the family as a whole. (+)

NEIGHBORHOOD: FACTOR I

1. I would like to live in a neighborhood where everybody knows everybody else. (+)
2. I have no desire to do things together with my neighbors. (—)
3. I couldn't stand living in a place where there were no neighbors for miles around. (+)
4. I prefer to stay out of neighborhood activities as much as possible. (—)

5. We should treat our neighbors as we treat our closest friends. (+)
6. Neighbors should take a personal interest in each other. (+)
7. People who are neighbors should feel free to borrow things from each other. (+)

NEIGHBORHOOD: FACTOR II

1. Juvenile delinquents usually come from neighborhoods in which everyone goes his own way and no one cares what anyone else does. (+)
2. Many of the ills of contemporary American society can be traced to the impersonal and atomistic character of urban life. (+)
3. I would guess that suicide rates are significantly lower in closely knit communities. (+)
4. Most people would find difficulty in adjusting to a life without neighbors. (+)
5. In the long run the only real answer to the juvenile delinquency problem is the small, cohesive community. (+)

NEIGHBORHOOD: FACTOR III

1. What I want most from my neighbors is respect for my privacy. (—)
2. I would prefer a neighborhood in which everyone pretty much goes his own way. (—)
3. As far as I am concerned, the fewer neighbors I have the better I like it. (—)
4. The ideal neighbor is the one who minds his own business. (—)
5. Neighbors should feel no social obligations towards each other. (—)
6. Good fences make good neighbors. (—)

CHURCH: FACTOR I

1. I like to go to church (Synagogue). (+)
2. I get more satisfaction from personal prayer than I do from attending formal worship services at church. (—)
3. I enjoy the feeling of fellowship I get from taking part in church activities. (+)
4. I would rather do my religious thinking at home than at church. (—)
5. I don't need a church to satisfy my religious needs. (—)
6. Going to church each week is about as enjoyable as any of the activities I engage in. (+)
7. To me, most religious services are a waste of time. (—)
8. I would rather worship God in private than in the midst of a large congregation. (—)
9. The church is the proper place for worship. (+)
10. Men should seek God together. (+)
11. It is only right and proper that men should congregate in a common setting to worship their common God. (+)
12. Every person who believes in God ought to belong to some sort of church. (+)

13. Any person who accepts God should attend church frequently. (+)
14. Community members should support their respective churches through active participation in church affairs. (+)
15. The gulf between God and man is more easily bridged in a church service than in private contemplation. (+)
16. We could cure many of the social ills plaguing modern society if we could get more people to go to church. (+)
17. Without the stabilizing influence of the churches, society would soon destroy itself. (+)
18. There are very few personal problems which can be resolved by going to church. (—)
19. Organized religion plays an important role in maintaining social order. (+)
20. People who attend church regularly are less likely to commit crimes than those who rarely or never go. (+)

MAN-GOD: FACTOR I*

1. In God's divine plan the fate of any particular individual depends less on what he himself does than on the behavior of mankind as a whole. (+)
2. Man can solve all his important problems without help from a Supreme Being. (+)
3. As human beings, we are all part of one divine scheme, sharing a common relationship to God. (—)
4. God is less concerned with the welfare of any specific individual than he is with the fate of mankind as a whole. (+)
5. Man is very much alone in the universe. (+)
6. Individuality is an illusion—we are all insignificant particles in an infinite universe. (+)
7. Each of us is a distinct entity, different from any others. (—)

GENERAL: FACTOR I

1. For the most part I get along quite well on my own—I don't need other people. (—)
2. My privacy means more to me than almost anything else. (—)
3. For me, life would be pretty empty without some kind of group to identify with, belong to, feel a part of. (+)
4. The independent spirit—spurning all aid, needing no one, self-reliant, and free—this is man at his best. (—)
5. In life, an individual should for the most part "go it alone," assuring himself of privacy, having much time to himself, attempting to control his own life. (—)
6. To be superior, a man must stand alone. (—)
7. One must avoid dependence upon persons or things—the center of life should be found within oneself. (—)

---

* The negative loading of item 3 and the positive loading of item 5 are somewhat puzzling in view of their inconsistency with the other items in the scale.

8. People should solve their problems by themselves. (—)
9. A man can learn better by striking out boldly on his own than he can by following the advice of others. (—)

GENERAL: FACTOR II

1. I find genuine pleasure in solitude. (—)
2. Whoever would be a man, must be a nonconformist. (—)
3. The spirit of togetherness can easily be overdone and lead to a stifling of individual initiative and creativity. (—)
4. The individualist is the man who is most likely to discover the best road to a new future. (—)
5. The independent, autonomous individual is society's major source of new ideas. (—)
6. One has to isolate himself from others in order to understand fully the meaning of life. (—)

CHAPTER 5

Equalitarianism—Authoritarianism

THE STUDY to be reported here was conducted shortly after the one described in the previous chapter and was similar to it in many respects. Both were laboratory studies of a very limited duration; the same task was used in each case; both involved a formalized trial and error sequence, and both tested for vertical and lateral generalization.

In other respects, however, the two studies were quite different, the major difference being that in this study we decided to experiment with another attitude dimension. Previously, we had sought to induce changes in attitudes dealing with the theme of individualism-collectivism. The attitude scales used in this study were all composed of items bearing some relationship to what is most appropriately called "equalitarianism-authoritarianism." This, it will be recalled, was the second of the two dimensions used in the Wisconsin study, the first being individualism-collectivism. One reason for the choice of equalitarianism-authoritarianism in this study was its relatively poor showing in the Wisconsin study and the possibility of improving upon this in a more controlled situation. In addition, this particular dimension seemed especially amenable to laboratory testing, given the nature of the Bales task (which was to be used again) and the need for control over performance feedback.

More broadly, however, our decision to change dimensions was governed by the desire to explore the generality of our theory. We had previously obtained promising results in two situations using the same dimension (individualism-collectivism) and were anxious to show that our theory had generality across attitude dimensions as well as generality across task situations.

There were other differences between this and our previous study. Among them was the decision to change the structure of the items in our attitude scales. Most of our new items were written in bipolar fashion, i.e., they involved a contrast between two presumably opposite orientations. In the past our items had taken the form of simple statements (e.g., "Anyone who believes in God should attend church frequently."); in the new format statements were deliberately made complex (e.g., "I would rather be in a group with a leader than a group where everyone shares equally in the decision making."). There were two reasons for this innovation. First, we felt it would contribute to scale homogeneity. We reasoned that unless the subject is "told" what the alternative to a statement he may wish to disagree with is, there is no guarantee that he will have this particular alternative in mind when he responds to the statement. If different subjects answer with different alternatives in mind, the items making up the scale will not be as highly correlated with each other. Since the scale reliabilities in our last study left something to be desired, this seemed like a reasonable way to improve upon them.

Secondly, in specifying the alternative to the sentiment presented in the stem of the statement, we hoped to reflect at the attitudinal level the "bipolarity" of the trial and error sequence at the behavioral level. The thought was that in posing the same basic contrast (e.g., between authority and equality) at each level (attitudes and experience alike), we would facilitate the induction of attitudes from experience.

A third difference between this present study and the previous one was the scheduling of subjects for one four-hour session rather than three two-hour sessions. In the previous study, students came for a total of six hours, but this was spread out over five to ten days. Under the present design, students spent a total of four hours in the experiment, the entire experience being concentrated in a single afternoon or evening. There were two reasons for making the change. First, it seemed likely, although we could not be sure, that spreading out the experiment over a whole week served to undermine the salience of what happened in the laboratory. In view of the difficulties involved in making the laboratory experience salient or important enough in the first place, there seemed to be good reason for concentrating the whole experiment in a single afternoon. The thought of running the whole experiment in a single session was attractive, secondly, because of the greater convenience involved in having subjects come only once.

There was a fourth difference closely related to the scheduling change. In the last study the pre-test questionnaire was administered in a psychology class approximately two weeks before the experiment began. This time the pre-test was administered right before the experiment, in the laboratory setting itself. Again there were two considerations involved. In the first place, the two week interim offered too many opportunities for subjects to change their attitudes for reasons unrelated to the experimental situation. This has already been commented upon. Secondly, the experimenters had too little control over the conditions under which the first questionnaire was administered. As a result, many of the questionnaires in the previous experiment were filled out in a careless, half-hearted manner. This undoubtedly contributed to the low reliabilities on some of our attitude scales. By administering the questionnaire right before and right after the experiment, we hoped to solve two problems at the same time: (1) the elimination of all nonexperimental factors as sources of attitude change and (2) the minimization of measurement error due to variation in questionnaire administration.

There was one further difference between this experiment and the one which preceded it. In the previous study, all subjects were males, most of them in their first year of college. The decision to use only males was based on the assumption that sex might make a difference in subjects' responses to the experimental situation. Given a limited budget and a shortage of girls at Cornell, only males were asked to participate. The sample was further limited to the younger males on the grounds that they would be more naïve with regard to the manipulations required in our procedure.

Having demonstrated that attitude induction in the laboratory was possible with this limited sample of subjects, it seemed appropriate to expand the sample to include females and upperclassmen. In the sample actually chosen we had students ranging in age from 16 to 45 and, in education, from junior year in high school to the final year of graduate school. Although it appeared unlikely that our theory would be valid only for freshmen males, we felt that we could add something to the generality of our findings by working in this second experiment with a more diverse population.

The general purpose of this study was identical to that of the one just reported in Chapter 4, namely to test the hypothesis that attitude change is a function of task experience. In this experiment subjects were asked to work on a task alternately with and without a leader. By virtue of feedback control, some subjects consistently performed better with a leader while others did better without one. We predicted that those who were rewarded for performing the task with a leader would become more authoritarian in their beliefs, values, and preferences and that those who were rewarded for performing without a leader would become more equalitarian in their attitudes. As in our previous experiment, it was expected that attitudes induced in the laboratory setting would generalize laterally to other specific task settings and vertically to more abstract categories of experience.

ATTITUDE QUESTIONNAIRE

In the Bales-Couch Value Profile there are two independent factors (I and III) which deal with equality and authority.[1] The first is called "Acceptance of Authority" and is made up primarily of items from the California F scale; the second is called "Equalitarianism." As in Wisconsin, the items written for this present study were designed to bear some relationship to factor III in the Value Profile, namely Equalitarianism. While we shall refer to our own scale as equalitarianism versus authoritarianism, it should be made clear at the outset that these terms are meant to specify the two poles of a single dimension, a dimension which we know to be empirically unrelated to the authoritarianism of the well-known F scale.[2] The decision to write items primarily oriented to the Bales-Couch Equalitarianism factor instead of the F scale was based on the assumption that the experience of working with and without a leader would be more relevant to the former than the latter. This, of course, was the same consideration involved in choosing what Bales and Couch call "Equalitarianism" as our second factor in the Wisconsin study.

Our initial questionnaire included 85 items dealing with the authority-equality theme in seven different areas. Three of these items were taken from the F scale (those with the highest loadings on the Value Profile factor I) to serve as marker variables, i.e., as aids in defining the factors which emerged from our correlation matrix. This proved to be a wise move since some of our items, although designed to measure what Bales and Couch called "Equalitarianism," turned out to be unrelated to that factor but closely related to the abbreviated F scale.

The remaining 82 items were all written around the central theme of investing authority in a leader (informal group leader, father, professor, government official, etc.) versus distributing it equally among group members. Put in normative terms, this involved the question of whether

---

[1] Robert F. Bales and Arthur S. Couch, "The Value Profile: A Factor Analytic Study of Value Statements," unpublished paper, 1959.

[2] We take the risk of confusing readers by using the term "authoritarianism" for something other than the F-scale for the simple reason that it is the only appropriate term for labeling the other end of the equalitarianism scale. The term "authoritarianism," we might add, is more appropriate here where it refers specifically to the centralization of control than in the F-scale where it is intended to cover a wide variety of loosely connected attitudes.

a single person or official should be given responsibility for making decisions or whether all members of the system should share equally in the decision-making process. Cognitively, the relevant question was which form of organization was generally the more effective. In cathectic terms, it was a question of which kind of relationship was to be preferred.

Areas were chosen so that we could test for both lateral and vertical generalization. By lateral generalization we mean generalization out from the experimental situation to other task settings of a relatively specific sort. They are specific in the sense that actual roles or positions can be identified (e.g., professor-student, father-child, representative-constituent, God-man) in each situation. For this purpose 48 items were written, 12 each dealing with equalitarianism-authoritarianism in the context of the classroom, the family, politics, and religion. Within each set of 12 items, four were expressed in the cathectic mode, four in the cognitive mode, and four in the evaluative or normative mode. Within each subset of four items, two were phrased in an equalitarian direction, two in an authoritarian direction. All items were bipolar in the sense that an equalitarian situation was always contrasted with an authoritarian one.

In an attempt to explore more systematically generalization of a vertical sort, we wrote items to measure equalitarianism-authoritarianism at three different levels of abstraction. Least abstract were 12 items dealing with the theme of equalitarianism-authoritarianism in *discussion groups.* We say least abstract because the experimental groups themselves were to be groups of a certain sort, namely discussion groups. The items were abstract, nevertheless, in that they failed to specify any of the particulars involved, e.g., the topic of discussion, the nature of the decision to be made, the size of the group, the kinds of people in the group, etc. The items forced the respondent to abstract from any number of concrete situations he might have had in mind—to answer with respect to discussion groups *in general.*

In composing a second set of items slightly more abstract than the first, we simply dropped the reference to discussion groups and made statements about *groups in general.* These we felt to be more abstract precisely because they failed to specify the nature of the group involved, i.e., discussion group, work group, friendship group, etc. In answering them, the subject was forced to generalize about a wide variety of groups, which may have been different with respect to goals, structure, composition, duration and the like. Again, 12 items were written, evenly divided among the cathectic, cognitive, and evaluative modes, with half phrased in an equalitarian and half in an authoritarian direction.

Discussion groups and groups in general represented the first two levels of abstraction in our series of measures designed to test for what we have called "vertical generalization." In an attempt to go one step further, we constructed a third scale which we called *equality in general*. Here the reference to groups was dropped altogether. The items referred instead to "people," "all men," "society," "everyone," etc. Some of these were taken from the Bales-Couch Profile (e.g., "Everyone should have an equal chance and an equal say."), some represented slightly edited versions of common cultural shibboleths (e.g., "In a very important sense, all men are created equal."), while others we made up ourselves (e.g., "People should be rewarded according to what they produce, even if this means that some people make a great deal more than others."). This scale was unlike our others in two respects: (1) it included no cathectic items, and (2) the items were not bipolar. The decision in each case was based on a desire to use statements common to most discussions of equalitarianism in the abstract. Statements of this sort are rarely couched in the cathectic mode and just as rarely phrased in a bipolar fashion.

The response format for all items was a nine-point graphic scale ranging from Strongly Disagree to Strongly Agree.[3] The first version of the questionnaire was administered to 80 of the more than 200 Cornell summer school students who responded to our invitation to sign up for a number of psychological experiments. These 80 students were used only to pretest the questionnaire; they were subsequently enrolled in an experiment unrelated to the one reported here. Of the remaining subjects 52 (23 females and 29 males) were signed up for the present experiment. These people did not take the pre-test questionnaire.

The item responses of the 80 students who were administered the pre-test were intercorrelated, factor analyzed using the centroid method, and rotated by the quartimax method.[4] Two factors were extracted. The first was clearly what we had in mind in writing the original items, i.e., an equalitarian-authoritarian dimension resembling factor III (Equalitarianism) in the Bales-Couch Value Profile. Practically all of

---

[3] The shift from ten categories (as in our previous study) to nine was prompted mainly by the fact that some of our previous subjects insisted on making a neutral point even where none existed (i.e., by placing an X between categories five and six).

[4] In the last study we were forced to do a factor analysis for each area separately (homework, family, etc.) since the computer routine at Cornell could handle a maximum of 40 items. By the time this study was in progress, however, the routine had been expanded to 85 items making it possible for us to do a single factor analysis for the whole questionnaire.

the discussion-group and groups-in-general items were highly loaded on this factor, as well as half of the classroom and politics items, and several of those dealing with equality in general. All of the religious and F-scales items and most of the family items were loaded on the second factor. The three F-scale items, included as marker variables, helped to make clear the difference between the two factors. Our factor II had much in common with Bales' first factor which he called "Acceptance of Authority." Religious and family items played a prominent role in each, suggesting the underlying theme of submission to traditional authority. Our first factor could best be conceptualized as a leadership dimension, dealing as it did with the problems of responsibility, consensus, and decision making. While both factors could be said to involve the problem of authority, factor I was primarily concerned with the role of leadership in problem solving, whereas factor II dealt with the authority issue in terms of yielding to more or less ascriptively defined authority *figures*.

In revising the questionnaire, all items that did not load .30 or better on either factor were rewritten to conform more closely to those items with high loadings on Factor I. In addition, all items with means greater than 7.0 or less than 3.0 were rephrased with an eye to bringing the means closer to the center of the scale (5.0), thus making attitude change in both directions equally possible.

The revised questionnaire again had 85 items, 12 in each of six areas (discussion groups, groups in general, classroom, family, politics, and religion), ten for equality in general, and three from the F scale. In each of the first six areas there were four belief, four value, and four preference items, with an equal number phrased in each direction. The ten equality in general items were not bipolar but were again phrased in both directions. The three F-scale items were left unchanged. The revised questionnaire is shown in Exhibit C at the end of this chapter.

There were two ways of making scales out of these items: (1) by putting together all items from a single area, e.g., family or politics), and (2) by putting together all items loaded on a single factor (factor I or factor II). Since we chose to analyze the data (from the "before" questionnaires of the 52 experimental subjects) both ways, the relevant information for each breakdown is given in Tables 5–1 and 5–2. Table 5–1 provides internal consistencies and test-retest reliabilities for each of the eight area scales.[5]

In making the second breakdown, i.e., by factor, only items which

---

[5] The internal consistency estimates and the test-retest reliabilities were computed the same way as before (see Chapter 3, footnote 18).

TABLE 5–1
Internal Consistencies and Reliabilities for Area Scales

Area	No. of Items	Internal Consistency	Test-Retest Reliability	
			AU	EQ
Discussion groups	12	.82	.01	.65
Groups in general	12	.88	.29	.80
Equality in general	10	.77	.85	.80
Classroom	12	.82	.71	.71
Family	12	.83	.76	.89
Politics	12	.90	.64	.73
Religion	12	.95	.92	.96
F scale	3	.72	.86	.93

loaded .30 or better on one of the two factors were included. If an item was loaded .30 or more on both factors, it was assigned to that factor on which it had the higher loading. Thirteen of the 85 items had loadings below .30 on both factors and were thus excluded from this part of the analysis. Table 5–2 shows the number of items from each area that were loaded .30 or better on each factor, as well as the internal consistency and test-retest reliability for each. The test-retest correlations are presented separately for the two experimental conditions (AU's and EQ's).

TABLE 5–2
Item Composition, Internal Consistencies, and Reliabilities for Factor Scales

Area	Factor I	Factor II
Discussion groups	12	0
Groups in general	12	0
Equality in general	7	0
Classroom	6	2
Family	1	8
Politics	6	3
Religion	0	12
F Scale	0	3
Total	44	28
Internal consistency	.93	.92
Test-retest reliability:		
AU	.32	.95
EQ	.79	.70

PROCEDURE

Fifty-two subjects were invited to participate in a laboratory experiment lasting approximately four hours. Groups were made up of six students each, in most cases three males and three females. Despite reminders over the phone and through the mail, a number of students failed to show up. Hence many of the groups were run with only five members and in two cases with only four.

When everyone thought to be coming had arrived, the 85-item "before" questionnaire was administered. The experiment was then introduced as a study designed to explore the relationship between leadership and performance. The experimenter explained that the object of the experiment was to learn more about the effects of different kinds of leadership on group performance, especially with tasks of a logical, problem-solving nature. It was emphasized that little was known about this area and that this particular study was purely exploratory, no predictions having been made.

The initial instructions for the task were identical to those used in the last experiment (Chapter 4, pp. 94–95). To summarize briefly, subjects were given the problem of predicting another student's responses to an attitude questionnaire. They were told how that student answered the first four items on the questionnaire, the object being to predict, as a group, how the student actually filled out the rest of the questionnaire. Poker chips ranging in value from one cent to ten cents were awarded depending on how close the group came to the right answer on each item. The experimenter pretended to check his master sheet for the right answers, although the amount of money to be awarded had already been decided in advance.

It was explained that the experiment would be divided into four phases. In the first phase the group was to have a leader, chosen from among the members present. In the second phase the leader would be asked to leave, the remaining members performing the task on their own. The third phase was to be conducted with the leader returning, the fourth once again with the leader absent. In the two "with-leader" periods, the leader would have the authority to make the final decision on each item prediction. While discussion of each item among all group members was encouraged, it was emphasized that the leader alone had the responsibility for making the final decision. In the two "without-leader" periods, the person acting as leader was asked to leave the room. The remaining members were then told that they must come to a unanimous decision for each item being predicted. To insure that everyone would participate, it was further explained that, prior to any discussion of the item, each member was to announce his or her estimate of the correct answer. Only after everyone had been heard from could the discussion begin. In all cases the decision was to be unanimous.

At this point the experimenter turned to the face sheet of the "before" questionnaire where subjects were asked to indicate age, sex, year in school, and a number of other things. Looking over the forms carefully, he finally selected one and turned to the group saying, "Mr. Sutherland, it appears that you are further along in your studies than any of the others. Would you mind acting as the group leader?" Sutherland was a paid confederate and as such took the role of leader in both "with-leader" phases of every group. There were several reasons for having a confederate play the role of leader. Most importantly, we felt it necessary to make very salient the difference between the two periods where the leader was present and the two where he was absent. Without a sharp contrast between "trial and error" it was unlikely that any attitude induction would take place. Pre-testing indicated that leaders chosen from among the naïve members were reluctant to exercise sufficient control over their peers. Consequently, his presence or absence seemed to make little difference to the others.

Sutherland was instructed to maintain control over both the discussion and the decisions throughout the two phases when he was present. It was deemed important, however, that he avoid making his decisions without consulting the others. If he were to enter his own personal guess as the final decision in every case, subjects would come to associate their success or failure with the leader's personal ability to solve logical problems of this sort. We wanted them, instead, to associate doing well or poorly with the fact that they were being led, not with the fact that they happened to get Sutherland as their leader. While in some cases Sutherland would enter his own personal estimate as the group decision, more often than not he abstained from making a public guess, concentrating instead on guiding the discussion and effecting compromises.

Twenty-four of the subjects were assigned to the "authoritarian" condition and 28 to the "equalitarian" condition. Those in the authoritarian condition were consistently rewarded more (by means of controlled results) for performing the task with a leader than without. The 28 subjects in the equalitarian condition always did better without a leader than when Sutherland was present. The experimenter saw to it that the ratio of earnings was approximately two to one, depending on which treatment the subjects were in. Subjects in the authoritarian condition, for example, earned approximately $1.50 in each of the two with-leader phases and $.75 in each of the other two, making a total of around $4.50 for the experiment as a whole.

At the end of the experiment, the experimenter passed out the "after" questionnaire (identical with the "before" questionnaire taken three and a half hours earlier) with the following comment: "Now that the experiment is over, we would like you to fill out another questionnaire. As you can see, this is the same questionnaire you completed earlier. We ask you to fill it out again in the belief that it may help us to understand some of the things that took place here today. We realize that this is a rather tedious thing to do, but would appreciate it if you took it seriously nevertheless. Please, no talking until everyone is finished."

When all the "after" questionnaires had been completed, subjects were given a timed 40-item vocabulary test.[6] The purpose behind giving the test was to see if there was any systematic relationship between verbal aptitude and amount of attitude change. Some previous studies had reported a negative correlation between IQ and *persuasibility*, others a positive correlation, and still others no relationship.[7] Although ours was not a persuasion study, it remained possible that intelligence would play a role here as well. There were, of course, many other individual differences we might have explored. It was decided, however, to limit ourselves at this time to the verbal IQ measure, leaving more systematic exploration for some future study.

Summary of Predictions

It was predicted that subjects who were rewarded more for performing the task with a leader than without (AU's) would become more authoritarian on each of the eight area scales: discussion groups, groups in general, equality in general, classroom, family, politics, religion, and the abbreviated F scale. Those who were rewarded more for performing the task without a leader (EQ's) were expected to become more equalitarian on the same eight scales. With respect to lateral generalization, our approach was again, as in the last chapter, primarily an exploratory one. Although no formal predictions were made, there was some reason to expect that the classroom items would change the most (on the basis of similarity to the experimental situation) and religion (presumably the furthest removed) the least, with family and politics

---

[6] J. P. Guilford and W. S. Zimmerman, *Guilford-Zimmerman Aptitude Survey: Manual* (Beverly Hills, Calif.: Sheridan Supply Co., 1956).

[7] C. I. Hovland, "Effects of the Mass Media of Communication," G. Lindzey (ed.), *Handbook of Social Psychology* (Reading, Mass.: Addison-Wesley, 1954), pp. 1086–87. See also, C. I. Hovland, I. L. Janis, and H. H. Kelley, *Communication and Persuasion* (New Haven: Yale University Press, 1953), p. 183. In general, the findings indicate that low IQ people will be more influenced by communications which contain unsupported generalities and invalid arguments, although they will be less influenced by communications involving complex arguments which require the drawing of valid inferences.

falling somewhere in between. With respect to vertical generalization we predicted that discussion groups (least abstract) would show the most change, groups in general second most, and equality in general (most abstract) the least amount of change.

The factor analysis provided another way of dividing up the questionnaire items. Factor I included those items (taken from a number of different areas) most closely concerned with the problems of leadership and decision making. The items loaded on factor II (mostly from family and religion but including several others as well) dealt mainly with authority in the traditional or conventional sense (or "authoritarianism" as defined by Adorno, et al). In comparing the content of the two factors, it was quite clear that factor I dealt with issues more closely related to the experimental situation than those involved in factor II. The most salient feature of the experimental situation was the problem of leadership. It was with this in mind that we originally tried to write items all of which would be loaded on factor I (taking factor III in the Bales-Couch Value Profile as our model). Even the religious items were written with the leadership concept in mind (e.g., "People should learn to rely on God for guidance in the conduct of their affairs rather than trying to decide everything for themselves."). The fact that the religious items were loaded instead on factor II is not too surprising, however, in view of the close relationship between conventional religious beliefs and the F-scale, as reported in both the Bales-Couch study and the *Authoritarian Personality*. With respect to factor differences in amount of change, then, we predicted that factor I would change more than factor II.

RESULTS

Item Differences. As in our previous study, our first step was to get an estimate of the success of the experiment as a whole by examining all items collectively, regardless of area or factor location. The relevant question is: on how many of the 85 items in the questionnaire was the difference between mean changes for the two groups of subjects (AU's and EQ's) in the predicted direction? The actual number is 68 (out of 85), which yields a χ^2 value of 29.41 which is significant at the .001 level.

Area Differences. Results are presented for changes on the eight area scales in Table 5-3 below. All scores are computed so that a *positive* change means subjects became more *equalitarian* in their attitudes, a *negative* score indicating change in the *authoritarian* direction. According to the predictions made, all numbers in the first column should be positive and those in the second column negative. This would indicate that subjects who were rewarded more for working without a leader became more equalitarian in their attitudes and that those who were rewarded more for performing the task with a leader became more authoritarian. The differences between the two changes (column

TABLE 5–3

Attitude Change by Area

Area	Mean Change		Diff.	t	p
	EQ	AU	(EQ − AU)		
Discussion groups	12.75	−15.12	27.87	5.73	.001
Groups in general	10.85	−9.16	20.01	4.56	.001
Equality in general	−0.61	−3.62	3.01	1.11	ns
Classroom	1.32	−4.25	5.57	1.64	ns
Family	1.78	−0.16	1.94	0.79	ns
Politics	3.96	−5.20	9.16	2.33	.05
Religion	−1.47	1.50	−1.97	−1.14	ns
F-scale	−0.04	1.42	−1.46	−1.99	.10

three) were computed by subtracting changes for the authoritarians from changes among the equalitarians. According to prediction, these should all be positive. The same, of course, is true for the t ratios listed in column four.[8]

The first three scales, representing different levels of abstraction, were designed to test our hypotheses with respect to what we have called "vertical generalization." In line with our expectations, the discussion group items changed the most, those dealing with equality in general the least. All changes are in the predicted direction, although equality in general falls far short of significance. In part, this latter fact reflects the extremely remote nature of the items in that scale. It may very well reflect the fact, moreover, that these items were worded differently from those in the other two scales (discussion groups and groups in general). Many were borrowed from other sources and none were phrased in the bipolar form used elsewhere.

In testing for lateral generalization, classroom items were expected to change the most and religion the least, with family and politics

---

[8] t-tests were also performed on "before" questionnaire data to see if AU's and EQ's were significantly different on any factors to begin with. The only significant t (.05) was for the religion scale where EQ's turned out to be more equalitarian than the AU's. On the basis of regression alone, we would predict that the EQ's would move in the AU direction and the AU's in the EQ direction. This, of course, is what did happen—to a slight and nonsignificant extent.

somewhere in between. As Table 5–3 indicates (from the *t* ratios in column four), politics changed the most, with classroom second, family third, and religion last. In fact, religion (along with the abbreviated F-scale) changed slightly in the direction opposite to that predicted. This last finding means that subjects who were rewarded more for performing the task *with* a leader were more likely at the end of the experiment to say that man should decide things for himself without God's help, that man's fate is in his own hands, not God's, etc. Interesting as this reversal might be, it can too easily be attributed to chance variation or regression (see footnote 8). In this respect, we have confirmed one of the Wisconsin findings, namely that leadership at the social structural level is unrelated to attitudes toward religious authority.

Before moving on to an analysis of changes by factor, it should be noted that in the three cases where differences proved to be significant (discussion groups, groups in general, and politics), the two groups (AU'S and EQ's) contributed about equally to the result. In other words, for those scales where significant attitude change did take place, both treatments (authoritarian and equalitarian) seemed to be working equally well.

Factor Differences. In Table 5–4 below, attitude change is analyzed by factor scales rather than our analytically defined area scales. A positive mean change again indicates change in the *equalitarian* direction. Factor I, it will be recalled, is made up primarily of items

TABLE 5–4
Attitude Change by Factor

| Factor | Mean Change | | Diff. | | |
	EQ	AU	(EQ − AU)	t	p
I	24.04	−33.54	57.58	5.23	.001
II	1.50	2.46	−0.96	−0.27	ns

from the following scales: discussion groups, groups in general, equality in general, classroom, and politics. Factor II includes all of the religious items, most of the family items and the three F-scale items. Knowing as we do (from Table 5–3) that discussion groups, groups in general, and politics changed significantly in the predicted direction and that religion and the three F-scale items changed slightly in the wrong direction, it is not surprising to find in Table 5–4 that factor I was the more successful of the two. The analysis by factors does more, however, than repeat what we found with our area scales. It tells us, in a sense, *why* some of the scales worked while others did not. Without the factor analysis, for example, we might be tempted to attribute the failure of our religious items to the fact that generalization from the experiment simply does not extend this far. This may be true, but can the same thing be said for the family items, which failed to show any significant change? And if both family and religion are too far removed from the experimental situation, how do we account for the significant change on politics? Can it be argued that community politics has more in common with our experimental setting than the family, itself a small group?

It would appear that religion and family failed to show any change, not because they were too far out for generalization to have any effect, but because they were on a different dimension altogether. Both were highly loaded on factor II (the F-scale factor) while the scales that worked best (discussion groups, groups in general, politics, and to some extent classroom) were all loaded on factor I (best thought of as a leadership dimension). Our own factor analysis simply confirmed what Bales and Couch found in their analysis of items in the Value Profile. Attitudes dealing with authority are of two distinct types—one concerning the role of leaders in decision making, the other involving relations with traditional sources of power (parents, God, convention, etc.). Given the salience of leadership and decision making in our experimental situation, it was not surprising that the attitudes induced there were generalized only to those scales loaded on factor I.

Subject Differences.   In view of the possibility that a minority of subjects were responsible for all the change appearing in the mean differences by area and factor, a separate analysis was done on the number of *subjects* changing in the predicted direction. As in the previous study, the tests were limited to those areas and factors showing a significant difference in mean change between experimental groups. Table 5–5 gives the results for the three area scales showing significant change (discussion groups, groups in general, and politics) as well as factor I. For any given test, only those subjects who changed in one direction or the other are included. A plus sign indicates change in the *equalitarian* direction. The results indicate that in three cases (discussion groups, groups in general and factor I) a significant majority of the subjects changed in the expected direction. In the case of politics, even though the *mean* changes were significantly different ($p < .05$), only slightly more than half of the *subjects* changed in the predicted direction. Some of those who did change apparently changed a great deal, enough so to produce a mean difference that reached significance.

TABLE 5–5
Changes by Subjects

Discussion Groups

	+	−
EQ	22	5
AU	3	20

$$\chi^2 = 20.62$$
$$p < .001$$

Groups in General

	+	−
EQ	21	6
AU	7	15

$$\chi^2 = 8.66$$
$$p < .01$$

Politics

	+	−
EQ	16	11
AU	10	11

$$\chi^2 = 0.26$$
ns

Factor I

	+	−
EQ	24	4
AU	5	19

$$\chi^2 = 19.49$$
$$p < .001$$

Sex Differences. In light of the fact that both males and females were used in this present study, it is of interest to see if sex made any difference in amount of attitude change. For the sake of simplicity, computations were done for factor scales only. On factor I, 25 of the

TABLE 5–6
Correlation between Verbal Intelligence and Amount of Attitude Change, by Condition and Area

	Condition	
Area	*EQ* (N = 22)*	*AU* (N = 20)*
Discussion groups	.35	−.22
Groups in general	−.22	−.15
Equality in general	−.26	−.40
Classroom	−.40	−.18
Family	−.33	−.10
Politics	−.23	−.40
Religion	−.17	.20
F-scale	−.36	.06

* The N's here are smaller than the total N's for each condition since some subjects were not given the vocabulary test.

29 males (or 86 per cent) and 18 of the 23 females (or 78 per cent) changed in the predicted direction. On factor II, where the subject population as a whole failed to change, 12 of the 29 males and 11 of the 23 females changed as predicted. It is quite clear, then, that where the experiment worked, it worked equally well for males and females alike.

Individual Differences. In testing for the relationship between verbal aptitude and attitude change, we found that, in the equalitarian groups, vocabulary scores correlated negatively with seven of the eight area change scores, and in the authoritarian groups negatively with six of the eight change scores, although none of the 16 correlation coefficients reached significance at the .05 level (see Table 5–6). In both groups the more verbally intelligent subjects changed somewhat less in the predicted direction than the less intelligent ones. It would appear that the relationship between verbal aptitude and attitude change, although consistently negative, is at best a modest one.

Original Position. In our last experiment, it was found that the subjects who changed the most were those whose original attitudes were most at variance with the treatment they were exposed to. A similar analysis was conducted on the data for this study, the results being shown in Table 5–7. Correlations between original position and change

TABLE 5–7

Correlations between Original Position and Attitude
Change in Predicted Direction, by Area and Condition

Area	AU (N = 24)	EQ (N = 28)
Discussion groups	$-.66\dagger$	$-.45*$
Groups in general	$-.57\dagger$	.12
Equality in general	.05	$-.31$
Classroom	$-.30$	$-.12$
Family	$-.29$	.02
Politics	$-.43*$	$-.20$
Religion	$-.05$	.13
F-scale	$-.33$	$-.37$
Total (all items)	$-.56\dagger$	$-.03$

* $p < .05$.
† $p < .01$.

in the predicted direction are listed for each treatment separately. Most of the correlations are negative, particularly so for subjects in the authoritarian condition. Among these same subjects, it is also true that original position is more highly correlated with change in those areas where *significant* change took place (discussion groups, groups in general, and politics) than in those areas where no significant change was obtained.

As was done in our first laboratory study, we plotted the scores graphically to see just how linear the relationship between initial position and amount of change was. The procedure was the same as that employed previously. As indicated in Figure 5–1, the relationship tends

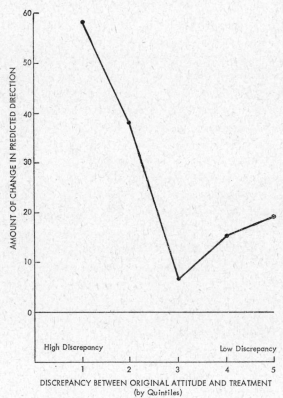

FIGURE 5–1

Amount of Change in Predicted Direction as a Function of
Amount of Discrepancy between Original Attitude and
Type of Treatment for AU's and EQ's Combined on Three Areas

to be negative (i.e., the greater the discrepancy between original attitude and treatment, the greater the change), although there is something in the way of a reversal in the fourth and fifth quintiles.

Preferences, Beliefs, and Values. Although no significance tests were performed for items written in the three different modes, casual inspection of the data showed there to be no systematic differences. This confirms the results of the previous two studies, namely that the mode of an item is irrelevant as far as change is concerned. To the extent that we were able to change one kind of orientation, we were successful in changing them all. When one failed, they all failed.

DISCUSSION

The original intent of this study was to explore the generality of our previous laboratory findings to another attitude dimension, in this case equalitarianism-authoritarianism. The findings would seem to indicate that we did somewhat better here than in the previous study (individualism-collectivism) which lasted two hours longer. Three of the eight t-tests for mean changes by area were significant at the .05 level or better in this study whereas only four out of 13 were significant at this level in the last study. Somewhat over 70 per cent of the subjects changed in the predicted direction on those areas showing significant t-ratios as opposed to around 60 per cent in the previous study. These results are especially encouraging in view of the relatively poor showing of the equalitarianism dimension in the Wisconsin study.

It should be remembered that this experiment lasted only four hours and that none of the attitudes involved was discussed by the subjects or even mentioned by the experimenter (except insofar as the explanation of the experiment required it). In no sense, therefore, could this be called a "communication-persuasion" study. It might be contended, however, that the subjects were aware of the experimenter's intent and responded to the "demand characteristics of the situation" by changing their attitudes in the predicted direction. While subjects were certainly aware of our interest in attitudes, they failed to indicate in postexperimental interviews any clear perception of our interest in *changing* those attitudes through the manipulation of performance feedback. Even when it was suggested that the experiment might have been "rigged," all but a handful denied that this was possible. Very few of those who were willing to entertain the possibility of deception guessed that the master sheet to which the experimenter referred in awarding chips was a dummy. When this was admitted, subjects were asked to hazard a guess as to our motivation in doing what we did. No one perceived that our efforts to control task results were designed to change subjects' responses to the before and after attitude questionnaire.

One feature of the experiment worth noting is the fact that generalization vertically to statements about authority and equality of an increasingly abstract sort seemed to work better than generalization laterally to the authority/equality issue as this appeared in other equally specific settings. The laboratory situation was a discussion group, but a very specific sort of discussion group. Yet subjects very clearly generalized from this specific group to discussion groups in general—and even beyond that to "groups" in general, whether discussion groups or not. They did relatively little generalizing, however, to other task settings like the classroom and the family where the authority/equality issue was presented in relatively concrete terms.

Just why there was so little lateral generalization can be explained partly in terms of the lack of *similarity* between the experimental situation (where decision making was prominent) and several of the task areas (where, according to our factor analysis, authority tended to be defined in more traditional terms). Beyond this, subjects were very *familiar* with certain of the areas (e.g., classroom and family) and hence more certain of their initial attitudes. Subjects who are very sure of their beliefs, preferences, and values are not likely to change significantly as the result of a very limited laboratory experience. The politics items were phrased in a rather unusual way and probably did not tap any deep ideological commitment. This might account for why they changed more than the others. In addition, they were oriented more directly than any of the others to the decision-making process as this was articulated in the laboratory.

CONCLUSIONS

In this, our third, study we achieved pretty much what we set out to achieve. The primary object of the study was to show that our theory had validity for more than one dimension of beliefs, values, and preferences. This was generally, although not completely, borne out by the data. We also made a number of methodological innovations which appeared to improve our results. While convinced that our theory and method were both basically sound, we remained disturbed by the fact that some of the scales which should have changed showed no change at all. Although we had managed to produce both lateral and vertical generalization, in neither case were the results entirely satisfactory. Vertical generalization did not extend to the most abstract scale (equality in general) while horizontal generalization extended to but one of several task settings.

At this point the thought occurred to us that we should try a different experimental task, or better yet a whole variety of tasks. A change in task would be worth trying for two reasons. Most simply, it might improve our results (i.e., yield more lateral and vertical generalization).

Even if our results were no better than before, however, it would tell us something about the generality of our theory across different task situations. This, we agreed, was an important consideration. What if we found that our theory was valid only for the Bales prediction task used in the two previous studies? While unlikely, the possibility seemed real enough to make us want to find out. The next experiment was designed with this thought in mind.

EXHIBIT C

DISCUSSION GROUPS*

1. I would rather participate in a small discussion group in which there is a definite leader than in one in which everybody is equal to everybody else. (I—)
2. I like small group discussions in which one person has final responsibility for making decisions more than those groups in which all decisions have to be unanimous. (I—)
3. I prefer discussion groups in which all members are equal to one another to those groups in which one person has authority over all the rest. (I+)
4. I would rather be in a discussion group in which everyone has an equal say in making decisions than in a group in which a leader or chairman always has the final say. (I+)
5. In general, discussion groups in which all members are equal tend to perform more effectively than groups in which authority is vested in a single person. (I+)
6. If a group has a decision to make, that decision is more apt to be a good one if all members get a chance to vote on it than if the members simply discuss the problem and the chairman decides on his own. (I+)
7. Discussion groups with a formal leader are more efficient than those in which members participate as equals. (I—)
8. In most discussion groups it is easier to get the work done and done well if one person takes charge than if everyone participates equally. (I—)
9. In most discussion groups there should be no leaders—everyone should have an equal say in all decisions. (I+)
10. In setting up a discussion group, someone should be given responsibility for making final decisions instead of leaving this up to the group as a whole. (I—)
11. Whenever possible, members of a discussion group should try to make their decisions unanimously rather than appointing a chairman to make the final decisions for them. (I+)
12. When people meet to work on a discussion problem, authority for making decisions should be vested in one or two people instead of giving everyone an equal say. (I—)

---

* Roman numerals indicate whether item loaded on factor I or factor II. (See text for explanation of factors.) If no roman numeral follows item, then item did not load above .30 on either factor. A (+) indicates item was weighted in the equalitarian direction, a (—) that it was weighted in the authoritarian direction.

CLASSROOM

1. I enjoy discussion sections in which I can give my opinions more than lectures in which I have to listen to a professor talk the whole time. (I+)
2. Other things being equal, I would rather be in a discussion section run by the professor than in one run by the students. (—)
3. I like professors who take charge of discussions more than those who let the students run the discussions themselves. (I—)
4. I like courses in which the professor lets the students do most of the talking better than those in which the professor does most of the talking himself. (+)
5. In the long run students are apt to learn more in classes in which everyone gets a chance to talk than in those classes in which the professor does most of the talking. (I+)
6. The professor is usually in a better position to judge what the students should learn than the students are themselves. (II—)
7. Students will learn more in a discussion section run by the professor in charge than in one run by the students themselves. (II—)
8. When students are given responsibility for organizing classroom discussions, they learn more than when the professor takes responsibility for organizing the discussions himself. (I+)
9. In a discussion section the professor should try to keep his own remarks to a minimum and let the students do most of the talking rather than attempting to control the discussions himself. (I+)
10. In discussion sections, it is the professor and not the students who should do most of the talking. (I—)
11. Under most conditions, a professor should take formal charge of his discussion section instead of letting the students run it themselves. (—)
12. In section meetings, the students rather than the professor should have major responsibility for organizing and maintaining the discussion. (+)

FAMILY

1. When I have children, I want them to look on me more as an equal than as a superior. (II+)
2. I would prefer a family in which teen-agers are consulted on all major family decisions to one in which the parents decided things pretty much on their own. (+)
3. I like families in which the parents assume responsibility for making the important decisions instead of leaving this up to the family as a whole. (II—)
4. I like the kind of family in which the parents exert guidance and control over their children better than families in which the children are left pretty much to do as they please. (II—)
5. Most teen-agers are incapable of solving the problems of adolescence without persistent advice and direction from their parents. (II—)
6. Delinquents are more likely to come from families in which the parents try to control their children too much rather than from families in which the parents exert too little control. (+)

7. The most well-adjusted children come from families in which the parents give their children as little guidance as possible rather than from families in which the parents exert a great deal of control. (II+)
8. An adolescent will mature more easily and more naturally if his parents continue to guide and direct his activities than if he is permitted to work things out pretty much on his own. (—)
9. A teen-ager should be allowed to decide most things for himself rather than having his parents make most of his decisions for him. (II+)
10. When it comes to a decision affecting the whole family (e.g., buying a new house), adolescents should have a voice in that decision rather than leaving it entirely up to the parents. (II+)
11. Parents should take an active role in guiding and directing the activities of their adolescent children instead of leaving the children to work out most things on their own. (II—)
12. Parents should assume responsibility for making decisions affecting the whole family rather than leaving such decisions up to the family as a whole. (I—)

POLITICS

1. I would prefer a political system in which the people themselves retain primary responsibility for making decisions instead of delegating this responsibility to appointed and elected officials. (I+)
2. Other things being equal, I would rather live in a community in which the elected leaders take responsibility for all major decisions than in a community in which the whole citizenry meets to decide such things by mutual consent. (I—)
3. The political system that appeals to me most is the completely democratic one in which almost all decisions are made by mutual agreement rather than by appointed or elected officials. (I+)
4. I prefer a system of government in which elected leaders take responsibility for all major decisions to a system in which the citizens are allowed to decide most things for themselves. (II—)
5. Our country could be run more effectively if leadership were somewhat more centralized. (I—)
6. Town hall democracy—where practically everybody participates in deciding issues—is a more effective way of solving community problems than a system under which most decisions are made by elected or appointed officials. (+)
7. Most communities are incapable of solving their problems by purely democratic methods—they need elected representatives to make their decisions for them. (I—)
8. The more decisions that can be made by the public itself rather than its elected officials, the more effective a system of government will be in meeting the needs of the people. (II+)
9. Community members should try to solve most of their problems through mutual agreement instead of relying on political leaders to make decisions for them. (+)

10. The members of a community should delegate decision-making responsibility to their elected or appointed officials rather than trying to work things out on their own. (—)
11. Community political leaders should take an active role in deciding local issues instead of leaving such decisions up to the people themselves. (I—)
12. Community members should insist on having an equal voice in most of the decisions that have to be made—instead of leaving such decisions up to their elected representatives. (II+)

RELIGION

1. I like to feel that man can think through his problems on his own rather than having to seek advice and help from a divine being. (II+)
2. I like the feeling that we can appeal to a higher being in times of crisis instead of having to solve our problems without any help at all. (II—)
3. I would prefer that man make his own decisions rather than relying on a divine being to make decisions for him. (II+)
4. I would rather feel that man's fate is in God's hands than in the hands of man himself. (II—)
5. Man is quite capable of deciding things for himself—he does not need God to do it for him. (II+)
6. Without God's guidance and infinite wisdom, mankind could not long endure. (II—)
7. Ultimately, man does not rule himself but is ruled by divine authority. (II—)
8. Man can solve all his problems by himself without the help of God. (II+)
9. People should learn to rely on God for guidance in the conduct of their affairs rather than trying to decide everything for themselves. (II—)
10. People should take responsibility for their own lives instead of depending on a supernatural being for direction. (II+)
11. Man should develop his own principles of moral conduct rather than relying on God to tell him how he should and should not behave. (II+)
12. People should take their important problems to God instead of attempting to work them out on their own. (II—)

GROUPS IN GENERAL

1. I like equalitarian groups better than groups with a definite authority structure. (I+)
2. I like groups in which the members decide what should be done unanimously better than groups in which a leader makes all the final decisions. (I+)
3. I prefer groups in which one person has the responsibility for making decisions to those groups in which all members have an equal say. (I—)
4. I would rather be in a group with an appointed leader than a group in which members treat each other strictly as equals. (I—)
5. A group of people who treat each other as equals will perform a lot better than a group with a formal leader. (I+)
6. In the long run, leaderless groups often produce more than groups where one person is in charge. (I+)

7. A group with a formal leader is more effective in solving problems than a group in which everyone has an equal say. (I—)
8. With one person responsible for making all decisions, a group is more apt to achieve its goals than it might if all decisions were required to be unanimous. (I—)
9. In just about any sort of group, someone should be given responsibility for making decisions instead of leaving this up to the group as a whole. (I—)
10. A good group is completely democratic—the members should decide things unanimously instead of giving any one person final authority. (I+)
11. In most groups, one person should be allowed to take charge—as opposed to requiring complete agreement among all group members. (I—)
12. In most groups, there should be no leaders—everyone should have an equal say in all decisions. (I+)

EQUALITY IN GENERAL

1. In a very important sense, all men are created equal. (I+)
2. There should be equality for everyone—because we are all human beings. (+)
3. In the ideal society, there would be no significant differences among men with respect to income, prestige, or power. (I+)
4. The assumption that all men are created equal is unrealistic and can only lead to confusion. (I—)
5. Everyone should have an equal chance and an equal say. (I+)
6. People should be rewarded according to what they produce, even if this means that some people make a great deal more than others. (I—)
7. Broadly speaking, inequality is a normal condition of human society and can never be eliminated. (I—)
8. People who contribute less to society than others have no right to expect the same kind of rewards. (—)
9. Each one should get what he needs—the things we have belong to all of us. (+)
10. In a variety of senses, all men are created quite unequal. (I—)

F-SCALE

1. Obedience and respect for authority are the most important virtues children should learn. (II—)
2. There is hardly anything lower than a person who does not feel a great love, gratitude, and respect for his parents. (II—)
3. What youth needs most is strict discipline, rugged determination, and the will to work and fight for family and country. (II—)

CHAPTER 6

Individualism—Collectivism (II)

AT THIS STAGE in our research, we felt that we had demonstrated at least three important things: first, that attitudes could be changed in a laboratory setting without the benefit of verbal persuasion; second, that change could be induced in beliefs, values, and preferences ranging far beyond the experimental situation; and third, that comparable results could be obtained with two distinct attitude dimensions (individualism-collectivism and equalitarianism-authoritarianism). Demonstrating the third point was, of course, the major intent behind the second laboratory study, reported in the last chapter. The fact remained, however, that despite some success in showing the generality of our predictions across attitude dimensions, all of the findings from both laboratory studies were based on the use of a single task. In trying to decide what steps to take next, it seemed reasonable to move in the direction of broadening the kinds of task experience to which our subjects were exposed. There were several reasons for doing so.

In the first place, there was the possibility, admittedly slight, that results of the sort we had obtained were unique to the Bales task in which subjects were asked to predict another student's responses to an attitude questionnaire. More importantly, we were reminded of the fact that in holding the task constant across treatment groups and varying, instead, the amount of reward received, we were not directly testing the theory which takes variation in task experience to be a major determinant of attitudes. According to the theory, it is the nature of the task, through the demands it makes upon its members, that helps to determine individual behavior and ultimately individual beliefs, values, and preferences. To test the theory more directly we should have exposed our subjects to different kinds of tasks, not the same task rewarded differentially. As explained at the opening of Chapter 4, we deliberately chose to hold the task constant and vary the rewards for performing it one way as opposed to another in the belief that this was the best way to make unequivocal the relative superiority of one form of organization over the other. The Bales task was especially suitable for this purpose. There can be no doubt, moreover, that we succeeded in this effort. From subjects' responses to the postmeeting reaction questionnaire in the first laboratory experiment (cf. Chapter 4, page 98), it is abundantly clear that half the sample (the CL's) perceived that the task could be done more effectively in groups, while the other half (the ID's) felt it could be done much better working alone.

It is true, nevertheless, that the task was the same in both cases, that it was only the rewards that were varied, some being rewarded more for performing the task together, others more for doing it alone. The same could be said for the second laboratory study in which the task was held constant while some subjects were rewarded more for working with a leader, others for working without a leader. At this point, in order to get a more direct test of the theory, we decided upon an experiment in which subjects would actually be exposed to different kinds of tasks. This meant giving up something in the way of control since no artificial (faked) results would be used. We would rely, instead, on the *natural* superiority, for a given task, of one organizational strategy over another.

While moving in the direction of a more naturalistic experiment, we were at the same time tempted to drop the idea of a formalized trial-and-error sequence as well. In brief, we felt that from the viewpoint of generalizing beyond the laboratory the ideal experiment would involve simply confronting half of our subjects with a task demanding one kind of organization (e.g., intense co-operation) and the other half a different task requiring an altogether different form of organization (e.g., independent activity). In this design, no one would be asked to work on the same task two different ways (e.g., first together and then alone). There would be no trial-and-error sequence such as we had used in the first two laboratory experiments. Subjects would simply be asked to work on a given task, organizing themselves in any way they saw fit. If trial and error were to take place, then, it would be spontaneous among group members rather than imposed by the experimenter. This "ideal" design was actually tried on a number of pre-test groups but failed to produce the desired results. As a consequence of this failure, we reverted to the built-in formalized trial-and-error sequence used in previous experiments. We did retain, however, the original idea of exposing our subjects to different kinds of tasks, relying on the natural reinforcing characteristics of each rather than the artificial feedback control previously employed.

This was one innovation, i.e., using different tasks for the two different treatment groups. In addition to this change, we decided to use more than one task in each of the two treatments. Within each treatment, that is, there would be a number of tasks, all similar in that they "required" the same organizational strategy. The reason for the change was simple. We felt intuitively that a task experience encompassing a variety of similar tasks would be more likely to lead to attitude change than an experience based upon a single task, as in our previous experiments. It is possible that our previous subjects resisted generalization to other areas because of the limited, unique, and isolated nature of the single task they were asked to work on. By broadening the experimental base, we hoped to facilitate the inductive leap from orientations developed in the laboratory setting to attitudes ranging throughout the universe of interpersonal relations.

For an attitude dimension in this experiment, we chose once more to work with individualism-collectivism. Among other considerations, we wanted to demonstrate, this time with a variety of tasks, the possibility of inducing change on a dimension previously employed in a study built around a single task with differential rewards.

In brief, our plan was as follows. Through pre-testing, we hoped to find a number of tasks some of which could clearly be done better by subjects working co-operatively in groups, others of which could be done more effectively working alone. In the experiment itself, then, half the subjects would be exposed exclusively to those tasks which we knew in advance could be performed more effectively in groups. As in previous experiments, the tasks would be performed alternately together and alone. The other half of the subject population would be asked to work on an entirely different set of tasks, those which pre-testing had indicated could be done better by individuals working independently of one another. Again for these subjects, the tasks would be performed alternately together and alone. The proposed effect in either case would be to make salient, through repeated trials across a number of tasks, the greater instrumental reward value of one of the two patterns of organization.

ATTITUDE QUESTIONNAIRE

Instead of using the same questionnaire employed in our first laboratory experiment, we decided to devise a new measure of individualism-collectivism. One reason for doing so was that the results of our second laboratory study seemed to indicate that bipolar items (e.g., "In general,

I would rather work in a group than by myself.") were helpful in anchoring each statement to a specific alternative whereas our first individualism-collectivism questionnaire was made up exclusively of unipolar items (e.g., "I enjoy doing things by myself.").

A second reason for starting anew was that we thought we could make finer distinctions among types of individualism-collectivism than had been made in our first questionnaire. Theoretically, we found it possible to distinguish among three basic levels of individualism-collectivism which we felt defined an intensity continuum for this dimension. At the simplest level, the relevant issue takes the form of doing things alone versus doing them together with other people. The question involved here is little more than whether or not interaction is to take place. If it can be assumed that interaction is taking place, a second question can be posed, namely, is the individual to co-operate with the others towards a common goal or is he to work pretty much on his own. It is, of course, possible to work in the presence of other people without co-operating with them; in this sense togetherness is a more primitive concept than co-operation. Assuming that co-operation does take place, we can ask still another question: Is the individual to assign priority to what he perceives to be in the best interests of the group or to what he thinks would be best for himself? This is what Parsons refers to as the "self-collectivity dilemma."[1] In Parsons' terms the issue may be resolved either "by giving primacy to interests, goals, and values shared with the other members of a given collective unit . . . or by giving primacy to . . . personal or private interests without considering their bearing on collective interests."[2] Since it is possible to co-operate with others without giving primacy to the interests of these others, we took the latter to be the more extreme of the two levels.

To summarize, three degrees or levels of individualism-collectivism were differentiated: (1) togetherness (versus aloneness), (2) co-operation (versus independence), and (3) collectivity orientation (versus self-orientation).

With these three levels in mind, we proceeded to write items dealing with five different areas. To test for vertical generalization, we wrote items involving (1) small work groups, (2) groups in general, and (3) way of life. The first two scales were roughly equivalent in form to the discussion-group and groups-in-general scales used in the previous study, the difference being that the latter all had something to do with

---

[1] Talcott Parsons and Edward A. Shils, *et al.*, *Toward a General Theory of Action* (Cambridge, Mass.: Harvard University Press, 1951), pp. 80–81.
[2] *Ibid.*

authority and equality. The way-of-life items written for this study were similar to the equality-in-general statements of the last study in that both were couched in relatively abstract terms. In the case of our equality-in-general scale, however, statements were borrowed from a number of sources, no attempt being made to rewrite items in the standard bipolar fashion used throughout the rest of the study. In view of the relatively poor performance of those items, care was taken this time in composing the way-of-life scale to use the same format employed in all the other items.

In order to test for lateral generalization, we wrote items dealing with the family and with fraternity life. The family was included mainly to give us a specific case for comparing the success of this experiment with the two previous laboratory studies in which items dealing with the family showed relatively little change. Items dealing with fraternity life were included partly because of a desire to try something new, partly because the subject seemed to lend itself well to statements at all three levels of analysis (togetherness, co-operation, and collectivity orientation).

Eighteen items were written for each of these five areas; six were phrased in the cathectic mode, six in the cognitive mode, and six in the evaluative mode. Although the results of our previous studies had indicated that the mode of expression was irrelevant as far as both item intercorrelations and propensity to change were concerned, it was decided to replicate these findings once more before giving up the distinctions involved.

Within each set of six items, two were designed to measure attitudes toward individual—group relations at the simplest level (aloneness versus togetherness), two at the second level (independence versus co-operation), and two at the third level (self-orientation versus collectivity orientation). In each of these three sets, one item was worded in an individual direction, the other in a group direction. The content of the questionnaire was thus perfectly balanced in terms of area, mode, level, and direction. Eventually nine more way-of-life items were added, making a total of 99 items in all. As in our previous study, the response format was a nine-point scale ranging from Strongly Disagree to Strongly Agree.

The original questionnaire was administered to a class of approximately 70 male and female students, none of whom were used later in the experiment itself. All items were intercorrelated, the matrix factor analyzed (centroid method), and the factors rotated (quartimax method). Since very few factor loadings over .40 were found on the third factor when three factors were extracted, it was concluded that two factors were adequate to account for most of the item intercorrelations. Factor I included 24 level-three items (collectivity orientation) and 13 level-two items (co-operation) with loadings of .40 or better. These 37 items were evenly distributed across the five content areas. In view of the heavy representation of level-three items, this first factor was labeled "self-orientation–collectivity orientation." Factor II included 19 items from level one (togetherness) and four from level two (co-operation), again evenly distributed across all five areas. By virtue of the prominent role of level-one statements in this factor, it was named "aloneness-togetherness." The remaining 39 items failed to load greater than .40 on either factor. As in previous studies, there was no tendency for items to cluster by cathectic, cognitive, and evaluative mode.

All items which were not loaded .40 or better on either factor I or factor II were discarded leaving a total of 60 items in the final questionnaire. There was no need to eliminate or rewrite items eliciting extreme responses since all item means ranged between 3.0 and 7.0 on our nine-point scale. In its final form, the questionnaire included statements quite evenly distributed across the five content areas and the three attitude modes. It can be seen in Exhibit D at the end of this chapter.

The final questionnaire was later factor analyzed using the "before" questionnaires of the 60 subjects who actually participated in the experiment. Rather surprisingly, the factor structure was not the same for this group. Most of the small work-group, groups-in-general, and family items loaded on factor I, whereas all of the fraternity and most of the way-of-life items loaded on factor II, regardless of level. We can think of no logical explanation for these differences except sampling error. Since these latter results made so little analytical sense, we decided, before looking at the actual results of the experiment, to violate good experimental technique and ignore the data from the second factor analysis, using instead the results of our first factor analysis.

As in our last study, then, questionnaire items were broken down two different ways (1) by area (small work groups, groups in general, way of life, family, and fraternity) and (2) by factor (factor I, self-orientation–collectivity orientation and factor II, aloneness-togetherness). The relevant information for each breakdown is given in the two tables below. Table 6–1 shows the number of items, internal consistencies, and test-retest reliabilities for each of the five area scales.[3]

---

[3] These were computed in the same manner as in the previous chapters (see Chapter 3, footnote 18).

TABLE 6–1
Internal Consistencies and Reliabilities for Area Scales

Area	No. of Items	Internal Consistency	Test-Retest Reliability	
			ID	CL
Small work groups	13	.75	.41	.36
Groups in general	11	.73	.40	.53
Way of life	16	.87	.82	.80
Family	10	.82	.83	.90
Fraternity	10	.76	.75	.80

All 60 items were used for the breakdown by factor, since in the first factor analysis all had loadings of .40 or better on at least one of the two dimensions. Where an item was loaded .40 or higher on both factors, it was assigned to the factor on which it had the higher loading. Table 6–2 shows the number of items from each area included in each of the two factors, as well as the corrected interitem and test-retest correlations.

TABLE 6–2
Internal Consistencies and Reliabilities for Factor Scales

	Factor I	Factor II
Small work groups	7	6
Groups in general	7	4
Way of life	11	5
Family	6	4
Fraternity	6	4
Total	37	23
Internal consistency	.88	.85
Test-retest:		
ID	.70	.74
CL	.74	.75

PROCEDURE

The subjects for this experiment were initially recruited at freshman registration (Cornell) in the fall of 1962 about two months before the experiment began. A sign was posted inviting all males to volunteer for a series of small group experiments, all participants to receive something in the neighborhood of $5.00 for an afternoon's work. From an initial pool of 125 males, about 80 were signed up for specific appointments. Additional male subjects were recruited from freshman courses later in the semester yielding a total of 93 subjects who actually participated in the experiment. Thirty-three of these were used for pre-testing the design, leaving 60 who took part in the final experiment to be described here.

Subjects were invited to the laboratory in groups of seven or eight. Once they had completed the "before" questionnaire, the experiment was introduced in the following manner.

Before we begin let me tell you a little about the purpose of the experiment. We are basically interested in finding out whether people ordinarily perform more effectively as members of a group or as individuals working independently of one another. There are a number of other things we shall be looking for, but will not mention at this time so as to avoid making you overly conscious of them. At the end of the experiment everything will be explained to you. You may ask any question you wish at that time.

We have a number of tasks we would like you to work on this afternoon. In each case you will have a chance to try the task once as a group and a second time working individually. Our position is somewhat akin to that of an employer who wants to know whether he can get better results by asking his employees to work on a problem together as a team or by having them work independently of one another. The manner of judging the superiority of one strategy over another will vary according to the task at hand. In some cases it will be appropriate to compare the group output with the *sum* of the individual outputs; at other times it will be more appropriate, from the employer's point of view, to compare the group output with the output of the most productive individual. Just why this should be the case will become clear to you as each task is explained.

Subjects were told that they would each receive $5.00 for the afternoon's work. Although we would have preferred to use incentive rates geared to actual performance, this proved to be impossible. Beyond the complexities involved (given an array of eight different tasks), an elaborate incentive system would have suggested to subjects that we knew from past experience approximately how well individuals and groups did on the tasks to be used, after they had just been told that this was what the experiment was designed to find out.[4]

Tasks for the CL's

Half the subjects (hereafter called the "CL's") were given four tasks which we knew ahead of time could be done more effectively by a group of people working closely together than by individuals working independently of one another. These were performed alternately by the group as a whole and by the same individuals working alone. The four tasks are described in detail below.

---

[4] In our final experiment (Chapter 9), however, we did find that we could use incentive rates in a design very similar to this one without arousing subjects' suspicions.

1. Crossword Puzzle. The seven or eight subjects present were seated around a table and given a single moderately difficult crossword puzzle with instructions to solve as much of it as they could in 20 minutes time. Performance was to be judged by the total number of letters solved correctly. Subjects were allowed to organize themselves in any way they wanted to, e.g., by dividing up the puzzle among group members, by having everyone work on the same word at the same time etc. When the 20 minutes were up, the experimenter added up the total number of correct letters and posted the figure on the board under the heading *group.*

Subjects were then moved to individual tables at the other end of the room where the experimenter distributed eight copies of another equally difficult crossword puzzle with the instructions that this time subjects were to work on the puzzle independently of one another. It was further explained that, in comparing the performance here with how well they did as a group, the number of correctly solved letters for all individuals combined (excluding duplications) would be used.

2. Memory Problem. In order, outwardly at least, to control for learning effect, half of the tasks were performed first in the group and then individually, the other half the other way around. Since the crossword puzzle was done with the group first, the memory problem was administered initially in the individual setting. One of the experimenters read a list of 30 adjectives and adverbs, the task being to write down as many as possible in the minute following the reading. The task was repeated five times using a list of different words in each case. Performance was judged by counting up the total number of unduplicated words remembered across the six trials.

Subjects were then moved back to the group table where six more word lists were ready, the difference being that in this setting they were free to talk with each other and organize the memory process by dividing up the labor among group members. It is not surprising, given the chance to assign limited portions of the list to individual members, that the group consistently made a higher score than the same people working individually.

3. Questionnaire Scoring. Starting as a group this time, subjects were given eight copies of a 75-item questionnaire, already filled out, their job being to compute scale scores according to a scoring key provided by the experimenter.[5] This involved giving positive weights to some responses and negative weights to others, and then summing across

---

[5] The questionnaire used was unrelated to the one the subjects themselves had filled out prior to the experiment.

items. Each questionnaire had eight subscales each with its own unique scoring key. A total score representing the sum of all the subscales was also required. Any score computed incorrectly had to be done over until all tallies were accurate. Performance was judged by the number of minutes taken before all scores for all questionnaires were done correctly.

In the group sessions each questionnaire was torn apart so that one group member could score the same scale for each of the eight questionnaires. Having but one scoring key to work with, subjects soon became quite expert at their computations. Later, when asked to perform the same task individually (with new questionnaires), subjects each received a whole questionnaire and were responsible for scoring all eight scales by themselves. With eight different scoring keys to work with, subjects were forced to work more slowly and made more mistakes in the process. The clock was not stopped until all subjects had correctly computed all eight scale scores plus a total.

4. Construction. For this task, subjects were required to build little two-wheeled wagons using parts and a diagram from an Erector Set. Starting individually, each subject was given his own parts and diagram and told to put together a complete wagon as quickly as possible. No one was allowed to help anyone else. All wagons had to pass inspection by the experimenter before being considered complete. Performance was evaluated in terms of the number of minutes required to complete seven wagons.

For the group session, subjects were organized on an assembly line basis, the details of which had been worked out in advance by the experimenter. Once assignments had been made and duties explained, subjects were left to improvise as they saw fit. Time was called when seven wagons had passed inspection.

Tasks for the ID's

Pre-testing (and in some cases, common sense) had indicated that the four tasks described above could be performed more effectively by people working in groups than by the same people working independently of each other. Approximately half of our subjects (31) were given these four tasks to work on. The remaining 29 subjects (the ID's) were confronted with a different series of tasks, each of which we knew to lend itself better to individual as opposed to group performance. These four tasks are described below.

1. Brainstorming. Starting in the group setting, subjects were given the name of a common object (pencil, chair, etc.), the task being to write down as many uses for the object as possible within a two-minute time limit. The task was repeated four times, using different objects in each case. One person was given the job of writing down all suggestions. At the end of each two-minute trial, the list was screened by the experimenter for inappropriate uses and duplications. The final score for the period was the total number of different uses across all five objects.

The subjects then moved to the other end of the room, took individual seats and performed the task once again, this time with five new objects. The same two-minute time limit was used here. Performance was judged in this case by totaling up the number of different uses across both subjects and objects. Where the same use for an object was listed by more than one subject, it was counted only once. In general, subjects produced about twice as many uses working individually as in a group.

2. *Word Game.* Starting individually this time, subjects were first asked to draw a 16-cell design, i.e., a 4×4 matrix of empty squares. The task consisted of placing letters one at a time in each of the cells as the experimenter read them off from a list so as to create as many three and four letter words in the matrix as possible. Thirteen letters were announced, subjects having one minute to decide where to put each one. The last three cells of the matrix were to be filled in at the end in any way subjects saw fit. No letters could be erased or moved once they had been entered in the matrix. Five points were given for each four-letter word and three points for each three-letter word. The score for this individual phase was taken to be the highest number of points achieved by any one subject. It was explained that since we (the hypothetical employer) were interested in getting the best matrix for our money, it would be meaningless to average or sum point values across eight different matrices.

In the group phase of this task, all subjects worked on the same matrix, which was drawn on the blackboard so that everyone could see it at the same time. One person was given the responsibility of writing in the letters as the group made its decisions. All other conditions were the same as before except that a different list of letters was used. Although on the surface it might seem that the group (with more brains to pick) would do better than the best individual, it did not work out this way. With so many conflicting strategies to choose from and so little time in which to make decisions, co-operation proved to be an ineffective way of approaching the task.

3. *Prediction.* This was the same Bales task described in the first

two laboratory experiments with the difference that here subjects could obtain the real answer from a stack of cards placed in front of them. In other words, there was no manipulation of results in this case. Two different questionnaires (both real) were used, one for each setting. In the group phase, all subjects had to agree on a single prediction before turning the answer card. The final score was based on the total number of points earned in 20 minutes.

When subjects worked on the task individually, each subject was given his own copy of the questionnaire and his own stack of answer cards. In comparing the performance of the group with that of the same subjects working independently, we again used the best individual performance as our reference. As with the word game, it was explained that a comparison of the group with the sum or average of individual scores would be meaningless since it was the best single set of predictions that we were looking for.

4. Construction. Having run out of ideas for ID tasks that were completely different from those given to the other subjects (the CL's), we decided to use the Erector Set again, with certain important modifications. The idea, of course, was to set up the task so that subjects would do better individually than in a group (the opposite of what we had for the CL's). The CL's did better in a group primarily because the experimenter provided them with a carefully worked out assembly line plan. Thus, for the ID's in the group phase, no instructions were given as to how to divide up the labor among group members, although they were always allowed to do so on their own.

In addition, only six wagons were required before the job was considered done. This again was designed with an eye to making things relatively easier in the individual phase. As noted previously, we could ordinarily count on one or two subjects out of eight who had absolutely no talent for work of this sort. By requiring only six units from the eight individuals present, we made it less likely that a small minority of subjects would inflate the total score. In addition, the fewer the units the less advantage there was to an assembly line in the group phase.

Finally, the task was always done in the group first, so that if any learning were to take place it would help subjects when working individually. With these three innovations, it turned out that subjects consistently did better when working alone than when co-operating as a group.

To summarize, half the subjects (the CL's) were asked to work alternately alone and together on four different tasks (crossword puzzle, memory problem, questionnaire scoring, and construction), which we knew in advance could be done more effectively together. In all but one isolated case, they actually did better as a group, although the group and individual scores were never very far apart. The other half of our subjects went through the same procedure only with a different set of tasks (brainstorming, word game, prediction, and construction), all of which pre-testing had indicated could be performed more effectively when subjects worked independently. Here again, pre-testing was borne out by the fact that in the experiment itself, subjects actually did better in every case when working independently of one another.

Summary of Predictions

With respect to attitude change, it was predicted that the CL's (those doing better together than alone) would become more collectivistic on each of the five area scales (small work groups, groups in general, way of life, family, and fraternity) and each of the two factor scales (self-orientation–collectivity orientation and aloneness-togetherness). The ID's (those doing better alone) were expected to become more individualistic on the same scales. In terms of vertical generalization, it was further predicted that the least abstract items (small work groups) would change the most, groups in general second, and way of life (the most abstract) the least. With regards to lateral generalization, no attempt was made to predict relative changes for family and fraternity. Finally, we made the prediction that factor II (aloneness-togetherness) would show more change than factor I (self versus collectivity orientation). This latter prediction was grounded on the assumption that in the experiment itself it was the alone-together contrast rather than the self-collectivity distinction that would be most salient to our subjects.

RESULTS

Change by Item. When all items were analyzed collectively, regardless of area or factor location, the results proved to be quite striking. Out of 60 items on the questionnaire, the differences between mean changes for CL's and ID's were in the predicted direction for 58, there being no change differences on the remaining two items. In other words, there was not a single reversal throughout the 60 item questionnaire. Omitting the two items which failed to change in either direction, this yields a chi-square value of 56.0 which is significant well beyond the .001 level. It is clear from this that, taken as a whole, the experiment had a very marked effect on subjects' attitudes.

Change by Area. Mean changes for CL's and ID's on each of the five area scales are shown in Table 6–3. All scales were scored so that a positive mean change indicates that subjects became more collectivistic, a negative change indicating movement in the individualistic direction. According to our predictions, all mean change scores in the CL column should be positive and all those in the ID column negative. This is in fact the case, without exception. As a result, all the between-group

TABLE 6–3

Attitude Change by Area Scales

| Area | Mean Change | | Diff. | | |
	CL	ID	(CL − ID)	t	p
Small work groups	17.39	−14.45	31.84	7.53	.001
Groups in general	7.84	−9.17	17.01	5.15	.001
Way of life	8.77	−6.90	15.67	4.53	.001
Family	4.32	−1.86	6.18	2.96	.01
Fraternity	5.97	−2.66	8.63	3.75	.001

differences (column three) and *t* ratios (column four) are in the expected direction. It is evident from the *p* values, moreover, that all five of the differences are highly significant, four of them beyond the .001 level.[6]

Turning to the *t* ratios in column four, there is evidence to suggest that generalization along the vertical axis conformed to expectations, in that the least abstract items (small work groups) changed the most while the most abstract items (way of life) changed the least. It is important to note, however, that the *t* ratio for the way-of-life scale, although smaller than the other two, is still a highly significant one.

Although we had already used items dealing with family life in both of our previous laboratory studies, this was the first time that we got clear-cut positive results. Even so, this scale has the smallest *t* ratio in Table 6–3, where all others reach the .001 level of significance.

The fraternity findings are especially interesting. It will be recalled that the experiment was conducted exclusively with males in the first term of their freshman year. Although fraternity rushing at Cornell does not begin formally until the end of the term, there is a good deal of thinking and talking about the decision to join in advance of that time. Assuming that our subjects were, in this respect, no different from their classmates, it is difficult to believe that, in four hours and with-

---

[6] A series of *t*-tests on scores taken from the "before" questionnaire revealed no significant differences between CL's and ID's on any of the five scales.

out a single verbal reference to fraternities, their attitudes toward fraternity life changed as significantly as they did. As indicated above, this is true of all the items in the fraternity scale. It is especially interesting, however, that subjects changed significantly on the most direct item in that scale—"I would rather belong to a fraternity than remain an independent." The changes are small, but systematic—and in the predicted direction.

Change by Factor. It is clear from Table 6–4 that both factors changed significantly in the predicted direction. On the grounds that the alone-together contrast was experimentally more salient than the self-collectivity dilemma, it had been predicted that factor II would show greater change than factor I. While there is some evidence for

TABLE 6–4
Attitude Change by Factor Scales

| Factor | Mean Change | | Diff. | | |
	CL	ID	(CL — ID)	t	p
I (Self-collectivity–orient.)	26.94	−13.07	40.01	5.64	.001
II (Aloneness–togetherness)	17.35	−21.90	39.25	8.09	.001

this in the two *t* ratios, (5.64 versus 8.09), the mean difference is very small and even slightly in the other direction. An alternative interpretation (post hoc) would have it that the experiment was oriented most closely to our level two (co-operation versus independence), thus falling halfway between togetherness (factor I) on the one hand and collectivity orientation (factor II) on the other. In this vein, it could be argued that the experiment involved something more than simply working alone versus together and yet failed to involve any real conflict between self-interests and group interests. Assuming the subjects' actual experience to be located somewhere in between the two, it would be reasonable to expect about the same amount of attitude generalization in both directions.

Change by People. Table 6–5 shows the number of subjects changing in each direction for all five area scales and both factor scales. All scales are scored so that a plus means change in the collectivistic direction. It is evident from the data that on all seven scales a significant majority of subjects changed in the predicted direction. On the average, something like 75 per cent of the subjects changed as expected. This is, of course, considerably better than what we found in our two previous

TABLE 6–5
People Changes by Area and Factor*

Small Work Groups

	+	−
ID	5	24
CL	28	3

$$\chi^2 = 29.45$$
$$p < .001$$

Groups in General

	+	−
ID	7	21
CL	24	7

$$\chi^2 = 14.16$$
$$p < .001$$

Family

	+	−
ID	10	18
CL	19	10

$$\chi^2 = 3.95$$
$$p < .05$$

Fraternity

	+	−
ID	10	16
CL	22	9

$$\chi^2 = 4.83$$
$$p < .05$$

Way of Life

	+	−
ID	9	20
CL	21	10

$$\chi^2 = 6.66$$
$$p < .01$$

Factor I
Self-collectivity

	+	−
ID	9	20
CL	24	6

$$\chi^2 = 10.66$$
$$p < .01$$

Factor II
Aloneness-Togetherness

	+	−
ID	3	26
CL	26	5

$$\chi^2 = 29.58$$
$$p < .001$$

* All tables do not sum to 60 since people who did not change were not included.

experiments and is in keeping with, although not identical to, the more significant mean and item changes reported above.

Preferences, Beliefs, and Values

Mean change scores for the CL and ID groups for each area and factor were computed separately for cathectic, cognitive, and evaluative items. Inspection of these means revealed no systematic differences. For some scales, the cathectic items changed the most, on others it was the cognitive items, and still others the evaluative items. Although no significance tests were performed, it is clear from these as well as previous results that the mode in which an item is phrased has no systematic effect on the amount of item change.

Initial Position and Amount of Change

The relationship between initial attitude position and amount of change in the predicted direction was computed the same way as in the two previous studies (see Chapter 4, pp. 103–4), although this time scores on all five areas were combined since all showed significant mean changes. It can be seen from Figure 6–1 that once more the relationship is negative, indicating that the greater the discrepancy between original position and treatment, the greater was the amount of attitude change in the direction of the treatment.

While different to some extent, the results of these last three studies appear to agree with each other well enough to justify the conclusion that in nonpersuasive laboratory studies such as these, *the greater the discrepancy between an individual's initial attitudes and the experience he undergoes, the greater will be the amount of attitude change induced.* The results seemed consistent enough at this point to render superfluous any further tests of this relationship in our subsequent experiments.

DISCUSSION

As the fourth in our series of studies dealing with task experience as a determinant of preferences, beliefs, and values, this was very clearly the most successful. There are a number of reasons for this. Most obviously, this was the first time that we had varied the kinds of task experience to which subjects were exposed, both between and within treatments. With reference to the latter, it would appear that the experience of doing better together or alone on four *different* tasks made it easier for subjects to generalize their immediate reactions to areas beyond the limits of the laboratory situation. The reader will recall that

FIGURE 6–1

Amount of Change in Predicted Direction as a Function of
Amount of Discrepancy between Original Attitude and
Type of Treatment for ID's and CL's Combined on Five Areas

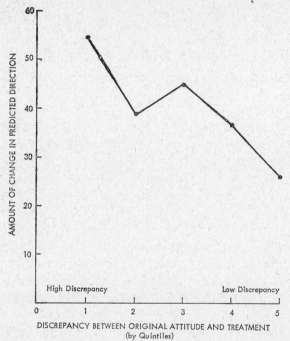

in our last study subjects changed very significantly on the discussion-group and groups-in-general items (both changes significant at the .001 level), but failed to generalize systematically beyond that. In the present study everything seemed to work, suggesting that both vertical and lateral generalization were facilitated by the greater breadth of the experience to which subjects were exposed in the laboratory.

There is, of course, no way of knowing at present that it was this innovation that made the difference. There are several alternative explanations. Among them, we could point to the actual tasks employed (as opposed to their variety). It is possible that in using tasks which could honestly be done better either together or alone, we eliminated some of the ambiguity involved in relying exclusively on faked results. The fact remains, however, that in our first laboratory experiment where results were completely faked, subjects were very clearly convinced that the task could be performed more effectively either together or alone, depending on how they were rewarded (cf. Chapter 4, page 98).

In searching for alternative explanations for the relative success of this experiment, we felt that it was more likely that the new questionnaire had something to do with it. Aside from the fact that all the items were new, the scales were more reliable, the factor loadings higher, and items were written in bipolar fashion throughout. Moreover, greater care was taken, in writing items, to stick to the main attitudinal theme. This, unfortunately, was not the case in the last study where, for example, in choosing items for the equality-in-general scale, we tended to wander away from the leadership/decision-making theme, ending instead with statements dealing with a variety of peripherally related issues ranging from whether or not men are created equal to questions of private property and income distribution. The comparable scale in this present study, way of life, was written very deliberately around the same themes used in all the other scales.

A further comment on the way-of-life scale is in order. We were frankly more interested in this scale than any of the others. As noted earlier (see page 142), nine extra items of this sort were added to the original questionnaire format in order to provide somewhat broader coverage of the area as well as to insure scale reliability. In its final version, the scale had 16 items, eleven of which dealt one way or another with what Parsons has called the "self-collectivity dilemma." In all eleven statements the dilemma was phrased in terms of the conflict between the individual's right to pursue his own self-interest and his obligations to the society in which he lives (e.g., "In the ideal society each individual would be willing to put the interests of society as a whole above his own personal needs" or, again, "A man's first duty should be to himself, and only secondarily to his fellow man."). These are very abstract sentiments. In the thinking of some, they are very sacred sentiments. To an extent, they also reflect one of the fundamental differences in the way present cultures have defined the role of the individual in society. Yet, for all of this, they underwent significant change in a four-hour laboratory experiment in which the experimenter confined himself to giving instructions for such things as solving crossword puzzles, playing word games, and building toy wagons with an Erector Set.

Despite the unequivocal significance of the changes reported here, it is clear from interviews with subjects at the end of the experiment that no one preceived this to be the object of the study. When asked about the purpose of the experiment, most repeated what they had been told at the beginning. When questioned further about the role of the attitude questionnaires, most of those who offered an opinion thought we might have been trying to predict performance from attitudes.

Only one or two out of 60 guessed that we were trying to change their attitudes, and this was only after their attention had been directed to the questionnaires. After the real purpose of the experiment had been explained, subjects were asked if they thought their attitudes changed at all. Some of them said they had changed slightly on the small-work-group items and a few thought they might have changed on the groups-in-general items, but none claimed to have changed on any of the other items. In fact, they thought it absurd that we ever expected them to do so. The fact that they actually did change, even on the very abstract way-of-life items, need not imply that unconscious forces were at work. Although the over-all changes were quite significant, very few individual subjects moved dramatically one way or the other. Items changes which are too small for the subject to be aware of can nevertheless yield significant *scale* changes if they are systematic enough. In view of the subjects' professed ignorance with respect to both the purpose of the experiment and the fact that attitude change did take place, it seems highly unlikely that the results of this study can be attributed to a conscious desire on the part of subjects to please the experimenter.

CONCLUSIONS

Unlike our earlier studies, this one proved to be everything we had hoped it would be. We achieved "complete" lateral and vertical generalization and at the same time showed that our findings were not tied to a single task. In view of the clear-cut success of the experiment, there seemed to be little point to continuing along the very same lines. It wasn't difficult to think of other avenues which still needed exploring. One of these was generality. Up to this point we had devoted most of our attention to two dimensions of culture: individualism-collectivism and equalitarianism-authoritarianism. Many others remained to be explored. Of these, two seemed especially interesting: religion and achievement. It was our hunch that in tracing the impact of task experience on each of these we would be led considerably beyond the limits of our theory as presented in Chapter 1.

EXHIBIT D

SMALL WORK GROUPS

1. Ordinarily I would rather work with others in a small group than work alone. (II+)*

---

* Roman numbers indicate whether item loaded on factor I or factor II (see text for explanation of factors). A + indicates that the item was weighted in the together or collectivistic direction, and a — indicates it was weighted in the alone or individualistic direction. In all cases the a priori direction coincided with the direction of the factor loading.

2. Given the choice, I would rather take on a task where I could work alone than one where I would have to work in a group with other people. (II—)

3. I prefer to be in groups in which everyone works for the good of the group as a whole rather than working simply for themselves. (I+)

4. People tend to work more efficiently when they are alone than when they are part of a small work group. (II—)

5. Generally speaking, it has been found that people working together in small groups are more productive than individuals working alone. (II+)

6. Work groups that allow the individual to pursue his own self-interests tend to be more productive than those which require the individual to work strictly for the group as a whole. (I—)

7. In general, a small work group can get more done if individual members consistently put the welfare of the group above their own personal interests and needs. (I+)

8. People should be encouraged to work alone instead of together in small groups. (II—)

9. Given the choice, people should do their work together in small groups rather than off by themselves. (II+)

10. In the work-group situation, people should do their best to co-operate with each other instead of trying to work out things on their own. (I+)

11. Members of small work groups should be encouraged to do their work as independently as possible rather than co-operating as members of a tightly knit group. (I—)

12. Members of small work groups should be given maximum freedom to pursue their own self-interests even if this sometimes conflicts with the goals of the group as a whole. (I—)

13. In small work groups, individual members should be encouraged to subordinate their private interests and desires to what is best for the group as a whole. (I+)

GROUPS IN GENERAL

1. In general, I would rather be by myself than with a group of other people. (II—)

2. In most cases, I would rather do something as part of a group than do it by myself. (II+)

3. The kind of group I like best is one in which there is intense co-operation among the group members rather than one in which each person does something independently of the others. (I+)

4. I would rather be in a group in which each member had certain group obligations to fulfill than in one in which everyone felt free to do whatever he pleased. (I+)

5. Groups which encourage intense co-operation among their members are more effective in getting things done than those which allow members to be relatively independent of one another. (I+)

6. In general, the most efficient way to organize a group is to allow each individual to work on his own rather than in close co-operation with other members. (I—)

7. Groups which emphasize the individual's responsibility to the group as a

whole are apt to be more effective in achieving their goals than those which grant the individual freedom to do what he thinks is best for himself. (I+)

8. People should spend more time alone and less time in groups. (II—)
9. Whenever possible, people should do things as part of a group rather than doing them alone. (II+)
10. Individuals in groups should do things on their own as much as possible rather than seeking the help and co-operation of other group members. (I—)
11. In any group, an individual's first responsibilities should be to himself, and only secondarily to his fellow group members. (I—)

FAMILY

1. I would prefer being part of a family in which everyone enjoys going places and doing things together to a family in which each person goes his own way. (II+)
2. I would prefer a family in which individual members are left pretty much to themselves to a family in which everyone is encouraged to do things together. (II—)
3. Families in which individual members feel free to engage in independent activities are more likely to develop productive citizens than those families which consistently encourage participation in co-operative activities. (I—)
4. Children should be trained to put their obligations to the family above their own personal interests. (I+)
5. An individual's first obligations should be to himself, and only secondarily to other members of his family. (I—)
6. Families which do a lot of things together are more apt to produce healthy, stable children than those in which everyone goes his or her own way. (II+)
7. The ideal family is one in which individual members co-operate in getting things done instead of working on their own. (II+)
8. Family tasks should be arranged so individual members can do as many things as possible on their own with a minimum of joint co-operation. (I—)
9. The families producing the most well-adjusted children are those which put a greater premium on altruistic, unselfish behavior than on individualistic self-oriented behavior. (I+)
10. Families which emphasize sticking up for one's own interests are more likely to produce socially useful citizens than families which encourage their members to do what is good for the family as a whole. (I—)

FRATERNITY

1. Given the choice I would rather be an independent than join a fraternity. (II—)
2. Generally speaking, a student will get more out of college if he joins a fraternity than if he remains an independent. (II+)
3. Students should be encouraged to join fraternities instead of going through college as independents. (II+)

4. In general, independents make better students than those who join fraternities. (II—)
5. I would rather belong to a fraternity that encouraged its members to accomplish things individually than one which demanded that its members work on a great many group activities together. (I—)
6. If I were to join a fraternity I would be willing to give up some of my personal interests and desires in order to work for the good of the fraternity as a whole. (I+)
7. I would prefer the kind of fraternity in which I would do whatever I felt like doing rather than the kind in which everyone is expected to go along with what the group decides. (I—)
8. The most dynamic fraternities are those that put stress on individual rather than co-operative accomplishments. (I—)
9. Fraternity members should co-operate as much as possible in joint activities involving the fraternity as a whole instead of pursuing their individual interests independently of one another. (I+)
10. A fraternity man's first obligations should be to himself and only secondarily to other members of his fraternity. (I—)

WAY OF LIFE

1. The way of life that appeals to me most is the independent life in which contacts with others are of secondary importance. (II—)
2. I prefer a way of life which calls for co-operation among men rather than independent achievement. (II+)
3. To me, a life dedicated to the welfare of one's fellow man is more satisfying than a life devoted to the pursuit of one's own private interests. (I+)
4. The life that appeals to me most is the one which minimizes my duty to others and maximizes my freedom to do what I like. (I—)
5. I prefer a way of life which emphasizes the supremacy of individual happiness to one which stresses our obligations to others. (I—)
6. People should spend more time in the company of others and less by themselves. (II+)
7. Societies should encourage their members to be more concerned with independent achievement and less concerned with group co-operation. (I—)
8. In the ideal society, men would willingly seek each other's help and co-operation instead of trying to go it alone. (II+)
9. The ideal life is that dedicated to the welfare of one's fellow man, even at the sacrifice of one's own personal happiness. (I+)
10. In the ideal society each individual would be willing to put the interests of society as a whole above his own personal needs. (I+)
11. Each individual should try to maximize his own personal happiness first, and concern himself only secondarily with the welfare of others. (I—)
12. A man's first duty should be to himself, and only secondarily to his fellow man. (I—)
13. Societies in which each person is encouraged to do what he can on his own will be more productive than those in which most things are done by people working closely together towards a common goal. (I—)

14. Other things being equal, societies which foster a spirit of social responsibility are apt to be more efficient and productive than those which grant the individual maximum freedom to do what he thinks is best for himself. (I+)

15. In the long run, the societies most likely to prosper are those which give the individual maximum freedom to pursue his own personal ends rather than those which stress the individual's obligations to work for the good of society as a whole. (I—)

16. The independent spirit—spurning all aid, needing no one, self-reliant, and free—this is man at his best. (II—)

CHAPTER 7

Religion

WITH THE reassuring results of the last study behind us, we decided to take another look at religion. Religion had already played a minor role in three of our previous experiments; in this study it was to occupy the center of the stage.

It is important here at the outset to realize that the study of religion takes us somewhat afield from the main body of our theory which deals with the role of task experience in the formation of those attitudes whose object is some form of behavior. Our previous experiments on individualism and equalitarianism represent direct tests of this theory. In each case, the attitude questionnaire was composed of items dealing in some way with the very kinds of behavior (e.g., alone versus together) which were involved in the experimental task situation. When we ask a subject whether he believes in God, however, it is clear that we are dealing with a set of attitudes many steps removed from anything that takes place in the laboratory.

Some of the religious scales used in previous experiments were not this far removed. In Chapter 4, for example, we included a scale dealing with the alone-together theme as this applied in the area of private versus public worship. In this case we made a very direct test of our theory. We took the area of divine worship to be just one more situation (the others being the family, neighborhood, and school) where the alone-together theme could be applied.

In our very first experiment (Chapter 3) we asked our subjects very directly whether they believed in God or not. It was assumed in the beginning that subjects who were confronted with conditions favoring the development of a highly centralized authority structure would become more authoritarian in their secular beliefs, values, and preferences and, by extension, more convinced that there was "a higher power above man." When the results failed to support this notion, we turned instead to the Miller-Swanson hypothesis which was couched in terms of group solidarity and the projection of a sense of collective or transcendent purpose.

Both of these ideas go considerably beyond our theory as this was presented in Chapter 1. In picking up the religion theme again in this chapter, we have tried to go beyond the theory once more. While we have continued to deal with the relationship between task experience and attitudes, we have made a deliberate attempt to explore certain features of that relationship which are not spelled out in our reinforcement-generalization model. In doing so, we have proceeded on the assumption that there is a great deal more to the relationship between task experience and attitudes than is implied in our original formulation.

THEORY

The primary impetus for this study came from our Wisconsin findings (Chapter 3) where both task and incentive system had a slight (and unexpected) impact on belief in God. According to those findings, students who were assigned to groups engaged in a disjunctive task (discussion) and operating on a competitive grading system were more likely than any others to give up their belief in God while those assigned to groups writing a blue-book essay (conjunctive task) and sharing a single-group grade showed the least tendency to fall. Neither task nor incentive system had an overwhelming impact on religion, one being significant at the .05 level and the other at the .10 level.

A post hoc attempt was made to explain these findings in terms of the notion that conventional theistic beliefs reflect "experiences of transcendent purpose encountered in the course of relations with other people."[1] The people most likely to believe that the world has purpose, that it was designed by some divine agency, are those who experience some sort of collective or transcendent purpose in their everyday lives. In applying this broadly defined hypothesis to our own research findings, we argued that the students most likely to feel some sense of joint or collective purpose were those who had to write a single blue-book essay each week and who were graded according to how well the group as a whole did.

Writing a single, joint essay requires a great deal of co-operation, especially when five to ten people are involved. In the process of developing a social structure, assigning positions, and defining expectations, it is to be expected that subjects will experience a sense of

---

[1] Daniel R. Miller and Guy E. Swanson, *The Changing American Parent* (New York: John Wiley & Sons, Inc., 1958), p. 277.

purpose which in some way is external to the individual and exercises constraint over him. It is this perception of group purpose, order, and interdependence that presumably gets projected onto a nonempirical reality where it takes the form of divine purpose and, by induction, divine being. Assuming that there is something to the idea, an even clearer case can be made for the impact of incentive system on religious beliefs. It is difficult *not* to feel a sense of collective purpose when each person's grade depends on what everyone else is doing, when everyone in the group receives the same grade depending on how well the group as a whole does. Conversely, it is unlikely that any such feelings or perceptions will emerge where individuals are competing for scarce rewards, i.e., where each individual's purpose or goal is at variance with everyone else's.

The first hint that the Miller-Swanson hypothesis might be appropriate to the Wisconsin findings came from an analysis of our interaction data. Both of the measures employed (the Bales index and the we/I ratio) showed blue-book sections to be higher on solidarity than discussion sections and single-grade sections higher than competitive ones. Solidarity, as measured this way, is presumably correlated with the less-easily measured "feelings of collective purpose" from which more formal religious beliefs are thought to flow. The fact that the groups which changed most in the atheistic direction were at the same time the least solidary certainly lends support to this notion.

In sum, the evidence seemed to indicate that both task and incentive system were causally related to group solidarity and, in turn, the religious beliefs of group members. While the relationship between each of the two situational variables and solidarity was statistically very significant (p's of .001), the relationship between situation and religious beliefs left much to be desired (*p*'s of .05 and .10). It was with the thought of exploring this latter relationship more thoroughly that we designed the experiment to be reported here.

On the continuing assumption that those aspects of the task situation which are important for solidarity are also important for religion, the decision was made to combine the two variables employed in the Wisconsin experiment so as to produce two contrasting conditions, one favoring high solidarity, the other low solidarity. To maximize solidarity, we asked subjects to work together and then paid them according to how well they did relative to the average group performance. To produce the opposite effect, we asked other subjects to work alone and paid them according to how well they did relative to each other. On the basis of the Wisconsin findings and the Miller-Swanson hypothesis, it was predicted that subjects in the former (Co-operative) condition would become *more* theistic while those assigned to the latter (Competitive) condition would become *less* theistic.

While designed in some ways as a "replication" of the Wisconsin study, this experiment differed from its predecessor in several important respects. Most of the differences are related to the fact that the Wisconsin experiment was carried out as part of a regularly scheduled college class, whereas the experiment to be described here was conducted in the laboratory. A detailed discussion of the specific differences involved is presented later on in the results section of this chapter.

While resembling in many ways the laboratory experiments described in Chapters 4–6, the experiment presented here is unique in three important respects. For one thing, it was the first laboratory study in which no attempt was made to formalize trial-and-error behavior by having subjects try each task two different ways (e.g., with and without a leader). The change was dictated less by the desire to see what would happen than by the fact that theism has little to say about the relative effectiveness, intrinsic enjoyabilty, or legitimacy of one form of behavior over another (e.g., working alone versus together). Strictly speaking, it is a set of beliefs concerning the existence and nature of God. As such, it does not lend itself to the same sort of contrast design that we had employed in previous laboratory studies.

In the second place, this was the first laboratory study in which an attempt was made to measure and change several different attitude dimensions rather than the same one in a variety of settings (e.g., individualism-collectivism in the family, community, school, etc.). Our primary interest, of course, was in religion—more specifically, belief in God. In view of the evidence indicating a substantial relationship between conventional religious beliefs and authoritarianism, we also included an abbreviated version of the *F-scale*. It was our hope that we could use the results here to clarify our understanding of the changes, if any, on the religous items. Despite our failure (pre-test, Chapter 6) to get any change on individualism-collectivism without a trial and error design, we decided to give it another chance in this study. For this purpose we included the *way-of-life* scale used in the previous experiment. A fourth scale, measuring attitudes toward *conformity*, was constructed and added on the hunch that those who were rewarded for co-operating with each other would become sensitized to each other's feelings and opinions, and thus more likely to accept conformity as a good thing, while those who were rewarded for "going it alone" would be more likely to insist that people should look to their own individual consciences in deciding what to do in any particular situation.

Thirdly, this study differed from all previous laboratory experiments in that subjects were invited back two to three weeks after the experiment to fill out the original questionnaire a third time. This was the first occasion when all conditions (including time and money) were appropriate for finding out whether the changes induced in the experiment itself would "wash out" right afterwards or whether the effect would wear off gradually as the laboratory experience became assimilated to a host of conflicting and competing experiences. Our own guess was that in testing two to three weeks after the experiment, we would find the changes still in effect but to a less significant degree.

ATTITUDE QUESTIONNAIRE

Since religion was our major concern, considerable care was taken to find or prepare items covering a variety of related religious themes. Forty-four statements dealing with belief in God, God's relationship to man, and similar themes were included in the final questionnaire. The first eight items were taken from the Bales-Couch Value Profile (some of them coming originally from the California F-scale).[2] The same eight items (plus two others) had been used to measure theism in the Wisconsin study. Some of the items referred specifically to a divine being (e.g., "Everyone should have complete faith in some supernatural power whose decisions he obeys without question.") while others spoke of related concepts (e.g., "Heaven and Hell are products of man's imagination and do not actually exist."). We knew from our own previous work that all eight items were highly intercorrelated.

Twelve additional statements were taken from the religion scale used in our leadership study (Chapter 5). All 12 were related in some way to the question of whether man should try to solve his problems on his own or whether he should look to a divine being to solve his problems for him. In the study for which they were originally written, we had expected that students rewarded for performing a task *with* a leader would be more apt to say that people should take their problems to God, while those who were rewarded for performing the task *without* a leader would be more likely to insist that man can and should solve his problems on his own. Neither prediction was borne out by

---

[2] Robert F. Bales and Arthur S. Couch, "The Value Profile: A Factor Analytic Study of Value Statements," unpublished paper, 1959.

the data; in fact, there was some evidence indicating a very slight change in the opposite direction. In including these 12 items here, we went on the assumption that although they were unrelated to leadership (authority), they might work in a design built around co-operation versus competition instead. The reasoning used was the same as that presented in our discussion of theism in general, namely that the belief in an orderly world made meaningful by man's relationship to God has its roots in the perception of collective purpose in everyday life.

In an attempt to broaden our coverage even more, we added six items dealing with the nature of God's interest in man (e.g., "God is more concerned with each person as an individual than he is with humanity as a whole."). All assume some belief in God and are written around the self-collectivity issue as this applies to the relationship between man and God. It was our hunch that subjects who worked together under a group incentive (the co-operatives) would be more willing to say that God is primarily interested in humanity as a whole, while subjects who competed with each other would be more apt to say that the relationship between man and God is a highly personal, individualistic one. Three of the items from this scale were taken from the God-man scale in our first laboratory experiment (Chapter 4); the other three were composed specifically for this study.

Another six items were included to measure the degree to which subjects attribute individualistic-collectivistic attitudes to God (e.g., "That life which is most pleasing to God is the life dedicated to the welfare of one's fellow man, even at the sacrifice of one's own personal happiness."). In constructing these items, we simply took statements from an old individualism-collectivism scale and prefaced each with a phrase to indicate that the thought expressed was divinely sanctioned. The hunch again was that subjects who were rewarded for going it alone would be more likely afterwards to say that God wants each individual to pursue his own private interests while those who worked together under a group incentive would be more apt to say that God "will love that person most who sacrifices himself most for his fellow man."

The final 12 items devoted to religion were taken from the questionnaire used in our first laboratory experiment (Chapter 4). All assume some belief in God and are directed to the issue of public versus private worship (e.g., "I would rather worship God in private than in the midst of a large congregation."). When used in the earlier study, this scale yielded significant changes. Less was to be expected here, however, because of the lack of any trial-and-error sequence in our experimental design.

In all, the questionnaire included 79 items. Forty-four of these were religious in content, leaving 35 for the other three scales: authoritarianism (F scale), way of life, and conformity. In constructing an abbreviated version of the F scale, we simply took the ten items with the highest discriminatory power.[3] The way-of-life items were borrowed from our previous study. Fifteen statements were selected to include several from each of three levels of individualism-collectivism (alone-together, independence-co-operation, and self versus collectivity orientation). All were phrased in a highly abstract manner. The last scale (conformity) was made up of ten new items, each of which posed a conflict between obeying the dictates of one's own conscience and yielding to the demands of a "generalized other."

All scales (with the exception of the F-scale) were balanced with approximately half the items phrased in each direction. No attempt was made to balance the number of beliefs, values, and preferences, since previous findings had shown the *mode* of the items to be irrelevant. All items were followed by the usual nine-point response format ranging from Strongly Disagree to Strongly Agree.

The 79-item questionnaire was administered for the first time to subjects actually participating in the experiment, there being no time to pre-test the items on another sample of students. The responses of 87 subjects to this "before" questionnaire were intercorrelated and then factor analyzed by the centroid method and rotated by the quartimax method. Two, three, four, and five factors were extracted. The five-factor solution seemed to make the most sense and thus was used for the purpose of developing factor scores. Only items loaded .40 or better were included in the computations; items loaded on two or more factors were assigned to the factor with the highest loading.

Factor I brought together all 20 of the purely theistic items, plus five of the six statements dealing with the nature of God's interest in man and two from the public versus private worship scale. A high score on this factor indicates belief in a Supreme Being, who takes a personal interest in each of us, and on whom we should learn to depend for guidance and emotional support. This complex can best be described as conventional theistic religion.

Factor II was clearly an F-scale factor with eight of the ten items from this scale loaded .40 or better. In addition, there were two items favoring public worship (e.g., "Any person who accepts God should attend church frequently.") and one describing God as wanting people

---

[3] T. W. Adorno *et al., The Authoritarian Personality* (New York: Harper & Bros., 1950), p. 260.

to be altruistic ("God will love that person most who sacrifices himself most for his fellow men.").

The remaining three factors can be described quite quickly. The third factor included ten of 15 individualism-collectivism (way-of-life) items and no others. The fourth factor included all ten of the conformity items and no others. Factor V included six of the 12 items from the public versus private worship scale plus a single item describing God as wanting people to be altruistic. These items are shown in Exhibit E at the end of this chapter.

To a great extent, then, we got out of the questionnaire pretty much what we put in. This was especially true with respect to factors II, III, and IV—which turned out to be F-scale, way of life (individualism-collectivism), and conformity respectively. Our religion items were divided into two major categories—a large 27-item cluster dealing with conventional, theistic (versus humanistic) beliefs and a smaller 6-item cluster focusing on the issue of organized (public) versus personal (private) worship. Because of the similarity between these factor scales and our a priori scales, there seemed little point to doing the analysis both ways (as we had in previous studies). On the grounds of maximizing scale reliability, we decided to work exclusively with the five factor scales.

Internal consistencies for each factor based on responses for the first 87 subjects and test-retest reliabilities based on responses for all 108 subjects are shown in Table 7-1[4].

TABLE 7-1
Internal Consistencies and Test-Retest Reliabilities
for Factor Scales

Factor	Name	No. of Items	Internal* Consistency	Test-Retest Reliability†	
				Co-op.	Comp.
I	Theism	27	.95	.95	.93
II	F-scale	11	.86	.87	.91
III	Individualism	10	.85	.92	.83
IV	Conformity	10	.84	.90	.81
V	Private worship	7	.82	.82	.85

* $N = 87$.
† $N = 108$.

[4] For computational formula, see Chapter 3, footnote 18. The discrepancy between the two N's (87 and 108) is due to the fact that the decision to add 21 more subjects was made after the internal consistencies had been computed but before we had gotten around to doing the test-retest correlations.

PROCEDURE

A total of 108 subjects (59 males and 49 females) participated in the experiment. The first 87 were recruited from classes at Cornell in the spring of 1963 and the remaining 21 at registration for summer school. The incentive offered was the possibility of making up to $6.50 for participating in a four-hour social psychology experiment. Most subjects were freshmen or sophomores and none had extensive exposure to courses in psychology.

In view of the tendency on the part of subjects to give more extreme responses to statements involving religious sentiments than to those dealing with other themes, we felt it necessary to exercise some control over the selection of subjects for this experiment.[5] It seemed clear that, no matter how good the experimental design was, extreme theists or atheists would resist change over the four-hour period. Given the low probability of getting significant results in the first place, the decision was made to accept only those subjects whose original religious beliefs might be classified as moderate.

At the time they originally signed up for the experiment, subjects were given a brief segment (the first eight items) of the before-after questionnaire. All those giving extreme answers (a one or a nine) to half or more of the items were rejected (and assigned instead to another experiment). This resulted in the loss of approximately 50 per cent of our initial subject pool. In view of this, the results of the experiment should only be generalized to that half of the student population with moderate religious beliefs.

Subjects were invited to the experiment in groups of four to six (all of the same sex). Before any explanation was given for the purpose of the experiment, they were asked to fill out the "before" questionnaire (with the exception of the first eight items which had already been filled out). In introducing the questionnaire, the experimenter sought to disassociate himself from it by explaining that the form had actually been prepared by a colleague who was interested in trying it out on a number of people before using it in a formal research project. The introduction to the experiment itself varied somewhat from one condition to the other. Sixty-four subjects (31 males and 33 females) were assigned (randomly) to the co-operative condition and 44 (28 males and 16 females) to the competitive condition. The procedures for each treatment are described separately below.

---

[5] In the last study involving religion (Chapter 5), we found quite a few subjects who gave extreme responses (1's or 9's) to all the items on the theism scale.

Co-operatives

When they had finished the "before" questionnaire, subjects in the co-operative condition were given the following instructions:

The purpose of this experiment is to find out something more about the effect of incentive rates, type of task, group size, and the like on work efficiency and performance. From day to day we vary the incentive system, the nature of the task, the number of students in each group, etc., to see in what way, if any, these variables affect performance. Our position is akin to that of a factory manager who is interested in finding out the best way to arrange work groups so as to get the most for his money. Today we are going to give you four different tasks to work on; how much money you earn depends on how well you do in each case. For each task we have computed a standard which represents the average score obtained by groups of this size on that task. If you beat the standard you will get a certain amount of money to be divided among you; if you fail to beat it you will receive a considerably smaller amount.

The four tasks used for this condition were as follows:

1. Jigsaw Puzzle. Subjects were given a 300-piece jigsaw puzzle and told to put together as many pieces as possible in the 40 minutes allowed. It was stipulated that only pieces joined together in one large mass would be counted at the end. The purpose of this was to guarantee that subjects would all work together rather than each working on a separate part of the puzzle. A typical group of six subjects received $9.00 (to be divided up equally) if they surpassed the standard of 220 pieces in 40 minutes and $6.00 if they did not.[6]

2. Prediction. This was the Bales task used in previous experiments. Here, as in the preceding study, no attempt was made to "doctor" the results. Subjects were given copies of a 58-item questionnaire with answers to the first four items, the object being to predict how the person who filled in the first four items answered the rest of the questionnaire. Five points were given for each correct guess and one point for each guess just one step off (e.g., Disagree instead of Slightly Disagree). For each item the group was required to come to a single, joint decision. Subjects received $9.00 if they scored 100 points or more, $6.00 for anything less than that. During this task, and only this one, an observer from behind the one-way glass scored subjects' behavior using the Bales 12-category system.

3. Tower. For the third task, subjects were given a Rig-a-Jig set (something like a Tinker Toy only with smaller pieces) and asked to

---

[6] Both the standard and the incentive were adjusted according to the size of the group (not everyone showed up for the experiment).

build the tallest tower they could in 40 minutes, with the requirement that the tower be study enough to stand unsupported for at least one minute. The standard was set at 77 inches for the male groups and 67 inches for the females. The incentive again was $9.00 for beating the standard, $6.00 for falling short.

4. Word Game. A 5×5 matrix was drawn on the blackboard, the object being to place one letter in each cell so as to make as many different words as possible. Ten points were given for five-letter words, five points for four-letter words, and two points for every three-letter word. Subjects were allowed 20 minutes for each of two separate matrices. The standard for the two matrices combined was 162 points.

Competitives

Subjects in the competitive condition came in groups of four to six, each group being homogeneous with respect to sex. The experiment was introduced in the same way as before up to the point where the incentive system was explained. The latter was presented in the following manner:

Today we are going to give you four different tasks to work on; how much money you earn depends on how well you do in each case. For each task, those who score in the top half of their group (e.g., first, second, or third in a group of six) will be given a plus, while those in the bottom half receive a minus. When all four tasks have been completed, the three people (in a group of six) with the most pluses will get $6.50 for the afternoon's work; those with the fewest pluses will receive $3.50.

The tasks used in the competitive condition were the same as those already described for the co-operative condition. Subjects in both conditions worked on a jigsaw puzzle, the prediction problem, the tower, and the word game. The difference lay in the fact that the co-operatives worked together (against a group standard) whereas the competitives worked alone (against each other). Given the immediate goal of creating one condition which was highly favorable to solidarity and another highly unfavorable, we decided that we could do better by having some subjects work together and some alone, rather than (as we did in the Wisconsin experiment) having everybody work in groups but on tasks which were either conjunctive or disjunctive. What we did, in effect, was to sacrifice something in the way of replication for the sake of sharpening the difference between the two conditions.

When the four tasks had been completed and subjects' earnings counted up, the original questionnaire was administered for the second time. In handing out the questionnaire, the experimenter said that he had been requested to do so by his colleague who wanted to find out something more about item means, variances, and scale homogeneity, etc., before using the instrument in a number of different research settings. The purpose of the ruse was to justify giving the questionnaire while at the same time maintaining its independence from the experiment per se. With respect to the latter, however, there seemed to be little chance that subjects would see any relationship between an experiment made up of jigsaw puzzles, towers, and word games on the one hand, and a questionnaire consisting primarily of statements concerning the nature and existence of God on the other.

Sometime later subjects were offered $1.00 to return for "another short test" at which time they were administered the identical questionnaire for a third time. The average lapse between second (after) and third (follow-up) administrations was three weeks. Ninety out of 108 subjects returned to take the follow-up questionnaire. The true purpose of the experiment was explained at that time. The remaining 18 subjects who did not show up were given the same information by mail.

RESULTS

Attitude Change: Before versus After

Changes by Factor.[7]   A glance at Table 7–2 is enough to indicate that only one of the five factors underwent significant change. Nothing at all happened in the other four cases. The factor showing the significant t ratio was, of course, the one we were most interested in. The experiment was expressly designed to change subjects' belief in God, and this is precisely what did happen.[8]

A closer look at the changes by condition, however, reveals that the co-operatives became less theistic while the competitives became more theistic, which is exactly the opposite of what we had predicted. Subjects who worked together under a group incentive system (the ones most likely to develop a sense of collective purpose) were expected to become more theistic in their beliefs; instead they became less so. Those

---

[7] A t-test on the "before" questionnaire scores revealed no significant difference between co-operatives and competitives on any of the five factors measured.

[8] Separate analyses by sex revealed that it was the males who did most of the changing. The t ratio for the females was only 0.60, compared to 2.94 for the males. This was unexpected in view of previous findings (Chapter 5) which indicated no relationship between sex and amount of change. Given the fact that the females were no more or less religious than the males to start with, we can think of no reason for the difference in change scores.

TABLE 7–2
Attitude Change, by Factor*

Factor	Name	Mean Change		d	t	p
		Co-op	Comp			
I	Theism	−3.03	5.11	8.14	2.75	.01
II	F-scale	−0.86	−1.11	0.25	0.18	ns
III	Individualism	1.67	2.18	0.51	0.46	ns
IV	Conformity	0.92	0.64	0.28	0.20	ns
V	Private worship	0.63	1.02	0.39	0.33	**ns**

* In each case, the factor label refers to the *positive* end of the scale.

who had been assigned to the competitive treatment where they worked alone and in competition with each other were expected to give up some of their belief in God; instead they became more religious.

Once the results were in, it was relatively easy to think of reasons for why it should have worked this way. In fact, it soon got to the point where we found it hard to explain why we had ever predicted the opposite in the first place. With the findings in front of us, it seemed quite reasonable that belief in God should be interpreted as a *substitute* for human solidarity rather than a *reflection* of it. From the viewpoint of a single individual, there are two alternative sources of emotional support, the human and the divine. Other things being equal, the more deeply the individual is embedded in a network of reciprocal ties with other human beings, the less urgent will be his need to seek help from God. The more rewarding he finds his interpersonal relationships, the easier he will find it to get along without God. Having been rewarded for taking his problems to other men rather than God, he will come to believe that man can solve his problems without help from God, and that people should try to solve their problems on their own rather than looking to God for help. If we can assume that believing in God is, in part at least, wish-fulfilling, the rest is clear. The less the individual's need for God's help, the less likely it is that he will believe that God even exists.

It can be safely assumed that most of our subjects, co-operatives and competitives alike, felt anxious throughout the experiment. Feeling anxious, they presumably were in need of emotional support. For the co-operatives, such support was available in the form of ties with other group members. Acts of solidarity (encouragement, approval, affection) were observed frequently in most groups. In light of the fact that members did help each other to feel less anxious, it is not surprising that they became more convinced that man could and should solve his problems without the help of some supernatural being. It is not enough to say they became less theistic; to put it positively, they became more humanistic. Humanism, according to Auer, is "a system of thought which assigns predominant interest to the affairs of man as compared with the superhuman, and which believes man to be capable of controlling those affairs."[9]

For our subjects in the competitive condition, there was no immediate source of emotional support. Each individual was strictly on his own; subjects were not even allowed to communicate with each other. Isolated as they were from their fellow human beings, subjects were more likely to turn to God for anxiety-reducing support. They became more convinced that there is a God and that man should go to Him for help. Whether they actually started thinking about God is not known. We never did ask them what they were thinking about. We do know from previous studies, however, that subjects often change their beliefs and values without being directly aware of it. It is very possible here that the combination of anxiety and isolation led to an intensification of dependency needs and in turn, the sharpening of theistic beliefs without any conscious perception of what was taking place.

We are still left with the problem, however, of accounting for the discrepancy between the results presented here and those which emerged from the Wisconsin study. The "contradiction" can best be handled by pointing to some of the ways in which the two studies differed. A discussion of those differences is postponed, however, until we have had a chance to look at all the data from this present experiment.

Although we had formulated no hypotheses with respect to the relationship between task success or failure and attitude change, it seemed like an appropriate area to explore. With this in mind, subjects were divided up according to how well they did in the experiment, i.e., how many times out of four they beat the standard. Three categories were used: high, medium, and low.[10] Mean changes on each of the five attitude factors were computed for highs, mediums, and lows in the co-operative condition, and then again for the highs, mediums, and lows in the competitive condition. The data are shown in Table 7–3.

---

[9] J. A. C. Fagginger Auer and Julian Hartt, *Humanism vs. Theism* (Antioch Press, 1951), p. 3.

[10] A certain amount of juggling was necessary to assure that all three categories were substantially represented. For the co-operatives, subjects winning four out of four tasks were assigned to the high category, those winning three or two out of four to the medium category, and those winning but once to the low category. Among the competitives, it was four out of four (rare) and three out of four in the high, two out of four in the medium, and one and zero out of four in the low.

TABLE 7–3

Attitude Change by Factor, Condition, and Success

		Co-operative			Competitive		
Factor	Name	H	M	L	H	M	L
I	....Theism	2.76	—7.53	0.00	7.50	—0.70	6.35
II	....F-scale	—2.12	—1.19	1.27	—3.43	2.00	—1.05
III	....Individualism	0.47	1.94	2.47	1.64	2.30	2.75
IV	....Conformity	—0.82	0.91	2.93	—2.79	0.30	3.15
V	....Private worship	0.24	0.28	1.80	—1.14	1.30	2.40

Somewhat to our surprise, changes on factor I (theism) showed a marked relationship to degree of success. In both the co-operative and competitive conditions subjects enjoying either a high or low degree of success were more likely to change in the theistic direction than those who performed moderately well. As can be seen from Figure 7–1, a plot of the scores yields two curves almost identical in shape. The only real difference is in the position of each curve relative to the base line of no change. As we know from the means in Table 7-2, subjects in the co-operative condition went down on theism (-3.03) while those in the competitive condition went up (5.11).

A trend analysis was performed to determine the significance of the trend of each curve in Figure 7–1. As indicated in Table 7–4, the quad-

TABLE 7–4

Trend Analysis of Effect of Success on Theism, by Condition

Condition	Between SS	Linear SS	Quadratic SS	F for Larger Trend	df	p
Competitive	448.28	3.44	444.84	2.24 (Q)	1;41	ns
Co-operative	1,356.91	88.15	1,268.76	5.67 (Q)	1;61	.05
Combined	2,661.60	10.38	2,651.22	12.17 (Q)	1;105	.001

ratic trend is significant ($p < .05$) for the co-operatives but not for the competitives. Combining the two, however, yields an over-all quadratic trend significant at the .001 level, suggesting that degree of success had an important nonlinear effect on religious beliefs independent of task or incentive system.[11]

It appears, then, that we have two main effects: condition (co-oper-

[11] A trend analysis on the "before" scores for religion revealed a significant quadratic trend just the reverse of what we found in our analysis of the changes. However, because there was no correlation between initial position and amount of change, no correction of the scores was necessary. Thus in doing the analysis reported in Table 7–4, we used the original scores.

ative versus competitive) and success (high, medium, and low). There
is no interaction between the two. An attempt has already been made
to explain the impact of condition on religious beliefs; it remains to
account for why degree of success played an equally important role.

Taking the lows first, it could be argued that failure arouses feelings
of helplessness which serve to strengthen or confirm the belief in a
personal, loving God. This would be especially true of those situations
in which the individual has no one but God to turn to (e.g., a highly

FIGURE 7–1

Change on Theism as a Function of Condition and Success

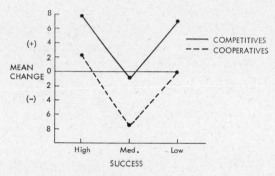

competitive situation like the one employed in the experiment). For
these people, believing in God represents an obvious way of reducing
anxiety.

Although the successful subjects (highs) were equally likely to
change in the theistic direction, they obviously did so for different reasons. Just what these reasons were is not at all clear. The "helplessness" explanation offered for the lows would lead us to expect a movement away from God among those subjects who did especially well on
the tasks. As we know, the opposite happened. In an attempt to make
some sense out of this finding, we came up with two speculations. In
the first place, it is possible that people who experience a very high
degree of task success turn to God not for emotional support but for
legitimation of their achievements. Believing in God serves to confirm the fact that this is an orderly, purposeful world in which everything that happens happens for some good reason. Succeeding in the
experiment was not an accident; while it might not have been specifically ordained by God, it was nevertheless in keeping with his over-all
design.

Alternatively, it could be argued that the successful subjects turned to God, not for legitimation of their achievements, but for recognition. This interpretation is based on the assumption that God serves (in part anyway) as a parental surrogate. The image brought to mind is that of a child running to its parents to win recognition for some recent success. When neither parents nor peers are available (as in our competitive condition), the individual is likely to seek out God. In this light, the difference between highs and lows can be thought of as the difference between a child running to its parents for recognition (following success) and a child running to its parents for help (following failure).

To continue the analysis, subjects who did moderately well (the mediums) felt neither helpless enough to seek God's help nor satisfied enough to want to tell anybody about it. Neither did they feel a need to confirm their achievements by placing them in the context of an orderly, purposeful universe in which God is responsible for everything that happens. Relative to the highs and lows, they had less need for God. Needing God less, they became less convinced of His existence.

To summarize, then, changes on factor I (theism) can be traced to two independent variables, experimental condition and degree of success. The fact that subjects in the co-operative condition became less theistic while those in the competitive condition became more theistic can be explained in terms of the availability of interpersonal means for the reduction of anxiety among those who worked together and the lack of such support for those who were required to work alone. The fact that, holding condition constant, highs and lows were more likely to change in a theistic direction than the mediums may be due to the relative helplessness of the lows and the greater need for recognition and/or legitimation on the part of the highs.

So much for factor I. An examination of the other four factors revealed one further instance in which degree of success seemed to have had a significant impact on attitude change, namely conformity (factor IV). As indicated in Figure 7–2 (based on data in Table 7–3), the relationship is very clearly a linear one. In both conditions (co-operative and competitive) the most successful subjects went down on conformity while the least successful subjects went up.

The results of a trend analysis performed on these data are shown in Table 7–5. There is a significant linear trend for the competitive condition ($p < .01$) but not for the co-operative condition. Combining the two conditions yields a linear trend significant at the .01 level.

The fact that the most successful subjects became less willing to endorse conformity as a good thing while the least successful went up on the same scale can be explained in terms of the effect of success on

TABLE 7–5

Trend Analysis of Effect of Success on Conformity, by Condition

Condition	Between SS	Linear SS	Quadratic SS	F for Larger Trend	df	p
Competitive	291.42	291.32	0.10	8.11 (L)	1;41	.01
Co-operative	112.49	112.11	0.38	2.01 (L)	1;61	ns
Combined	373.62	372.27	1.35	7.98 (L)	1;105	.01

self-confidence. People who have succeeded often and are thus very confident of their own abilities have less to gain from going along with others than those who have failed often and are thus unsure of themselves. It is the latter for whom conformity is apt to be most rewarding. It is among the least self-confident that we are most likely to find conformity behavior as well as beliefs, values, and preferences stressing the importance and desirability of conforming.

FIGURE 7–2

Change on Conformity as a Function of Condition and Success

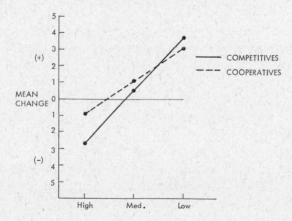

Changes by People. In keeping with previous practice those scales showing significant *mean* differences between conditions and/or degree of success were reanalyzed in terms of the number of subjects changing in each direction. Table 7–6 shows the number of subjects in each condition going up and down on factor I (theism). Confirming the results of our previous *t*-test, we find that the co-operatives were more likely to go down on theism while the competitives were more apt to go up.

In Table 7–7, the same data are broken down by degree of success. Again the chi-square is significant at the .01 level supporting the results of our earlier trend analysis. Pooling across conditions, we find that a majority of both highs and lows became more theistic while well over one half of the mediums went down on theism.

The only other scale showing significant change was conformity (factor IV), and this was true only when the data were broken down by degree of success. In Table 7–8 we present data indicating the

TABLE 7–6

Number of Subjects Changing on Theism, by Condition

	+	−
Co-operative	25	36
Competitive	28	16

$$\chi^2 = 4.38$$
$$p < .05$$

TABLE 7–7

Number of Subjects Changing on Theism, by Success

	+	−
High	21	9
Medium	13	28
Low	19	15

$$\chi^2 = 10.74$$
$$p < .01$$

TABLE 7–8

Number of Subjects Changing on Conformity, by Success

	+	−
High	10	19
Medium	20	19
Low	24	10

$$\chi^2 = 8.25$$
$$p < .05$$

number of subjects changing on this factor, again according to degree of success. The distribution of scores supports the earlier trend analysis in which we found a negative linear relationship between success and change in the conformity direction.

Attitude Change: Before versus Follow-up

Changes by Factor. Tests identical to those already described were performed on data provided by the 90 subjects (out of 108) who returned two to four weeks after the experiment to fill out the questionnaire a third time. Whereas previously we had compared "before" scores with "after" scores, we here compared the "before" scores with those from the third or follow-up administration. Once again t ratios were computed for each of the five factor scales in order to test for the significance of the difference between mean changes for the two conditions. The appropriate data are given in Table 7–9.

TABLE 7–9
Attitude Change, by Factor (Before versus Follow-up)

		Mean Change				
Factor	Name	Co-op	Comp.	d	t	p
I	Theism	−5.35	0.12	5.47	1.82	.10
II	F-scale	−1.65	−2.59	0.94	0.52	ns
III	Individualism	2.45	4.37	1.92	1.29	ns
IV	Conformity	0.43	0.83	0.40	0.25	ns
V	Private worship	0.90	2.07	1.17	0.73	ns

A comparison of this table with Table 7–2 (before versus after) indicates that while subjects in the competitive condition underwent a marked increase in theism immediately following the experiment, they had regressed to their original positions by the time the follow-up questionnaire was administered three weeks later. Member of the co-operative condition, on the contrary, changed even further in the atheistic or humanistic direction (−5.35 versus −3.03). There is no obvious reason for why all the change among the competitives got "washed out" while the co-operatives changed even more in the original direction. The end result of all the shifting is, of course, that the difference between the two conditions is now significant at only the .10 level, compared with the p of .01 found earlier. This is not entirely surprising in light of the many competing and conflicting experiences that must have intervened subsequent to the experiment to offset the impact of the laboratory experience.

In Table 7–10 below the data are broken down according to degree of success.

Upon testing, factor I proved to be the only factor showing changes significantly related to degree of success. The earlier finding for factor IV (conformity) got washed out due to a major reversal among the lows in the co-operative condition. Plotting the data for religion reveals

TABLE 7–10

Attitude Change by Factor, Condition and Success
(Before versus Follow-up)

		Co-operative			Competitive		
Factor	Name	H	M	L	H	M	L
I	Theism	−3.92	−8.52	0.18	0.43	−5.10	2.94
II	F-scale	−3.46	−1.10	−1.09	−4.64	1.00	−2.18
III	Individualism	1.77	3.35	3.09	5.64	3.00	4.12
IV	Conformity	0.62	3.25	−4.73	−1.50	2.00	2.06
V	Private worship	0.00	0.00	3.91	0.79	2.40	3.76

two curves (Figure 7–3) very similar in shape to those seen before for the same factor. Neither is significantly quadratic although the combined trend reaches the .05 level (see Table 7–11). In view of the smaller mean difference involved, the two curves are, of course, closer together than was the case with the before-after data. It is interesting to note as well that both curves have shifted downward in a humanistic direction, a move which may reflect the secularizing influence of college itself (for a similar finding see Chapter 3, page 78).

Changes by People. The number of subjects in each condition changing in a theistic (+) or a humanistic (−) direction is given in

FIGURE 7–3

Change on Theism as a Function of Condition and Success
(Before versus Follow-up)

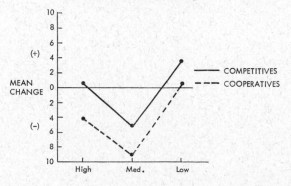

Table 7–12. The distribution shows competitive subjects more likely to go up on factor I and co-operatives more apt to go down. The chi-square value for this table is significant at the .10 level, thus agreeing exactly with the t-test reported in Table 7–9.

Changes by subject are shown as a function of degree of success in Table 7–13. The quadratic trend is still apparent in the data although the chi-square value just reaches the .05 level of significance.

TABLE 7–11
Trend Analysis of Effect of Success on Theism, by Condition
(Before versus Follow-up)

Condition	Between SS	Linear SS	Quadratic SS	F for Larger Trend	df	p
Competitive	409.12	61.87	347.25	1.64 (Q)	1;38	ns
Co-operative	614.29	77.19	537.10	2.74 (Q)	1;46	ns
Combined	1,429.00	181.36	1,247.64	6.27 (Q)	1;87	.05

TABLE 7–12
Number of Subjects Changing on Theism, by Condition
(Before versus Follow-up)

	+	—
Co-operative	17	32
Competitive	23	18

$$\chi^2 = 3.32$$
$$p < .10$$

TABLE 7–13
Number of Subjects Changing on Theism, by Success
(Before versus Follow-up)

	+	—
High	14	13
Medium	10	25
Low	16	12

$$\chi^2 = 6.00$$
$$p < .05$$

Whether based on mean differences or subject differences, the results would appear to indicate a gradual attenuation rather than an immediate washing out of the attitude change induced at the time of the experiment. While p values for the before-after changes ranged between .01 and .05 similar tests performed on the before-follow-up changes yielded values ranging between .05 and .10.

DISCUSSION

It remains to be explained why the findings reported here contradict those which emerged from our Wisconsin study. At Wisconsin, it will be recalled, we found that the most solidary groups (joint essay and single-grade group) retained their theistic beliefs over the four-month period, while the least solidary groups (discussion and curved grades) became considerably less theistic. In the laboratory experiment reported here, it was the co-operatives who became less theistic and the competitives who went up on theism. In view of the fact that the laboratory experiment was designed as an approximate replication of the earlier classroom study, it is difficult to understand how the results could be so different. It must be remembered, however, that the two studies were dissimilar in several important respects.

For one thing, religion was talked about in the Wisconsin study, whereas it was never even mentioned in the laboratory experiment. This is relevant because it points to persuasion as a possible source of change in the earlier study. While all students heard the same set of lectures (two of which were devoted to religion), they were exposed to different instructors in their weekly discussion sections. One of the instructors was an atheist, the second a lukewarm Protestant, and the third a devout Catholic. While an attempt was made to distribute instructors evenly throughout the four-variable design, the fact that there were only three instructors made a perfectly symmetrical solution impossible. With instructor variation imperfectly controlled, it remains possible that *student* differences in attitude change were caused by *instructor* differences in implicit or explicit persuasion.

There is an even more striking difference between the two studies. While the Wisconsin study lasted a whole term (from February to May), the laboratory experiment was completed in four hours. This raises the interesting possibility that the two sets of results are not contradictory at all but simply indicative of a temporal effect in which two changes are involved: a short-run change which gets washed out soon after the experiment is over and a long-run "sleeper" effect which doesn't show up until considerable time has elapsed. This would imply that in the initial stages, it is anxiety and the means available for reducing it that account for the direction of change in religious beliefs, and that in the long-run it is the sense of collective purpose or the lack of same which determines whether or not one will believe in God. This is a highly speculative idea for which there is no theoretical or empirical support. Our own data show, moreover, that the original, "short-run" changes were still in effect three weeks after the experiment took place. In view of this fact, it seems unlikely that time itself would account for the difference between the two sets of findings.

There is another factor that might be mentioned. Most of the subjects in the laboratory experiment were fairly moderate in their religious beliefs, the theistic and atheistic extremes having been eliminated through a pre-test screening device. In the Wisconsin study all volunteers were accepted regardless of religious beliefs. The result, of course, was that we ended up with a good many extremes. This would explain everything if we could show that the extremes changed one way and the moderates another. A plotting of the changes in terms of original position and amount of change, however, reveals that while the extremes changed somewhat less than the moderates, they changed in the same direction.

In the fourth place, the two measures of theism were not identical. Of the ten items used in the Wisconsin study, eight were included in the questionnaire used in the laboratory study. These eight were then combined with 19 others to yield a single, homogeneous, theism factor. The results reported in this chapter were based on factor scores computed by summing across all 27 items, including the eight borrowed from the Wisconsin questionnaire. On the chance that these eight were working one way and the remaining 19 another, we analyzed the two sets of items separately. No important differences were found.

There are several other differences that might be mentioned: (1) the nature of the tasks employed (discussion and essay writing versus a variety of games and puzzles, (2) the kind of rewards involved (course grades versus money), (3) opportunities for interaction (in the laboratory experiment, the competitives were not even allowed to talk to each other), and (4) the presence of a formal leader (section instructor versus experimenter). While these all seem important, it is difficult to see how any one of them could account for the difference in results.

It is our hunch that replication will bear out the results of the laboratory experiment, leaving the Wisconsin findings to be explained in terms of some of the variables mentioned above, notably uncontrolled for variation in exposure to persuasion. In the laboratory, there was no opportunity for anyone to persuade anyone else to accept his religious beliefs; the subject of religion was never mentioned at any time during the experiment. Moreover, the questionnaire containing the religious items was introduced as part of another, unrelated research project. While there was plenty of opportunity at the end of the experiment for subjects to ask about the questionnaire, no one thought it important or relevant enough to mention. The subject of religion was brought up for the first time *after* subjects had filled out the questionnaire for a *third* time. It was clear at that time that no one suspected that the real purpose of the experiment was to change religious beliefs.

CONCLUSIONS

In this study it might properly be said that we raised more questions than we answered. This was due partly to the fact that the results in this experiment reversed those found earlier at Wisconsin. It was due again to the fact that the findings were but tenuously related to the reinforcement-generalization model on which all previous studies had been based. While the reversal in findings was unexpected, the decision to explore aspects of the task-attitude relationship not explicitly covered by the theory was quite deliberate. In the process of exploring, we learned (among other things) that task success and failure can have a significant impact on beliefs and values independently of the nature of the task itself. This idea is taken up again in the next study where it is analyzed in conjunction with attitudes toward achievement.

EXHIBIT E

FACTOR I: THEISM*

1. Heaven and Hell are products of man's imagination and do not actually exist. (—)
2. Every explanation of man and the world is incomplete unless it takes into account God's will. (+)
3. There is no supernatural world and no supernatural rewards and punishments. (—)
4. Man can solve all his important problems without help from a Supreme Being. (—)
5. Every person should have complete faith in some supernatural power whose decisions he obeys without question. (+)

---

* In factor I a (+) indicates item was weighted in the "theistic" direction, and a (—) that it was weighted in the "atheistic" direction.

6. There is a higher power above man. (+)
7. All the evidence goes to show that the universe has evolved in accordance with natural principles, so there is no necessity to assume a God behind it. (−)
8. Many events in human history took place only because a Supreme Being stepped in to make them happen. (+)
9. I like to feel that man can think through his problems on his own rather than having to seek advice from a divine being. (−)
10. I like the feeling that we can appeal to a higher being in times of crisis instead of having to solve our problems without any help at all. (+)
11. I would prefer that man make his own decisions rather than relying on a divine being to make decisions for him. (−)
12. I would rather feel that man's fate is in God's hands than in the hands of man himself. (+)
13. Man is quite capable of deciding things for himself—he does not need God to do it for him. (−)
14. Without God's guidance and infinite wisdom, mankind could not long endure. (+)
15. Ultimately, mankind does not rule itself but is ruled by divine authority. (+)
16. Man can solve all his problems himself without the help of God. (−)
17. People should learn to rely on God for guidance in the conduct of their affairs rather than trying to decide everything for themselves. (+)
18. People should take responsibility for their own lives instead of depending on a supernatural being for direction. (−)
19. Man should develop his own principles of moral conduct rather than relying on God to tell him how he should and should not behave. (−)
20. People should take their important problems to God instead of attempting to work them out on their own. (+)
21. As human beings, we are all part of one divine scheme, sharing a common relationship to God. (+)
22. God is less concerned with the welfare of any specific individual than he is with the fate of mankind as a whole. (−)
23. No matter how insignificant the individual may feel in God's eyes, each one of us plays a very vital part in God's over-all plan. (+)
24. God is more concerned with each person as an individual than he is with humanity as a whole. (+)
25. Each of us is related to God in a very personal, unique way. (+)
26. I don't need a church to satisfy my religious needs. (−)
27. To me, most religious services are a waste of time. (−)

FACTOR II: AUTHORITARIANISM (F-SCALE)†

1. God will love that person most who sacrifices himself most for his fellow men. (+)
2. Every person who believes in God ought to belong to some sort of church. (+)

---

† All items in factor II are weighted in a "high authoritarian" (+) direction.

3. Any person who accepts God should attend church frequently. (+)
4. Obedience and respect for authority are the most important virtues children should learn. (+)
5. What youth needs most is strict discipline, rugged determination, and the will to work and fight for family and country. (+)
6. An insult to our honor should always be punished. (+)
7. Young people sometimes get rebellious ideas, but as they grow up they ought to get over them and settle down. (+)
8. Sex crimes, such as rape and attacks on children, deserve more than mere imprisonment; such criminals ought to be publicly whipped, or worse. (+)
9. People can be divided into two distinct classes; the weak and the strong. (+)
10. There is hardly anything lower than a person who does not feel a great love, gratitude, and respect for his parents. (+)
11. No sane, normal, decent person could ever think of hurting a close friend or relative. (+)

FACTOR III: INDIVIDUALISM-COLLECTIVISM‡

1. The way of life that appeals to me most is the independent life in which contacts with others are of secondary importance. (—)
2. I prefer a way of life which calls for co-operation among men rather than independent achievement. (+)
3. The independent spirit—spurning all aid, needing no one, self-reliant, and free—this is man at his best. (—)
4. To me, a life dedicated to the welfare of one's fellow man is more satisfying than a life devoted to the pursuit of one's own private interests. (+)
5. The life that appeals to me the most is the one which minimizes my duty to others and maximizes my freedom to do what I like. (—)
6. I prefer a way of life which emphasizes the supremacy of individual happiness to one which stresses our obligations to others. (—)
7. Societies should encourage their members to be more concerned with independent achievement and less concerned with group co-operation. (—)
8. Each individual should try to maximize his own personal happiness first, and concern himself only secondarily with the welfare of others. (—)
9. A man's first duty should be to himself, and only secondarily to his fellow man. (—)
10. Societies in which each person is encouraged to do what he can on his own will be more productive than those in which most things are done by people working closely together towards a common goal. (—)

FACTOR IV: CONFORMITY§

1. One should avoid doing things in public that appear wrong to others even if one knows that these things are really all right. (+)

---

‡ A (+) for factor III indicates item was weighted in the "collectivistic" direction; a (—) that it was weighted in the "individualistic" direction.

§ A (+) for factor IV indicates item was weighted in the "conformity" direction; a (—) that it was weighted in the "nonconformity" direction.

2. No matter what the consequences, a person should insist on doing what he thinks is right even if it goes against what everyone else thinks. (—)
3. In general, a person should say what he thinks even if he knows that others will disagree very strongly. (—)
4. The ultimate decisions as to what is proper must come from the individual conscience rather than from an examination of the social customs of the time. (—)
5. When in doubt about the right thing to do, it is best to find out how other people think about it. (+)
6. We should avoid doing things that other people disapprove of, even if we personally think they are all right. (+)
7. A person should govern his conduct strictly in terms of what he thinks is right no matter what other people might say. (—)
8. Before deciding what to do, a person should always take into consideration how he thinks other people would act if they were in the same situation. (+)
9. The best way to judge what is appropriate in a given situation is to look at what other people are doing. (+)
10. In general, a person should do things the way that seems best to him even when this conflicts with what most people around him think is right. (—)

FACTOR V: PUBLIC VERSUS PRIVATE PRAYER‖

1. That life which is most pleasing to God is the life dedicated to the welfare of one's fellow man, even at the sacrifice of one's own personal happiness. (+)
2. I get more satisfaction from personal prayer than I do from attending formal worship services at church (synagogue). (—)
3. I would rather do my religious thinking at home than at church. (—)
4. I would rather worship God in private than in the midst of a large congregation. (—)
5. Men should seek God together. (+)
6. It is only right and proper that men should congregate in a common setting to worship their common God. (+)
7. The gulf between God and man is more easily bridged in a church service than in private contemplation. (+)

‖ A (+) for factor V indicates item was weighted in the "public prayer" direction:
a (—) indicates that it was weighted in the "private prayer" direction.

CHAPTER 8

Achievement

Up to this point we had directed our research efforts to three major dimensions of culture: individualism, equalitarianism, and theism. While not all of our findings were significant, the over-all results left little doubt that task experience could play an important role in shaping the beliefs, values, and preferences which subjects held with respect to the world around them. The possibility remained, however, that the findings reported were unique to the particular dimensions studied. While this seemed unlikely, it was obvious that further demonstrations of the generality of the theory across attitude dimensions would give us greater confidence in it.

It was with this in mind that, in this sixth study, we decided to extend our analysis to still another cultural theme, namely achievement. This is a more complex dimension than any of those studied thus far, including individualism-collectivism which we saw (Chapter 6) could be broken down analytically into at least three different subtypes. At the level of cultural beliefs, values, and preferences, achievement can best be thought of as a syndrome of related themes rather than a single unitary dimension. Within this syndrome it is possible to differentiate themes dealing with level of aspiration, striving, activity, luck, ability, time orientation, and mastery over nature. There are presumably other themes like these, many of which are associated with what is commonly known as the "Protestant ethic."[1]

Achievement is not only a more complex dimension; in many ways it is also a more interesting dimension than any we have dealt with previously. It has already been the subject of numerous studies in psychology and sociology; more recently it has invaded some of the other social sciences, notably economics.[2] In view of the importance tradition-

[1] Max Weber, *The Protestant Ethic and the Spirit of Capitalism* (London: George Allen & Unwin Ltd., 1930).
[2] David C. McClelland, *The Achieving Society* (Princeton, N.J.: Van Nostrand Co., Inc., 1961).

ally assigned to achievement in American culture, it is not surprising that many scholars have found it an interesting area to study.

Many of these studies are purely descriptive in nature; they are concerned with showing that some people are more achievement-oriented than others. No systematic attempt is made to explain why this should be the case. Social class is a popular variable in correlational studies of this sort.[3] In other research, achievement attitudes are taken as given and then used to explain variation in something else, e.g., economic growth rates. The goal here is to demonstrate that the presence or absence of achievement themes is causally related to other aspects of the social system, e.g., the level and nature of economic activity.[4] In still other studies, achievement is treated as a dependent variable, as something to be explained in terms of other elements in the culture or social structure. Directly stated, the question here asks why some people are more achievement-oriented than others. Most of the research done thus far has focused on child-rearing practices, particularly independence and mastery training.[5]

The study to be reported here was designed to test the general notion that attitudes toward achievement are in part a reflection of task experience. As in our previous research, we hoped to demonstrate that by confronting subjects with different kinds of task experience, we could induce systematic attitude change. Despite the many significant findings reported, our previous studies were of little help in suggesting what kinds of achievement attitudes would be affected by what kinds of task experience. Our major hypothesis linking the two emerged instead from what we had read elsewhere, in psychology and the philosophy of history.

In a laboratory study stemming from McClelland's earlier work on the achievement motive, Atkinson found that individuals who have a moderate (50–50) probability of success on any given task will produce more or expend more effort on the task than those who have either a very high (e.g., 75 per cent) or very low (e.g., 25 per cent) probability of succeeding.[6] In other words, tasks which are either too easy or too hard will be less motivating than tasks which are of moderate difficulty.

---

[3] For example, see Bernard C. Rosen, "Race, Ethnicity, and the Achievement Syndrome," *American Sociological Review*, Vol. 24 (1959), pp. 47–60.

[4] McClelland, *op. cit.*

[5] See, for example, M. R. Winterbottom, "The Relation of Need for Achievement to Learning Experiences in Independence and Mastery," in J. W. Atkinson (ed.), *Motives in Fantasy, Action, and Society* (Princeton, N.J.: Van Nostrand Co., Inc., 1958), pp. 453–78.

[6] J. W. Atkinson, "Towards Experimental Analysis of Human Motivation in Terms of Motives, Expectancies, and Incentives," in Atkinson (ed.), *op. cit.*, pp. 288–305.

Although it is directed to a much broader class of phenomena, Toynbee's notion of "challenge and response" involves the same basic idea.[7] According to the author, societies which are *moderately* challenged by their environments (both natural and social) will be driven to greater achievements than those which are stimulated either too little or too much. To produce a vigorous, creative response, the stimulus must be neither too strong or too weak, but "just right."

Whether we talk about probabilities of success or challenge and response, the same principle is involved: in problem-solving situations, the most vigorous response can be expected when the problem (task) is neither very easy nor very hard, but of moderate difficulty. It is important to note that the proposition refers not to the method of organizing the task (as in past studies) but to its difficulty. It should be noted as well that the proposition deals with the relationship between task difficulty and *behavior,* but has nothing to say about attitude formation or change.

It is part of our theory, however, that behavior is but one of several responses elicited by a task stimulus. An individual engaged in a task will also develop a set of beliefs, preferences, and values specific to the task at hand. These situationally specific orientations will then be generalized to other tasks or classes of tasks, according to the principles of similarity, familiarity, and specificity. Assuming this to be the case, we would expect to find that tasks which evoke a vigorous behavioral response will also evoke beliefs, preferences, and values stressing the importance and desirability of working hard, making an effort, and getting the job done. Conversely, tasks which are either too easy or too hard will evoke an apathetic behavioral response and a set of orientations de-emphasizing the importance of achievement.

With a very easy task, it is not necessary to work hard in order to achieve task success. When confronted with a situation of this sort, the individual will respond (1) cognitively, by perceiving that hard work has low instrumental reward value, (2) cathectically, by withholding commitment to his work, and (3) evaluatively, by refusing to define hard work as morally desirable. For the person faced with an impossibly difficult task, much the same can be said. Hard work may be rejected here not because it is unnecessary but because it is inadequate to achieve task success. No matter how much of an effort the individual may make, it is never enough. When effort fails to pay off, the individual will respond by de-emphasizing its importance.

---

[7] Arnold J. Toynbee, *A Study of History* (New York: Oxford Press, 1962).

When facing a task of moderate difficulty, things tend to look quite different. By definition, such a task cannot be performed successfully without considerable effort. Just as important, however, is the fact that success *can* be attained if the effort is made. For a person facing such a task, hard work will have considerable instrumental reward value. This should be reflected in his *behavior* as well as his *beliefs* about the importance of hard work, his *liking* for hard work, and the *value* that people, in a situation like this, should work hard. Once established, these positive orientations to the task at hand will presumably get generalized laterally to a variety of other task situations and vertically to increasingly inclusive classes of experience.

It was not difficult to translate this model into an actual experimental design, although considerable pre-testing was done before the final design was decided upon. Three conditions were established by varying the difficulty of the task, the actual degree of success to be achieved being predetermined for each group. The "easy" condition was deliberately arranged so as to make it possible for everyone to succeed with very little effort. In the "medum" condition task norms were set so as to give the average subject a 50–50 chance of succeeding. The "hard" condition was designed to make success on the task virtually impossible.

This part of the design was relatively simple. Much more difficult was the problem of deciding what kinds of scales to use in the attitude questionnaire. It was obvious from the beginning that there was no one dimension we could call achievement. A number of related themes seemed to be involved. Some of the scales finally decided upon were suggested by readings we had done in anthropology and sociology (especially the work of F. Kluckhohn[8]); some of the others were suggested by the experiment itself. Six scales were included in the final questionnaire.

Two of these scales were made up of items dealing with effort, an achievement theme which seemed particularly relevant to the easy-medium-hard experimental design we had decided upon. In one of these scales, effort was contrasted with *ability* (e.g., "In the long run, ability is probably more important than hard work in deciding who succeeds in life"). In the other scale, effort was contrasted with *luck* (e.g., "Compared to hard work, luck plays a minor role in determining success"). Luck and ability are two separate alternatives to hard work as an explanation of success or failure, hence the two different scales in the questionnaire.

---

[8] Florence Rockwood Kluckhohn and Fred L. Strodtbeck, *Variations in Value Orientations* (Evanston, Ill.: Row, Peterson & Co., 1961).

A third scale (*future versus present*) was suggested by Kluckhohn's time-orientation factor.[9] Items here dealt with the problem of postponing immediate gratification for the sake of long-term satisfactions. The time dimension is often included in discussions of achievement, the Protestant ethic, and, more generally, the role of culture in economic growth. While less obviously related to the experimental design than those scales dealing with hard work, it is clearly part of the over-all achievement syndrome and was included for that reason. A fourth scale was devoted to *level of aspiration*. The items here involved the issue of whether one should set his goals very high or be satisfied with more modest, easily achieved successes.

Activity versus passivity was the theme of the fifth scale. The item content revolved around the issue of taking the initiative in getting what you want out of life versus accepting things pretty much as they come (e.g., "The secret of happiness is not expecting too much out of life and being content with what comes your way."). Our final scale (*man versus nature*) was again suggested by one of Kluckhohn's dimensions.[10] Each item dealt with the question of man's ability to control the environment in which he lives (e.g., "Given time, the natural environment can be changed to fit whatever pattern man may wish to impose upon it."). Like several of those already mentioned, the man-nature scale was only indirectly related to the kind of experience subjects were to undergo in the laboratory. It was included, first, because it is generally associated with the achievement syndrome and, second, because it seemed no further removed from the laboratory setting than some of the abstract scales used in our previous studies.

Despite the obvious variation in item content, the same basic prediction was made for all six scales, namely that subjects in the medium condition would go up on achievement orientation while those in both the easy and hard conditions would go down. "Up" refers to attitude change in the direction indicated by the first part of the scale label. Thus, for those in the medium condition, we predicted change in the direction of effort (both kinds), future orientation, high level of aspiration, activity, and man (indicating man *over* nature). Change in the opposite direction was predicted for subjects in both the easy and hard conditions. A graphic plot of the predicted changes by condition would look something like Figure 8–1 below.

All of these scales are quite abstract in nature. No attempt was made, as in previous chapters, to compose scales in different areas

---

[9] *Ibid.*, pp. 13–15.
[10] *Ibid.*, p. 13.

(lateral generalization) and at different levels of abstraction (vertical generalization). The objective of this study was simply to explore a new attitude dimension (achievement) without getting too formal in the process. This is why we chose to work with several different themes (effort, time-orientation, man versus nature, etc.), each one treated broadly, rather than one major theme broken down into different areas and levels of abstraction. Although the same prediction was made for

FIGURE 8–1

Predicted Relationship between Attitude Change and Task Difficulty

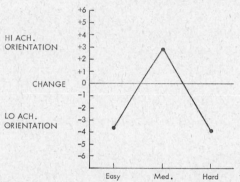

all six scales, we never really believed that things would be so simple. The pyramid-shaped prediction seemed most appropriate for those scales dealing with effort since the experiment itself was designed to make salient the instrumentality or futility of hard work. Some of the other scales, e.g., man versus nature, go considerably beyond this to speak of issues only tangentially related to the task experience proper. These scales are not simply more abstract than the others; they are quite different in subject matter. They were included along with the others because they seemed to bear some relationship to the over-all theme of achievement. Although we did not expect them to change in precisely the same way as the rest, there was nothing in our theory that would help us to predict exactly what would happen. In this sense, our efforts could best be thought of as exploratory.

The fact that we chose to deal broadly with six related but different dimensions rather than with one dimension in depth clearly distinguishes this study from most of those reported in previous chapters. There is another difference which should be noted. In the earlier laboratory studies, we tried to make up for the limited amount of time available in a laboratory experiment by formalizing the trial-and-error process which we felt to be so important for attitude formation and change. In Chapter 6, for example, we had subjects try each task alone, then together, the assumption being that the immediate contrast would facilitate the crystallization of new beliefs, preferences, and values. Pre-testing in that experiment had indicated that, without the contrast, little attitude change could be expected. The religion study, however, was run without any formalized trial and error, and yielded some rather impressive (if confusing) results. This we felt to be encouraging since in the present study (achievement) there seemed to be no convenient way of building a contrast into the experiment even if we wanted to.

A contrast design similar to those used previously would have involved asking subjects to try each task two different ways, working hard once and taking it easy the other time. It would have been necessary to confront half of the subjects (those we wanted to make more achievement-oriented) with tasks that could in fact be done better if they worked hard than if they took it easy. The other half (those we wanted to go down on achievement) would have been put to work on a series of tasks which we knew ahead of time could be performed more efficiently by taking it easy than by making a real effort.

There were at least two things that made this design unworkable: (1) the problem of operationalizing what was meant by working hard and taking it easy, and (2) the difficulty in finding tasks which could actually be done *better* taking it easy than working hard. Combined, the two problems argued strongly for omitting any trial-and-error sequence from the experimental design.

What we ended up with instead was a design in which subjects were free to engage in any trial-and-error behavior they wanted to. No attempt was made to regulate the amount of effort put into the task. Subjects were simply assigned to one of three task conditions (easy, medium, or hard) where some, we assumed, would find hard work highly instrumental to task success (the mediums) while others would find it either insufficient (hards) or unnecessary (easies) for success. It was expected that each individual would engage in some trial-and-error behavior on his own, settling down eventually to a level of effort in keeping with the difficulty of the task.

ATTITUDE QUESTIONNAIRE

Ten items were written for each of six different attitude themes: effort-ability, level of aspiration, activity-passivity, effort-luck, future-present, and man-nature. All items were written at an abstract level, in bipolar fashion, and were phrased equally in both directions so that all scales were balanced. No effort was made to equalize the number of belief, preference, and value items since previous results had made it clear that mode was irrelevant to both factor structure and amount of change. As in the past, all items were followed by a nine-point response format ranging from Strongly Disagree to Strongly Agree.

There was no opportunity to pre-test the questionnaire, thus it was administered for the first time to our 78 experimental subjects just prior to the experiment. A number of different factor analyses were performed on the "before" scores (for fuller explanation see page 202), the last of which (principal components with varimax rotation) yielded the following six factors: (1) *effort-luck* (made up exclusively of items from the *a priori* scale with the same name), (2) *future-present* (included nine out of ten future-present items), (3) *man-nature* (all of the man-nature items plus one level-of-aspiration and one future-present item), (4) *achievement through effort* (a combination of one effort-ability item, three level-of-aspiration items, and four items from the activity-passivity scale—all endorsing, in varied form, the notion of actively and energetically pursuing goals which have been set high), (5) *control-acceptance* (made up of one effort-ability item, three level-of-aspiration items, and six activity-passivity items—all representing variations around the theme of taking life as it comes as opposed to shaping it to fit our own needs), and (6) *effort-ability* (eight effort-ability items plus two items from the level-of-aspiration scale). All items, grouped by factor, can be seen in Exhibit F at the end of the chapter.

Factor scores were computed by summing responses to all items loaded .30 or better, each item receiving equal weight regardless of loading. Items which were loaded .30 or better on two or more factors were assigned to the factor with the highest loading. Internal consistencies and test-retest reliabilities are shown for each of the six factors in Table 8–1 below.[11]

PROCEDURE

This experiment required fairly extensive pre-testing before yielding significant results. Seven different pre-test designs using one group each were run in the spring of 1963 without apparent success. In the summer of that same year a new design was tried, found to be working, and adopted for the study reported here.

---

[11] For the method used in computing these estimates, see Chapter 3, footnote 18.

TABLE 8–1

Internal Consistencies and Test-Retest Reliabilities for Factor Scales

Factor	Number of Items	Internal Consistency	Test-Retest Reliability		
			Easy	Medium	Hard
I Effort-luck	10	.88	.85	.84	.85
II Future-present	9	.87	.91	.89	.87
III Man-nature	12	.85	.87	**.78**	**.92**
IV Achievement through effort	8	.76	.79	**.75**	**.82**
V Control-acceptance	10	.80	.96	.82	**.79**
VI Effort-ability	10	.80	.82	.72	.74

Subjects for the final study were 78 in number (38 males and 40 females) and were recruited both at Summer School registration and the Student Union. They were subsequently invited to the experiment in groups ranging from five to twelve. Once there, they first filled out the attitude questionnaire and then heard the experimenter introduce the experiment in the following manner:

The purpose of this study is to help us learn more about the effects of task success or failure on an individual's subjective probability (personal estimate of his chances) of doing well in subsequent trials. What we are going to do is give you a number of different tasks to work on, the idea being to surpass the standard of success which will be posted on the board. The standard in each case constitutes what we consider to be a successful performance, based on how well other students like you have done in the past. It should be noted that on each task the standard we shall put on the board represents a score *somewhat above the average performance*. After every few tasks we shall ask you to rate your probability of surpassing the standard on the next group of tasks. Although you will be paid five dollars for the experiment regardless of how you do, we want you to try to do as well as you can.

Two forms were then passed out to each individual present. The first (Scoring Sheet) contained a list of numbers running from 1 to 48, with a plus and a minus opposite each number. Subjects were told that there would be 48 different tasks and that for each one they were to circle either a plus or minus to indicate whether or not they had beaten the standard posted on the board. Each subject was also provided with 14 subjective probability forms. The experimenter explained that the 48 tasks would be broken down into 14 sets, and that for each set subjects were to indicate their subjective probability of beating the standard. This was done by circling any one of 20 percentages ranging from 05 to 1.00.

Subjects were randomly assigned to one of three conditions: easy (24), medium (29), and hard (25). All members of all conditions received the same instructions and worked on the same tasks. The major difference was that the standard of success was set artificially low for the easy condition and high for the hard condition, with the mediums falling about half way between. In an attempt to maximize the difference between the mediums and the other two, we told subjects in the medium condition to record their *actual task scores* each time (as well as circling a plus or minus), while those in the easy and hard conditions were told that all we were interested in was whether they beat the standard or not. This, we assumed, would minimize the reinforcing effects of gradual improvement in the easy and hard conditions. In addition, subjects in the easy condition were instructed to *stop working,* on any given task, when they had surpassed the standard of success. This was done to prevent them from substituting personal goals (e.g., scoring *as high as possible* on each task) for the stated experimental goals (surpassing the standard on each task). Only in this way could we guarantee that everyone in the easy condition would find that hard work was unnecessary for task success.

In concluding the instructions, the experimenter pointed out to subjects that as they proceeded from one task to the other, they should keep in mind how well they were doing as a whole. Subjects in the easy condition were told that, according to our experience with previous groups, the average person surpassed the standard on 15 of the 48 tasks. For subjects in the medium condition this was changed to 20 out of 48, and for those in the hard condition 25 out of 48. The reason for presenting this information was to make things seem even easier for those in the easy condition and harder for those in the hard condition.

Tasks

The first task (referred to as *uses*) was identical to the brainstorming task employed in previous experiments.[12] Subjects were asked to give as many uses as they could think of for a common object (e.g., red brick) in the space of one minute. In the easy condition the standard was set at 4, in the medium condition at 9, and in the hard condition at 14. The task was run in three sets of five objects each. Before each set of five, subjects were asked to fill out a probability sheet indicating their perceived chances of beating the standard on the trials coming up. After

---

[12] The idea for this task came from the *AC Test of Creative Ability,* Harris & Simberg, AC Spark Plug Division, General Motors Corp. (no date given).

each individual trial, of course, a plus or minus was circled, indicating whether in fact the standard had been surpassed.

In the second task (*consequences*), subjects were given a hypothetical state of affairs and asked to list all the consequences that might follow if the conditions described were to come true (e.g., "What would happen if nobody needed food anymore to live?").[13] Nine such situations were used, two minutes being given for each. The standards once again were set at 4, 9, and 14. Subjective probability sheets were filled out for each set of three.

The third task was called *reasons,* the object being to give as many logical reasons as possible why a certain hypothetical fact (stated by the experimenter) might be true (e.g., "There are more fat men in jail than any other physical type.").[14] Six trials were run (two minutes each) with standards of 2, 5, and 8 reasons for the easy, medium, and hard conditions respectively.

For the fourth task, (*categories*), subjects were given an adjective (e.g., round) and allowed one minute to list as many things as they could that might appropriately be described by that adjective.[15] The standards were the same as those used in the first two tasks.

This is also true of our last task (*ideas*) in which subjects were presented with an event (e.g., a man going up a ladder) and asked to list all the questions they could think of that would help to define the situation (e.g., what rung is he on, is someone chasing him, etc.).[16]

To summarize, essentially the same instructions were given to all subjects with the exception that the standards of success were set artificially low for those in the easy condition and artificially high for those in the hard condition. In setting the standards, care was taken to see that subjects in the medium condition scored about half pluses and half minuses, while the easies scored almost all pluses and the hards close to all minuses. It was expected that the subjective probability ratings would average close to .50 for the mediums, over .75 for the easies, and under .25 for the hards, reflecting a variety of experiences ranging from complete security (and perhaps boredom) at the top to unrelieved frustration at the bottom.

At the end of the experiment, subjects were told to add up the

---

[13] This task was taken from the "Consequences" test designed by Christensen, Merrifield & Guilford, Sheridan Supply Co., Beverly Hills, Calif., 1958.

[14] This task was similar to one part of the *AC Test of Creative Ability, op. cit.*

[15] This task was based on the "Thing Categories" test in J. W. French (ed.), *Manual for Kit of Selected Tests for Reference Aptitude and Achievement Factors* (Princeton, N.J.: Educational Testing Service, 1954).

[16] Based on the "Topics Test," *Ibid.*

number of pluses they got for surpassing the standard and to enter that number at the bottom of their Scoring Sheet. When this was done, the attitude questionnaire was administered for the second time. As in the previous experiment, subjects were told that a colleague was developing the questionnaire for use in another study and had asked the experimenters to administer it a second time as this was standard procedure in constructing an instrument of this nature.

RESULTS

Performance and Probability of Success. To the extent that our experimental manipulations were successful, we should expect to find differences between conditions in (1) subjective probability of success and (2) actual degree of success attained. In computing the first figure, all probability ratings (14 for each subject) were averaged within each condition; for the success figure, we averaged the individual percentages indicating the number of times out of 48 that the standard had been surpassed. The appropriate data are presented in Table 8–2 below.

TABLE 8–2
Subjective Probability and Performance Means, by Condition

	Easy	Medium	Hard
Subjective Probability of Success Rating	.82	.53	.29
Actual Proportion Success Achieved	.96	.54	.14

The data in Table 8–2 indicate that the conditions we hoped to establish did in fact materialize. At both levels (subjective probability and actual performance) the mediums hovered around the 50 per cent mark, while the easies and hards were approximately equidistant high and low respectively. It is clear from the performance figures that the easies really had it easy whereas the hards never had a chance. In light of the fact that there was very little overlap between conditions, significant tests on these measures seemed gratuitous.

Attitude Change

Changes by Factor. A significant test for item (rather than scale) changes was not computed in this study due to both the small number of items involved in each scale and the complexity of the analysis with three instead of the usual two conditions.

Our first step in analyzing the scale changes was to factor analyze the "before" questionnaire responses. As indicated earlier (page 197), a number of different analyses were performed. The first time around we tried a centroid analysis with quartimax rotation, as in all previous studies. In the process of examining the results, it became evident that some of the factors extracted were quite heterogeneous with respect to the way in which items were changing. Items similarly loaded on the same factor were behaving differently, some changing one way, some the other. In the hopes of getting a more efficient factor structure, one which would put together items changing in the same fashion, we subjected our item correlations to a principal components analysis followed by varimax rotation. Six factors were extracted.

The results were much more satisfactory. With few exceptions (mainly in the last factor extracted), items which changed in the same way ended up on the same factor. As indicated in our earlier discussion of the questionnaire, some factors were made up of items drawn exclusively from *one* of the a priori scales (e.g., effort-luck). Other factors, however, tended to attract items from a number of different a priori scales (the fifth factor, for example, included significantly loaded items from three different scales—effort-ability, level of aspiration, and activity-passivity). In both cases, items which changed in the same way tended to end up on the same factor.

It should be made clear that, in preparing the data for testing, we deliberately picked that factor analysis (principal components) which did the best job of grouping items according to the way they changed. In doing so, we had to look at the individual item changes before deciding which factor analysis to use. All of this bears testimony to the fact that the whole study was a highly inductive one, that we were more interested in finding out what kinds of achievement themes were likely to change than in testing propositions formulated in advance.

Once factor scores had been computed for all "before" and "after" questionnaires, mean changes were calculated separately for easies, mediums, and hards. These mean changes are plotted in Figure 8–2 below. A trend analysis was performed on the changes for each of the six factors using the experimental condition as the independent variable. The appropriate data are shown in Table 8–3.[17]

---

[17] For the second time in our research (see Chapter 7) we found that our practice of assigning subjects randomly had failed to match groups sufficiently with respect to initial attitudes. Significant differences (in trend) were found on the "before" scores for four

A significant *quadratic* (curvilinear) trend was found for factor I (effort-luck), with mediums going up on effort and both easies and hards going down. Factor IV (achievement through effort) suggests a similar profile, although the F is far from significant.

FIGURE 8–2

Mean Changes for Factor Scales, by Condition

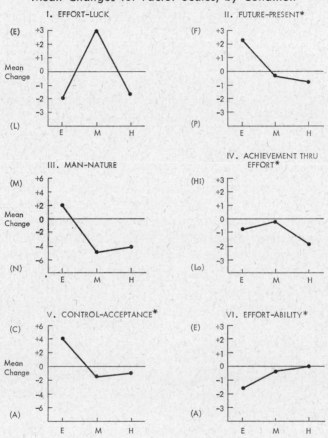

*Adjusted by covariance analysis for initial position. See footnote 17.

A significant *linear* trend, on the other hand, emerged in factor V (control-acceptance), with strong hints to the same effect in factors II (future-present) and III (man-nature). In all three cases, subjects in the easy condition went up (in the direction of future, man, and

of the six factor scales. In order to eliminate the possibility of attitude change due simply to differential regression, the means and sums of squares were corrected by an analysis of covariance. Because of significant correlations between initial position and amount of change, this procedure had a considerable effect on some of the scores.

control) while both mediums and hards went down (in the direction of present, nature, and acceptance). Although the three factors are empirically orthogonal to one another, they share an obvious analytic resemblance. The theme common to all three is man's ability and obligation to control himself and the environment in which he lives. In abstract terms, the issue is between control, mastery, and planning on the one hand and acceptance, fatalism, and acquiescence on the

TABLE 8–3

Trend Analysis of Effects of Condition on Attitudes, by Factor

| Factor | | Sums of Squares | | F for Larger | |
	Between	Linear (L)	Quadratic (Q)	Trend†	p
I Effort-luck	396.24	0.34	395.90	6.39 (Q)	.05
II Future-present*	119.15	93.29	25.86	2.50 (L)	ns
III Man-nature	498.49	341.44	157.05	3.03 (L)	.10
IV Achievement through effort*	45.45	23.02	22.43	1.07 (L)	ns
V Control-acceptance*	480.94	342.22	138.72	10.22 (L)	.01
VI Effort-ability*	31.61	25.70	5.91	0.46 (L)	ns

* ss after adjusting for initial position by covariance analysis;
† d.f. = 1 ; 75

other. Factor V is already defined by two of these terms: control-acceptance. The mastery-fatalism theme is most salient in factor III (e.g., "There is little man can do to master the world around him in view of the immense power of nature compared to his own."). Most of the items in factor II (future-present) are concerned with whether it is better to acquiesce in the face of impulses demanding immediate gratification or to postpone such gratification for the sake of achieving longer-term goals.

In view of the similarities involved, factors II, III, and V were combined to produce an a posteriori second-order factor which was then subjected to the same kind of trend analysis used previously. As might be expected the linear trend for this new summary factor was a highly significant one ($F = 12.47$, $p < .001$). A plot of the mean changes by condition is shown in Figure 8–3.

Changes by People. Table 8–4 indicates how many subjects in each condition changed in each direction. As in previous studies, this was done only for those factors showing significant differences (trends) by condition, in this case factors I and V. A similar analysis was performed on factors II, III, and V combined. According to Table 8–4,

FIGURE 8–3
Mean Changes by Condition for Factors II, III, and V Combined

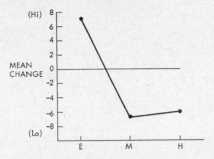

two of the three chi-square values are significant at the .05 level or better.[18]

In looking back over the results reported in Figure 8–2 and Table 8–3, it is evident that our predictions were only partially borne out. The only factor clearly showing the expected pyramidal distribution was factor I (effort-luck). Confronted with a series of tasks of moderate difficulty, subjects in the medium condition changed their attitudes in the direction of favoring effort over luck as an explanation of worldly success. Subjects, on the contrary, who found their tasks extremely easy or hard were more willing after the experiment to attribute success in life to "getting the breaks."

The only other factors reaching or approaching significance (II, III, and V) all revealed a pattern of changes markedly different from what had been predicted. In each case it was the subjects in the easy condi-

---

[18] One further analysis should be noted, despite the fact that it failed to turn up anything of interest. In all of our analyses thus far, subjects were divided up by condition (easy, medium, and hard) on the assumption that *all* those in the easy condition found the tasks very easy, that all those in the hard condition found the tasks very hard, etc. However, due to individual differences in the abilities required for success on these tasks, some subjects did better or worse than they "were supposed" to, e.g., several subjects in the medium condition actually did better than some of those in the easy condition. The same kind of anomaly was found in the probability rating data.

It seemed reasonable to assume that better results could be obtained by breaking down subjects in terms of (1) actual amount of success (number of tasks on which standard was surpassed) and/or (2) rated probability of succeeding. Either variable could be seen as *intervening* between the objective situation (as determined by the experimenter) and attitude change. Moreover, in their role as intervening variables, actual success and subjective probability of success should constitute better predictors of attitude change than the antecedent conditions on which they in turn depend. With this in mind, a move was made to reclassify subjects according to how well they did and how well they thought they would do. In the process of dividing up the subjects this way, however, it became clear that while some individuals were getting shifted around (e.g., from medium to easy), the vast majority were getting put back in the same categories. The project was dropped when it became obvious that reordering subjects would make no difference in the over-all attitude change scores.

TABLE 8–4
Changes by People for Factors Showing Significant Trends

I (effort-luck)

	E	M	H
+	9	17	12
−	13	11	12

$\chi^2 = 2.11$ ns

V (control-acceptance)

	E	M	H
+	16	12	7
−	5	16	18

$\chi^2 = 10.99$ $p < .01$

II, II, and V (combined)

	E	M	H
+	16	10	6
−	8	17	17

$\chi^2 = 8.55$ $p < .05$

tion who differed from the other two, there being little or no difference between mediums and hards. In each case, moreover, the easies did what we expected the mediums to do; they became more future-oriented, more convinced of man's ability to master his natural environment, and more insistent that we should try to control life rather than letting things take their own course. If it were not for the pyramid in factor I, we might be tempted to conclude that our easy condition was more nearly a medium-type situation, and that our medium and hard conditions should both be classified as hard. This we decided was extremely unlikely not only because mediums and hards differed so radically on factor I, but because the performance and subjective probability data attest to the "easiness" of the easy condition as well as the real difference between the other two.

On reflection, it seemed much more likely that we had two distinct change patterns on our hands, the curvilinear one which we had predicted and the linear one which we had not. The curvilinear pattern was typical of at least one effort factor (effort-luck) and suggestive of one other (factor IV—achievement through effort). The results here seemed to reflect more than anything else *the instrumentality of hard work* in the experiment itself. Hard work had little reward value outside of the medium condition; among the easies it was unnecessary for success, among the hards it was inadequate for success.

The *linear* patterns (future-present, man-nature, and control-acceptance), on the other hand, seemed to reflect *the degree of success attained* rather than the importance of effort in attaining it. The easies, it is clear, achieved a very high degree of success. We can surmise that after the opening moments they felt quite relaxed, confident, optimistic, and free from the anxiety so characteristic of subjects in the medium and hard conditions. It is likely that the movement away from acceptance, fatalism and acquiescence, in the direction of control, mastery, and planning had its roots in this very sense of confidence and security. The fact that they were so successful would account for why they became more forceful and confident in their conception of man's ability to control the world around him. The fact that they were successful with a minimum of effort explains why they became less convinced of the importance of hard work in getting ahead in life.

It is not entirely clear why, in the three factors showing a linear trend, there was a very sigificant difference between easies and the other two, but no difference between mediums and hards. Conceivably the mediums considered themselves to be failures, in terms of the expectations they brought into the situation. This is unlikely, however, in view of the fact that they did just about as well on the whole as the average student, a fact that they were familiar with throughout the experiment. It remains possible, of course, that our subjects interpreted doing as well as their peers (but no better) as failure, in which case they could be expected to act more like the hards than the easies.

The tendency for the easies to get differentiated from the other two can more easily be explained, we feel, in terms of the fact that while mediums and hards were under a good deal of strain and anxiety, the easies were a relaxed and light-hearted bunch throughout the experiment. It will be recalled that subjects in the easy condition were told to *stop* working as soon as they surpassed the standard on any given task. This meant that most subjects finished each task considerably before the time was up, which gave them ample time to relax and reflect on their past successes. Subjects in the other two conditions tended to keep on working right up to the buzzer, although as the experiment progressed more and more of the hards seemed to be going through the motions without making a real effort. Unlike the easies who did a lot of smiling and generally looked confident, most of the hards and mediums wore very serious expressions, suggesting a high level of tension and anxiety. This is consistent with the fact that the easies became *more* confident of man's ability to control his environment, while both mediums and hards became *less* so.

It seems reasonable to conclude from all of this that we have at least two syndromes of achievement-related attitudes, each bearing its own relationship to task experience. Beliefs and values dealing generally with the importance of hard work in achieving success are clearly affected by the probability of succeeding in a specific task situation. This can be explained in terms of the fact that hard work has greater instrumental reward value where the task is of moderate difficulty than when the task is either very easy or very hard. The pyramidal distribution of changes on factor I (effort-luck) is consistent with this reasoning and, in fact, was predicted on the basis *of* it.

Findings relevant to the second achievement syndrome cannot be explained in the same terms. The syndrome, once again, represents a combination of themes dealing with control, time, and mastery over nature. In content, this second syndrome is clearly different from the first which was concerned exclusively with the instrumentality of hard work. According to the results, subjects in the easy condition went up on control, mastery, etc. while both mediums and hards went down.

While this finding is certainly interesting and statistically quite significant, it does not follow directly from anything in our theory. The theory is based on the notion that, in any task situation, some behaviors will have greater instrumental reward value than others. Attitude formation is seen as a process in which the individual responds cognitively, cathectically, and evaluatively to the exigencies of the situation and, in turn, generalizes these responses to other task settings and to increasingly abstract classes of experience. As indicated above, the pyramidal distribution of changes on factor I (effort-luck) can easily be explained in terms of reinforcement and generalization. There is nothing in our second syndrome, however, which is analagous to hard work; there is no behavior which we can speak of as having higher instrumental reward value in one condition than in the others. Factors in the second syndrome speak of control, mastery over nature, planning, and their opposites. There is no reason to assume, however, that the easies (who went up on these factors) were rewarded more for controlling, mastering, and planning than the mediums and hards who went down on the same scales.

There *is* reason to believe, however, that the easies felt considerably more relaxed, confident, and secure in their ability to handle the tasks successfully than subjects from either of the other two conditions. We suspect that it is this confidence in solving specific problems that got generalized to the abstract notion that man has the capacity (and obligation) to shape his environment to fit his own human needs. If this is the case, it is not so much a matter of reinforcing behavior but of changing one's perception of one's own abilities. By virtue of close to four hours of "controlled" success and failure, subjects in the easy condition presumably came to see themselves in an increasingly favorable light, while those in the medium and hard conditions were forced throughout to consider the possibility that they might not be as good as they thought they were. With this in mind, it is perhaps not surprising that the easies became more convinced of man's ability to dominate his surroundings at the same time that the others were growing increasingly doubtful.

DISCUSSION

In view of the relatively small changes obtained and the *post hoc* nature of much of the analysis, we hesitate to generalize these findings to task settings outside the laboratory. It is difficult nevertheless to refrain from pointing out the implications of what we have learned here for our understanding of cross-cultural and subcultural differences in achievement-orientation. Much has been written about the impact of achievement values on behavior (striving, mobility, etc.); much less has been written about where such values come from in the first place.

We are so accustomed in this society to invoking achievement values to explain class differences in aspiration and performance, that we rarely bother to ask why middle-class and lower-class values are so different in the first place. The answer we have hypothesized here, namely that achievement values have their roots in task success and failure, is not meant to be an original one. It is not uncommon to hear social scientists talk in these terms and then in the next breath add that, since success and failure are products (as well as determinants) of achievement attitudes, the whole relationship is a circular one, meaning that there is little that can be done beyond admitting that "it probably works both ways."

While it very likely does work both ways, we shall never know for certain until we do more testing. Our own experiment, despite its many obvious limitations, is a step in this direction. Given the experimental controls, there can be little doubt as to the direction of the causal relationships involved. Subjecting a person to a series of tasks which are either extremely easy or impossibly difficult has the effect of weakening his belief in the importance of hard work for success. If you subject him instead to a series of tasks in which he has more nearly a 50-50 chance of succeeding, his evaluation of hard work will go up.

While we do not wish to maintain that our three experimental conditions represent the three social classes (upper, middle, and lower) in miniature, we would argue that, by virtue of the important role which success and failure play in both, there is something to be gained from looking at the two together. Members of the lower class have something in common with the subjects in our hard condition in that both have little chance of achieving success as this is defined by others. The easies bear more resemblance to members of the upper class who can count on certain rewards (though ascription) without having to make any real effort to get them. Like those in the middle class, subjects in the medium condition found themselves in a position to achieve success, but only if they made an all-out effort to do so.

If we are to make any real headway in explaining why people have different achievement attitudes in the first place, we must go beyond the handy but inefficient concept of social class and talk about the kinds of experiences that upper-, middle-, and lower-class people actually have. The experiment reported here is suggestive of one approach that might be taken. In this experiment we examined one specific and important kind of experience, namely task success or failure. We found that by exposing some subjects to greater success than others, we could produce systematic differences in before-after changes on items dealing with effort, luck, control, fatalism, time orientation, and mastery over nature. While the results remain sketchy at best, they do indicate that success and failure experience can play an influential role in the shaping of achievement-related values and beliefs.

EXHIBIT F

FACTOR I: EFFORT VERSUS LUCK*

1. It is impossible to get ahead in life on hard work alone; what you really need is a few lucky breaks. (—)
2. In the long run luck is probably more important than effort in deciding who succeeds in life. (—)
3. Hard work is no guarantee that you will get what you want in life; more important, you need the right breaks at the right time. (—)

---

* On factor I, (+) means that the item was weighted in the "effort" direction, (—) that it was weighted in the "luck" direction.

4. A person who works hard at what he is doing will succeed whether he gets any breaks or not. (+)
5. Persistent effort and striving will generally get you what you want in life, regardless of whether the breaks come your way or not. (+)
6. Compared to hard work, luck plays a minor role in determining success. (+)
7. Without some lucky breaks along the way, it is impossible to succeed in life, no matter how hard you work. (—)
8. In most situations, if you work hard enough you can count on doing well; getting breaks is relatively unimportant. (+)
9. In most task settings, success depends more on making an effort than on getting the breaks. (+)
10. No matter how hard you might work, you have to get the breaks in order to achieve success. (—)

FACTOR II: FUTURE VERSUS PRESENT†

1. It is better to get what you can out of life in the present, since you can never tell what the future might bring. (—)
2. To attain real happiness in life, one must be willing to give up immediate satisfactions for the sake of longer-term future goals. (+)
3. It is the wise man who learns to forego immediate pleasures in order to achieve more lasting satisfactions sometime in the future. (+)
4. Man's lot would be a happier one if people concerned themselves less with the present and spent more time planning for the future. (+)
5. People should always plan their activities in terms of how they relate to future goals rather than in terms of how much short-run enjoyment they will bring. (+)
6. Man's life should be guided more by the demands of the present than by his visions of the future. (—)
7. It is impossible to achieve any kind of lasting satisfaction in life unless you are willing to subordinate the needs of the present to considerations of what is best for the future. (+)
8. It is generally better to plan your activities in terms of how they relate to immediate goals than in terms of goals which cannot be achieved until some time in the future. (—)
9. People would be better off if they spent more time thinking about the immediate present and less time making plans for the future. (—)

FACTOR III: MAN VERSUS NATURE‡

1. People should be content with an average level of performance rather than always trying to be the best at everything. (—)
2. An individual should be more concerned with what he is right now than what he might become sometime in the future. (+)

---

† On factor II, (+) means that the item was weighted in the "future" direction, (—) that it was weighted in the "present" direction.

‡ On factor III, (+) means that the item was weighted in the "man" direction, (—) that it was weighted in the "nature" direction.

3. It is clear from his past achievements that man is capable of completely reshaping the world around him to suit his own human needs. (+)
4. Given time, the natural environment can be changed to fit whatever pattern man may wish to impose upon it. (+●)
5. There is little man can do to master the world around him in view of the immense power of nature compared to his own. (—)
6. There is no secret of nature that man will not eventually discover and no power of nature that he will not eventually master. (+)
7. In spite of man's best efforts he can never completely master his environment. (—)
8. There is nothing in the natural environment that mankind will not someday be able to understand and utilize for his own ends. (+)
9. There are some aspects of man's environment which he can never hope to comprehend or control. (—)
10. Despite his many achievements, man will always be dominated by the natural environment in which he lives. (—)
11. In the long run, there is no reason why man cannot completely alter his environment to fit his own purposes. (+)
12. There are mysteries in nature which man is innately incapable of solving. (—)

FACTOR IV: ACHIEVEMENT THROUGH EFFORT§

1. No matter how much ability you might have, you have to work hard in order to achieve success. (+)
2. People should set their goals high rather than being satisfied with modest achievements. (+)
3. People ought to try to achieve every bit as much as they are capable of rather than being content with just getting by. (+)
4. The happiest people are those who set the sky as the limit and try their best to reach the highest possible goals rather than setting their sights low where they will be sure of making it. (+)
5. The happy man is the man who makes things happen for him rather than letting things happen to him. (+)
6. If you want anything out of life, you have to go get it because it probably won't come to you. (+)
7. To achieve lasting satisfaction in life, one must actively and energetically pursue one's goals instead of resting content with what comes one's way. (+)
8. Happiness rarely comes to those who wait for it; if you want something in this life you have to go out and get it. (+)

FACTOR V: CONTROL-ACCEPTANCE‖

1. Persistent effort will usually get you what you want in life whether you have ability or not. (—)

---

§ On factor IV, (+) means that the item was weighted in the "high achievement through effort" direction.

‖ On factor V, (+) means that the item was weighted in the "control" direction, and (—) that it was weighted in the "acceptance" direction.

2. A person ought to set his goals as high as possible rather than playing it safe by setting them so low he is sure of reaching them. (+)
3. People should set goals for themselves which they can achieve fairly easily rather than goals which they may never attain. (—)
4. Setting your sights high often leads to disappointment; it is better to set more modest goals which you can be sure of reaching. (—)
5. The secret of happiness is not expecting too much out of life and being content with what comes your way. (—)
6. It is best to let things come as they will rather than always trying to control what happens to you. (—)
7. People should always go out and get what they want in life rather than letting things take their own course. (+)
8. People who accept life pretty much as it is tend to be happier than those who go out of their way to influence the course of events. (—)
9. People would be a lot happier if they took life for what it is instead of trying to shape the course of things to fit their own ends. (—)
10. People should try to accept life as they find it instead of constantly trying to change it to suit their own needs. (—)

FACTOR VI: EFFORT VERSUS ABILITY¶

1. In the long run, ability is probably more important than hard work in deciding who succeeds in life. (—)
2. It is impossible to get ahead in life on hard work alone; you have to have a lot of ability if you want to make it. (—)
3. A person who works hard at what he is doing will generally succeed even if he has very little ability. (+)
4. Compared to hard work, ability plays a relatively minor role in determining success. (+)
5. Without unusual ability, it is impossible to succeed in life, no matter how hard you work. (—)
6. In most task settings, success depends more on effort than ability. (+)
7. Hard work is no guarantee that you will succeed at what you do; in the long run it is ability that counts. (—)
8. In most situations, success depends more on having exceptional ability than on working unusually hard. (—)
9. Setting one's own goals high only leads to disappointment; it is better to set them at a modest level and be sure of making them. (—)
10. The happy man is the man who sets his goals as high as he dares rather than playing it safe by setting them so low there is no risk of failure. (+)

¶ On factor VI, (+) means that the item was weighted in the "effort" direction, (—) that it was weighted in the "ability" direction.

CHAPTER 9

Individualism-Collectivism (III)

THE STUDY reported in the last chapter was specifically designed to test the applicability of our thesis to an area of thought (achievement) which was at once unrelated to anything we had previously explored and at the same time very closely related to the interests of our fellow sociologists and psychologists. The results of that study gave additional support to the idea that the beliefs and values we entertain with respect to the world around us have their roots in task experience. Like the religion study which preceded it, however, the achievement experiment contributed little to the elaboration of our formal theory. With regard to theory development, nothing of central importance had been added since Chapter 6 where we left the issue of lateral and vertical generalization. It was with this in mind that we decided, in our seventh and final experiment, to return to the problem of generalization and the theme of individualism-collectivism.

There were several considerations involved in planning this final experiment. First of all, we were anxious to do a single study which would incorporate all of the major elements in our theoretical scheme. These include behavior, situationally specific orientations, and the two kinds of generalization (lateral and vertical). While measures of behavior had occupied much of our attention in the original Wisconsin experiment, no formal attempt was made to test this feature of the theory in subsequent studies. Starting with the first Cornell study, we decided that we could maximize the effect of experience on attitudes by exercising systematic control over subjects' behavior. Subjects were *told* to work alone or together, with a leader or without one, etc. There was never any choice, thus no opportunity to get a systematic measure of behavioral differences. With this in mind, this last experiment was deliberately designed to give subjects the chance to decide for themselves how they would perform the tasks involved. The actual choices made (in this case between doing the task together versus doing it alone) provided the desired measure of behavior.

There was another consideration involved in our decision to let subjects do their own choosing. In a natural setting where a number of people are confronted with a task to be solved, trial-and-error learning rarely proceeds as systematically and rigidly as it did in our previous experiments where subjects alternated between doing each task together, then alone, then together, etc. While there is admittedly much to be learned from a highly controlled and often artificial experiment, we decided in favor of the more flexible arrangement here on the assumption that the more natural we made the situation, (1) the more difficult it would be to dismiss the findings as an artifact of the laboratory, and (2) the more attitude generalization we would get to areas outside the laboratory.

Critical to our theory is the notion that, in working on a task, people respond not only behaviorally but attitudinally by developing cognitive, cathectic, and evaluative orientations specific to the task at hand. It is from these situationally specific orientations that lateral and vertical generalization proceed. In only one previous study, however, did we actually get a formal measure of these specific orientations (Chapter 4, cf. page 98). The results there were so significant (statistically) that no effort was made to replicate the finding in subsequent experiments. Given our goal here of incorporating in this final study all the elements of our theory, it was decided to include a measure of task-specific orientations similar to the one previously used.

The next set of propositions in our theory involves the generalization of these specific orientations laterally to other concrete task situations and vertically to increasingly abstract categories of experience. In our last individualism-collectivism experiment (Chapter 6) we found very clear evidence to the effect that both kinds of generalization were operating. The study was limited, however, by the rather informal, ad hoc nature of that part of the analysis dealing with lateral generalization. Only two scales (family and fraternity) were used and no predictions were made for the relative amount of change on each. Our basic concern was with showing simply that some kind of lateral generalization did take place. A specific set of principles detailing the conditions under which generalization would occur had not yet been formulated. On the basis of that study and those that preceded it, we drew the tentative conclusion that there were at least two major principles involved.

In planning this present study, we decided to subject each of these two principles to a more formal test. We hypothesized that attitude generalization from situation X to situation Y would be most likely to occur where (1) X is similar to Y and (2) the subject is unfamiliar with Y (and thus uncertain in his attitudes toward Y). To test these hypotheses we picked four areas (factory, school, neighborhood, and family) which we felt to be quite different with respect to (1) similarity to the laboratory situation, and (2) familiarity to subjects. The laboratory situation was to be very much like the one reported in Chapter 6, i.e., a series of intellectual and motor tasks which could be done either alone or together.

We made the assumption that factory and school were more similar to the experimental situation than either neighborhood or family. Both factory and school (college) involve a high degree of purely instrumental activity (work) while neighborhood and family constitute settings where social-emotional or expressive activities tend to predominate. On the grounds of similarity alone, then, we predicted greater generalization to factory and school than to either neighborhood or family.

Looking at the same four settings again in terms of familiarity to subjects, it seemed reasonable to assume that college undergraduates would be more familiar with school and family life than with either factory or neighborhood activities (though there may be some doubt about the latter). Given the general rule that subjects will generalize more to areas they know little about, we predicted more change on the factory and neighborhood scales than on those dealing with school or the family. Putting the two sets of predictions together, we concluded that attitudes toward factory life would change the most, family the least, with school and neighborhood falling somewhere in between. The relationships involved can more easily be seen in Table 9–1.

Previously, in writing items covering a given area (family, classroom, politics, etc.), we made no attempt to distinguish among categories of tasks within each area. Most of the items were quite general in nature. In composing a family scale, for example, we usually phrased our items in terms of "doing things together as a family versus doing things on your own" or some variation on this theme. No reference was made to any specific kind of family task or activity. In the process of composing scales for each of the four areas described above (factory, school, family, neighborhood), the thought occurred to us that we might carry our similarity principle one step further by exploring generalization to different kinds of tasks *within* each area. Having made the distinction between instrumental and expressive activity in our analysis of area differences, we decided to use it again to describe task differences within each area.

Within each of the four areas, we constructed one scale dealing exclusively with instrumental tasks (work), a second scale dealing exclusively with expressive tasks (in this case, leisure), and a third deal-

TABLE 9–1

Classification of Task Areas in Terms of Similarity and Familiarity

		Similarity	
		High	Low
Familiarity	High	School (++)	Family (+)
	Low	Factory (+++)	Neighborhood (++)

ing with tasks in general. The latter scale was included in order to facilitate comparison with our earlier studies in which most of the area items had been phrased in a general fashion. As in the past, these items referred to doing things together or alone but failed to specify what "things" were involved.

Given the highly instrumental nature of the laboratory setting, we predicted that, *within each area,* subjects would show the greatest change on the instrumental scale, the least on the expressive scale, with the general scale (in some ways a combination of the other two) falling somewhere in between. These predictions were based on the same similarity principle invoked in predicting differences in the amount of change *between* areas. In the latter case we proposed (holding familiarity constant) that factory and school would change more than either family or neighborhood on the grounds that factory and school, being generally more instrumental in nature, were more similar to the laboratory setting.

Aside from the fact that it incorporates all the major elements of our theory, this final study differs from what was done before primarily in that it attempts to extend our understanding of lateral generalization. There are several other features of the design, however, which should be mentioned.

For one thing, we decided to administer our questionnaire three times, once right before the experiment, immediately afterwards, and again two to three weeks later. This had been done only once before (the religion study). In view of our desire to include everything we could in this final effort, it seemed highly appropriate to find out something more about the "life span" of our anticipated attitude changes.

A minor innovation involved the ordering of items on the questionnaire. In two of our previous studies we had put the scales most likely to change at the beginning of the questionnaire (see Chapters 5 and 6). This left open the possibility that the initial scales had evoked some sort of generalized response set which was then carried over to the less obvious scales, scales which might not have shown any change if they had come first on the questionnaire. With this possibility in mind, we deliberately put our new neighborhood and family scales first on the assumption that they were less likely to change than any of the others in the questionnaire.

As in the religion and achievement studies, an attempt was made to minimize the "demand characteristics" of the situation by disassociating the questionnaire as much as possible from the experiment itself. Again, the questionnaire was introduced (in both the before and after administrations) as part of someone else's dissertation research. We mention this here because it was not done in the last individualism-collectivism study (the one most comparable to this one).

ATTITUDE QUESTIONNAIRE

As already indicated, the attitude dimension chosen for this study was individualism-collectivism. This is a very broad theme which can be dealt with at any one of several different levels. For reasons of convenience in writing items, we decided to work with the simplest version of the individualism-collectivism theme, namely alone versus together. Evidence from Chapter 6 had indicated that, despite the analytical distinctions made between togetherness, co-operation, and collectivism, items at all levels worked equally well.

Taking the general theme of doing things alone versus together, we wrote 18 items for each of the four areas previously mentioned, namely neighborhood, family, factory, and school. The first six items in each set of 18 referred to tasks in general, the next six to instrumental tasks, and the final six to expressive tasks (recreation). All of these scales were designed to test for lateral generalization.

With respect to vertical generalization (induction), we decided to try something a little bit different from what we had done in the previous individualism-collectivism study. There are many ways of testing for vertical generalization, precisely because there are so many ways of abstracting from experience. In the previous ID-CL study, we used three scales which presumably defined a continuum running from a relatively specific set of items dealing with small work groups, up through another set dealing with groups in general, reaching finally to a third set dealing with the relationship between individual and society (way of life). In part, this series of scales constituted a gradient defined in terms of *size,* with small groups at one end, groups of all sorts in the middle, and society at the other end.

There are other gradients we might have used. Instead of size, for example, we could have taken task content as our criterion. This is, in fact, what we did do for the study reported here. In keeping with the instrumental-expressive breakdown used in our lateral generalization scales, we decided upon three related scales, the least abstract of which was made up of six items dealing with the alone-together theme as this applied to instrumental tasks in general. Unlike the instrumental scales already mentioned, no reference was made here to any specific situation such as neighborhood, factory, school, etc. To distinguish this scale from the specific ones, we called it the *working* scale. All six of the items refer to working together versus working alone. In constructing the scale, we took many of the items from the *small-work-groups* scale of our last individualism-collectivism study, deleting the reference to small groups. In their new form, the items refer simply to working alone versus together in any kind of setting.

In making up the second scale in this series, we again borrowed heavily from our previous study. From the old *groups-in-general* scale, we selected six items written around the theme of doing things together versus doing them alone. These we considered to be more abstract than the items in our working scale, for the obvious reason that *doing* is a more inclusive category than *working.* Among other things, doing includes engaging in expressive activities such as playing games, entertaining friends, etc.

For our most abstract scale, we composed six new items around the theme of *being* together or alone. This represented a slight departure from the previous individualism-collectivism study where we took way of life as the third and most abstract level. The reason for the change was that we considered the *being* scale to represent a logically purer extension of the first two (working and doing) than the more heterogeneous way-of-life scale. Being includes more than doing; it includes spending time "doing nothing." The scale items pose the question of whether it is better to spend time in the presence of others or off by oneself. No mention is ever made of *doing* anything.

All 90 items in the questionnaire were phrased in a bipolar fashion and were followed by the usual nine-point response format. Within each set of six items three were worded in the "alone" direction and three in the "together" direction.

Since our previous studies had shown that the mode of the item was irrelevant insofar as change was concerned, no attempt was made this time to balance the number of items written in the cognitive, cathectic, and evaluative modes. As it turned out, most of the general activity and expressive activity items tended to be either cathectic or evaluative whereas most of the instrumental activity items were cognitive.

Since there was no opportunity for pre-testing this questionnaire, it was administered for the first time to our 68 experimental subjects. The "before" questionnaires were used to obtain item intercorrelations, which were then factor analyzed (centroid method) and rotated (quartimax method). The first of two factors extracted contained primarily general-activity and expressive-activity (leisure time) items while the second was made up almost entirely of instrumental-activity items. In both cases the four areas (neighborhood, family, factory, and school) were represented equally well. This particular structure would seem to suggest that the general-activity items were most often interpreted as referring to the use of leisure time.[1]

Since we had already decided to do separate tests on the different kinds of activity (general, instrumental, and expressive) across all four areas combined, it was clear that the factor analysis would add nothing to our understanding of the findings. For this reason we decided to ignore it and work directly with our a priori scales. We did, however, exclude from further consideration all items (seven) whose means were either less than 3.0 or greater than 7.0.

The internal consistencies and test-retest reliabilities of all scales used in the analysis are presented in Table 9–2 below.[2] All items are shown in Exhibit G at the end of this chapter.

PROCEDURE

The subjects for this experiment were 34 females and 34 males who

---

[1] A third factor was also extracted which had very few items with loadings over .40 and which did not lend itself to any obvious interpretation.

[2] These estimates were computed in the same manner as in previous studies (see Chapter 3, footnote 18).

TABLE 9–2
Internal Consistencies and Test-Retest Reliabilities

Scale	No. of Items	Internal Consistency	Test-Retest Reliability	
			ID	CL
Neighborhood-general	5	.85	.72	.73
Neighborhood-instrumental	3	.84	.66	.74
Neighborhood-expressive	6	.84	.85	.73
Family-general	6	.88	.83	.76
Family-instrumental	6	.85	.67	.69
Family-expressive	6	.90	.88	.86
Factory-general	6	.82	.52	.48
Factory-instrumental	6	.86	.54	.45
Factory-expressive	5	.92	.64	.79
School-general	5	.80	.84	.79
School-instrumental	6	.88	.75	.84
School-expressive	5	.78	.86	.82
Working	6	.81	.90	.91
Doing	6	.71	.58	.52
Being	6	.85	.77	.72
All neighborhood	14	.90	.88	.80
All family	18	.92	.86	.83
All factory	17	.87	.68	.52
All school	16	.90	.88	.86
All general	22	.90	.88	.86
All instrumental	21	.88	.66	.81
All expressive	22	.92	.93	.87

had registered for the 1963 Cornell summer school session. Subjects were recruited at registration, the student union, and in one of the dormitories. The incentive offered was the possibility of making up to $6.50 for participation in a social psychology experiment. Subjects ranged in age from 17 to 55.[3]

Students were invited to the experiment in groups of five or six. Each of the 12 groups was made up of either all males or all females. When it appeared that all had arrived who intended to, subjects were asked to fill out the "before" questionnaire.

When all had finished, the experiment was introduced in the following manner:

Before we begin, let me tell you something about the purpose of the experiment. We are interested in learning more about the way people go about solving problems under different task and incentive conditions. Of the many kinds of strategy involved, we are primarily concerned with the question of how people organize themselves in working on the task. Given the very limited nature of

[3] In working out the procedure for this experiment, we ran one pre-test group. The results are described briefly in the discussion section (pp. 241–42).

our experimental setting, we have decided to focus on one major variable—the choice between working on a task as a group or as a set of independent individuals. From day to day students in the experiment are asked to work on a variety of tasks under a number of different incentive conditions. What we want to know is how each of these variables is related to the organizational strategies employed and the degree of success attained.

Subjects were then told that they would be given three different tasks to work on (about an hour each) and that their earnings for the experiment would depend on how well they did on each. It was further explained that on each task they would have a chance to vote on whether they would do it individually or as a group. To make the choice more meaningful, several practice trials were to be run with each task before doing it for money. During the practice trials as well as the paid trials, subjects were to be given the chance to vote on which way they wanted to try it (i.e., individually or as a group). This meant that at any time, even during the paid trials, subjects could, if they wanted to, switch from one strategy to the other. In all cases the choice was limited to the two alternatives—either everyone worked together or everyone worked alone. No compromises (e.g., two three-man groups) were allowed. All decisions were to be made according to majority rule. The precise incentive rates (number of cents for each unit produced) were explained in detail prior to each of the three tasks.

Thirty-five subjects (17 females and 18 males) were assigned (at random) to the individualistic (ID) condition, and 33 (17 females and 16 males) to the collectivistic (CL) condition. The ID's were given three tasks to perform which we knew from previous testing could be done better if subjects worked independently than if they worked as a group. They, of course, were not aware of this. The CL's, on the other hand, were given three different tasks which pre-testing had indicated could be performed more efficiently if subjects worked together than if each worked on his own. It was assumed that, on the basis of their practice trials, subjects would draw the same conclusions we had. Assuming again that subjects wanted to maximize their earnings, we expected the ID's to choose to perform their tasks individually, with the CL's deciding in favor of the group.

The tasks, scoring systems and incentive rates for each condition are described below:

Tasks for ID's

1. Brainstorming. Subjects were given one minute to write down as many uses as they could think of for each of several common objects.

They were told that if they chose to work together, their score would be determined by the total number of uses given; in this case, one person was asked to do the writing for the whole group. If they chose to work individually (separate tables with no talking allowed), the total score was computed by pooling all the individual uses given and then crossing out the duplications.

Subjects were given two practice trials (several objects in each trial) and then three trials for pay. Before each trial (whether practice or pay), subjects were asked to vote on whether they wanted to do it individually or as a group. A record was kept on the board indicating how well they did on each trial. Subjects were told that if they averaged 30 or more uses per object they would receive $9.00 plus 25 cents for every use over that average. If they averaged less than 30 uses per object, they would receive a flat $6.00. The payment was to be divided equally among the group members regardless of how they chose to perform the task.[4]

2. Prediction. This was the Bales task that we had used in several previous experiments. Subjects were given several answers to a questionnaire and then asked to predict how the person filling out the questionnaire answered the remaining items. Five different questionnaires of 20 items each were used, with subjects getting 10 minutes to work on each one. Before passing out a questionnaire, the experimenter revealed the sex, age, and occupational role of the person who had previously filled it out. In scoring, five points were awarded for each prediction "on the nose" and one point for those that were "one off" (see Chapter 4, page 94). The first two questionnaires were for practice and the last three for pay. A vote was taken before each of the five questionnaires.

If the subjects chose to work as a group, they were seated around a single table and told that they must come to a joint decision on each item being predicted. The total score in this case was simply the total number of points earned by the group. If they chose instead to work individually, each subject was given a copy of the questionnaire to work on at a separate table. In this case the best individual score was taken as the score for the whole group. The rationale given was that since we were interested in the best single set of predictions we could get, it would be meaningless to sum or average the individual scores and compare this with the group performance.

---

[4] The standards given here and for all tasks described below are for a typical six-person group. Appropriate adjustments were made when less than six people showed up for the experiment.

Subjects were told that if they averaged 30 or more points per questionnaire (in the three pay trials), they would receive $9.00 plus 25 cents for each additional point above that average. If they failed to reach the standard, they would receive $6.00.

3a. Tractor. This task was used for the first two groups in the ID condition and then abandoned for a different task when it appeared that the groups were doing almost as well as the individuals.

The task involved making a number of small tractors (shown in a diagram) from a toy construction set (Rig-a-Jig). If the subjects worked as a group, they were allowed to set up an assembly line whereas if they chose to try it individually each was given his own set of parts and a separate table to work at. There were two practice trials and two trials for pay, again with voting before each trial.

Scoring was the same whether subjects chose to do the task individually or as a group. If they produced an average of ten or more tractors in the two pay sessions (13 minutes each), they received $9.00 plus 50 cents for each tractor beyond that average. If they failed to produce an average of ten tractors, they received $6.00.

Due to the difficulty in setting up an assembly line with such a small piece (and in a very short period of time), subjects did slightly better working alone than together, but the difference was not salient enough to create the impression that one strategy was clearly superior to the other. For this reason the construction task was replaced (after two groups had been run) with the one described below.

3b. Word Game. Subjects had to fill in a blank 4×4 matrix with at least six different four-letter words. The letter to be inserted in the upper left hand corner was always given in advance by the experimenter.[5] If they made six or more words, all the words in the matrix counted.[6] But if they made less than six, none of them counted. The object was to make as many matrices with six or more four-letter words as possible (time limit of four minutes). If subjects chose to work as a group, they all had to work on the same matrix at the same time (blank matrices were drawn on the blackboard). Scoring here was simply a matter of adding up all the four-letter words across matrices (the same word could not be used more than once.) If they chose to work alone, the total score was computed by adding up all the *different* four-letter words across the individuals present. There were three

---

[5] This rule was designed to keep subjects from using the same words over and over again from trial to trial.

[6] Less than six words (out of the ten possible) would have made the task too easy; more than six would have made it too hard.

practice trials and three more for pay, with voting before each trial (in one group we were forced by lack of time to omit one practice and one pay trial).

Subjects were told in advance that if they produced a total of 60 or more four-letter words (according to the rules already specified) they would receive $9.00 plus 25 cents for each word above that standard. For anything less than 60 they would receive $6.00.

Tasks for CL's

1. Memory. The experimenter read a list of 30 randomly ordered nouns and adjectives, the object being for subjects to recall on paper as many of these as they could after the list had been read. If subjects chose to work as a group, they were allowed to divide up the labor in any way they saw fit, although no suggestion to this effect was ever made by the experimenter. The group's score was determined by simply adding up the number of different words remembered (out of a total of 30). In those cases where subjects voted to work individually, scoring was done by totaling the number of different words remembered by all persons present. There were two practice sessions (two lists of 30 words in each) and three more for pay.

If subjects recalled an average of 26 or more words in the three pay trials, they received $9.00 plus 50 cents for each word above this standard. If they failed to average at least 26 words, they received $6.00 dollars.

2. Tower. The task here was to build the highest tower possible in 20 minutes using parts from the same Rig-a-Jig set described earlier. Any kind of structure was allowed, the only condition being that the tower had to stand unsupported for one minute at the end of the 20-minute period. If the subjects worked as a group they could pool their parts and work on the tower together. If they chose to work individually, each person was given his own set of parts and told not to help or ask for help from any of the others. In scoring, we simply measured the height of the tower—in the group setting the tower that everybody worked on together, in the individual setting, the highest single tower constructed. The rationale given for the latter was that we (in the hypothetical role of managers) only wanted one tower, the tallest one we could get, and that to sum or average a number of individual towers would be meaningless.

Subjects were given two practice sessions and one trial for pay. For a tower 70 or more inches high (60 for females), subjects received $9.00 plus 25 cents for every inch beyond the standard. For a tower less than the standard, they received $6.00. The same incentive was used whether subjects worked alone or together. In either case, as with all of our tasks, the money was to be divided equally among the persons present.

3. Crossword. Subjects were asked to work a set of five relatively easy crossword puzzles, the object being to complete as much of each puzzle as possible in the time allowed. When the decision was made to work as a group, subjects were allowed to set up any sort of co-operative arrangement they desired. When they chose instead to work individually, each person was given his own copy of the puzzle and taken to a separate table where he worked completely on his own. In scoring, we counted up the number of correct *letters* entered. For those cases where subjects voted to work alone, the score was computed by totaling the number of *different* correctly entered letters for all individuals combined.

Subjects were given two ten-minute practice puzzles and three ten-minute puzzles for pay, all of roughly equal difficulty (in two groups we had to omit the third trial for pay). A vote was taken prior to each trial. Each puzzle had approximately 138 letters to be filled in. If subjects averaged 125 letters or more in the three trials for pay, they were given $9.00 plus 25 cents for every letter beyond that. If they failed to reach the standard, they received $6.00.

After finishing each task, all subjects were asked to fill out a brief, three-item questionnaire on which they were given the opportunity to indicate which way they *preferred* doing the task, which way they *believed* it could be done more effectively, and which way they thought people *should* do it if given a choice. These forms, given at the end of each task, were designed to measure what we have referred to as situationally specific orientations, i.e., preferences, beliefs, and values vis-à-vis the task itself. A nine-point response format anchored at each end by the words "alone" and "together" was used for each of the three items in the questionnaire.

Throughout the experiment, in both conditions (ID and CL), a record was kept on the blackboard indicating for each trial of every task the way it was performed (alone or together) and the score achieved, as well as the amount of money earned for each task as a whole. At all times the experimenters studiously refrained from making any comments with respect to which strategy seemed to be working better.

At the end of the experiment, the amount of money won was figured out and posted on the blackboard. The "after" questionnaire was then introduced with the explanation that the same colleague who had prevailed upon the experimenter to administer it in the first place wanted it administered again, a "standard practice in the development of an instrument of this sort." Subjects were told that this was definitely not meant to be a test of consistency and that they should, to the extent possible, try to forget how they answered it the first time.

All subjects were asked back to participate in another brief experiment, unrelated to this one. At that time (from one to three weeks later) they were administered the same questionnaire for the third time. Fifty-six of our original 68 subjects returned to participate in this other experiment and take our follow-up questionnaire. After they had finished, the true purpose of the original experiment was explained to them.

RESULTS

Behavior

Choice. In terms of our theory, the first thing to be looked at is behavior. Half of our subjects (the ID's) were confronted with a task situation in which co-operation had very little or no instrumental reward value, while the others (CL's) were faced with a situation in which co-operation had very high instrumental reward value. We would expect that, given the freedom to choose whichever strategy they wanted to, the ID's would more often choose to work alone and the CL's together. That this is actually what did happen can be seen from Table 9–3, which deals exclusively with those trials in which subjects worked for money.

TABLE 9–3

Choice Behavior in the ID and CL Conditions

| | | No. of Choices in Trials for Pay | |
		Alone	Together
Experimental Condition	ID	50	1
	CL	0	40

$$\chi^2 = 83.1$$
$$p < .001$$

One group in the ID condition chose to work together once during a trial for pay. This was on the construction task which we later replaced with the word game. No group in the CL condition ever chose to work alone during a paid trial. The chi-square for Table 9–3 is 83.1, with p considerably less than .001.

Learning. It is also of interest to see how much learning (defined as a change in behavior) took place during the experiment. More specifically, to what extent did subjects change their behavior (choices) from the practice trials to the trials for pay? Also, did the amount of shifting that took place differ between ID's and CL's? With reference to the latter, we had the hunch that the more learning that took place, the more attitude change we would find, although this hypothesis was never formally incorporated into our theory. The relevant data on choice behavior are given in Table 9–4.

TABLE 9–4

Choice Behavior in Practice and Paid Trials
for ID and CL Conditions

		ID				*CL*	
		Number of Choices				*Number of Choices*	
		Alone	Together			Alone	Together
	Practice	24	15		Practice	6	30
Trial				Trial			
	Paid	50	1		Paid	0	40

$$\chi^2 = 17.43 \qquad\qquad \chi^2 = 5.19$$
$$p < .001 \qquad\qquad\quad p < .05$$

It is evident that a significant change in behavior occurred in both conditions, although more so among the ID's than the CL's. Not a single CL group voted to try the memory task alone, even in practice. And only a few CL groups bothered to try either of the other two tasks (tower and crossword puzzle) alone. It appears, then, that our CL tasks were more "obvious" than our ID tasks, the result being that the CL's did less learning than the ID's. The implications of this difference will be seen later on.

Rewards. All male groups in the CL condition and all but one in the ID condidition made the standard on all three tasks. Two female groups in the CL condition failed to reach standard on the tower, but all other female groups made it on all tasks. No group ever reached the standard on any task by doing it the "wrong" way, i.e., wrong so far as our predictions were concerned. It is clear, then, that the ID's were actually rewarded more for doing their tasks alone, while the CL's were rewarded more for doing theirs as a group. With this in

mind, it is not surprising that once the practice trials were over the
ID's, with one exception, chose to do their tasks individually, while the
CL's chose to do theirs as a group.

Task Ratings

The task rating forms (filled out by each person after each task)
were scored by numbering the nine response spaces one to nine, with
nine indicating an extreme "together" response and *one* an extreme
"alone" response. Mean ratings for each of the four ID tasks (including the tractor task which was later replaced by the word game)
and the three CL tasks were obtained by averaging the means of each
person's responses to the three items for each task. These over-all
means are shown in Table 9–5.[7]

TABLE 9–5
Ratings for ID and CL Tasks, by Individual Task*

ID Tasks	Means	CL Tasks	Means
Brainstorming	1.46	Memory	8.91
Prediction	2.26	Tower	7.91
Tractor	2.08	Crossword	7.94
Word game	1.22		

* A high mean indicates endorsement of a "together" strategy; a low mean an endorsement of an "alone" strategy.

There seems to be little doubt that ID's and CL's differed radically
in their orientations to the tasks they were asked to perform. In Table
9–5, cognitive, cathectic, and evaluative orientations were combined so
that we might do a breakdown by the specific tasks involved. In computing scores for the following table (9–6), the procedure was reversed;
tasks were combined so that we could test each orientation separately.

The results are unequivocal. The fact that the cognitive items seemed

TABLE 9–6
Ratings for ID and CL Tasks, by Orientation

Orientation	All ID Tasks	All CL Tasks	d	t	p
Cathectic (preferences)	1.74	8.25	6.51	19.9	.001
Cognitive (beliefs)	1.66	8.53	6.87	26.4	.001
Evaluative (values)	1.75	8.39	6.64	22.5	.001
Total (all orientations)	5.15	25.17	20.02	26.1	.001

[7] Significance tests on this data are deferred until Table 9–6 below.

to have done the best and the cathectic items the worst can be attributed to the larger variance of the latter, rather than to the mean differences.[8]

Attitude Change (Before versus After)

Changes by Item. To find out whether the experiment as a whole was successful or not, it is relevant to see how many items on the entire questionnaire actually changed in the predicted direction. There were originally 90 items in the questionnaire. Seven of these had extreme means (over 7.0 or under 3.0) and were thus excluded from further analysis. Of the remaining 83, the difference between changes for ID's and CL's was in the predicted direction on 77, which yields a highly significant chi-square of 59.0.

Changes by Area, Type of Activity, and Level of Abstraction. To test the predictions made for changes by area (neighborhood, family, factory, and school), type of activity (general, instrumental, and expressive), and level of abstraction (working, doing, and being), *t* tests were performed on the differences between mean changes for ID's and CL's for 22 different scales. Some of these represent combinations of others. In Table 9–7 we start by presenting mean changes, differences,

TABLE 9–7
Mean Changes and *t* Ratios for Types of Activity, by Area

Area	Type of Activity	Mean Change ID	CL	d	t	p
Neighborhood ...	general	−2.69	1.97	4.66	2.93	.01
	instrumental	−2.62	0.97	3.59	3.70	.001
	expressive	−1.83	2.09	3.92	2.55	.05
Family	general	−5.20	−0.73	4.47	2.71	.01
	instrumental	−5.57	2.55	8.12	4.14	.001
	expressive	0.03	1.45	1.42	1.08	ns
Factory	general	−6.31	6.00	12.31	5.35	.001
	instrumental	−9.97	11.36	21.33	8.53	.001
	expressive	−0.06	0.94	1.00	0.60	ns
School	general	−0.71	1.52	2.23	1.83	ns
	instrumental	−1.34	2.52	3.86	2.12	.05
	expressive	−1.28	2.24	3.52	3.53	.001

and *t* ratios for each of the four areas broken down by the three types of activity within each area. All scales were arranged so that a positive score indicates a change in the *together* direction. According to our predictions, all scores in the ID column should be negative and all

---

[8] An F-test indicates that the variance of the cathectic orientations was significantly greater ($p < .05$) than the variance of the cognitive orientations.

those in the CL column positive. In computing the difference between the two, the ID's are subtracted from the CL's which means that if our predictions are accurate, all the differences listed in column three should be positive. The same is, of course, true of the t ratios in column four.[9]

With two exceptions, all mean changes are in the expected direction. Most of the differences (9 out of 12) are significant at the .05 level or beyond. It was predicted that in each of the four areas the instrumental items would show the most change, general second most, and expressive the least. Looking at the t ratios, this is clearly the case with respect to neighborhood, family, and factory, but not school. With regards to the latter, it is possible that subjects perceived the experiment as recreation with respect to school work, since they had taken time off from their studies in order to participate in the experiment. Thus the experience might have been interpreted as expressive activity in the context of school and as instrumental activity in the other three settings (family, factory, and neighborhood).

A better test of our predictions with respect to change by type of activity can be obtained by computing mean changes for each type of activity summed across all four areas. The results are shown in Table 9–8. Once again, a positive score means change in the *together* direction.

TABLE 9–8
Mean Changes and t Ratios for Type of Activity Scales

Type of Activity	Mean Change		d	t	p
	ID	CL			
General	−14.91	8.76	23.67	6.74	.001
Instrumental	−19.51	17.39	36.90	7.99	.001
Expressive	−3.14	6.73	9.87	3.25	.01

The results from Table 9–8 help to clarify what we found in the previous table. Combining changes across areas, we see that subjects changed most on the instrumental items, second most on the general items, and least on those dealing with expressive activity, although even this last difference is significant at the .01 level.

It is possible to combine our data once again, this time by summing across types of activity to get total scores for each of the four areas. This enables us to test the prediction (based on similarity and familiarity) that factory would change the most, family the least, with

---

[9] t-tests performed on the "before" questionnaires revealed no significant differences between ID's and CL's on any of the 22 scales.

school and neighborhood falling somewhere in between. The relevant statistics are given in Table 9–9.

TABLE 9–9
Mean Changes and *t* Ratios for Area Scales

| Area | Mean Change | | *d* | *t* | *p* |
	ID	CL			
Neighborhood	−7.14	5.03	12.17	4.38	.001
Family	−10.74	3.27	14.01	4.28	.001
Factory	−16.34	18.30	34.64	7.80	.001
School	−3.34	6.27	9.61	3.44	.01

Although we were successful in producing highly significant changes in all four areas, our predictions about the relative amount of change in each were not completely borne out. As expected, factory changed the most but family did too well and school not well enough. In terms of our two basic principles (similarity and familiarity), the relatively poor showing of the school items may be attributed to the fact that they were either less similar to the experimental situation than we had assumed, or that they were more familiar to the subjects than anticipated. Without empirical measures of similarity and familiarity, there is little we can do to pinpoint the answer.

All of the data presented thus far deal with what we have called "lateral generalization." The remaining three scales in the questionnaire (working, doing, and being) were designed to test for vertical generalization, i.e. induction from the specific to the increasingly abstract or inclusive. We predicted that *working* (the least inclusive category) would change the most, *doing* (which is somewhat more inclusive) second most, and *being* the least. The results are presented in Table 9–10.

TABLE 9–10
Mean Changes and *t* Ratios for Abstract Scales

| Scale | Mean Change | | *d* | *t* | *p* |
	ID	CL			
Working	−4.82	6.45	11.27	5.61	.001
Doing	−0.94	0.73	1.67	1.09	ns
Being	−2.94	1.30	4.24	3.89	.001

While the simplest scale (working) changed as predicted, and the most abstract (being) did even better than expected, the one we thought would fall somewhere in between (doing) did not even approach significance.[10] This is especially strange in light of the fact that most of the items were taken, with little change, from the groups-in-general scale in our last individualism-collectivism experiment where they underwent very significant change. It is possible that the items in this scale (phrased in terms of "doing things" alone or together) were interpreted by subjects as referring to leisure-time activities. In our culture the phrase "doing things" often carries that connotation. This explanation is also supported by the results of our factor analysis where we found expressive activity items and general activity items loaded on the same dimension. The complicating fact remains, however, that the same scale underwent significant change in our previous individualism-collectivism experiment.

Changes by People. The number of subjects changing in the predicted direction was determined for all the summary scales shown in Tables 9–8 and 9–9 (three types of activity and four areas). The distributions are shown in Table 9–11. A plus indicates a change in the together direction and a minus a change in the alone direction. People who did not change in either direction were not included in the tables.

All seven chi-square values are significant at the .05 level or better, with four reaching the .001 level and two others the .01 level. In keeping with the *t* tests already reported, the instrumental activity items showed the largest chi-square with the general activity items next and expressive activity last. As for the area scales, factory was the most significant, school second, family third, and neighborhood fourth. This ordering is somewhat closer to our original predictions than were the mean changes presented earlier, although family and neighborhood are still reversed.

Taking the seven tables collectively, we find that approximately 76 per cent of the subjects who changed, changed in the predicted direction. If we include those few subjects who did not change in either direction, the figure drops to 74 per cent. On the whole, we can say that analyzing the data by the *number* of people who changed their attitudes yields results highly comparable to the previous analysis which was based on *how much* they changed.

An examination of all the change data presented thus far reveals that the ID's changed slightly more than the CL's, although this difference is within the range of chance expectancies.

---

[10] The *working* scale (Table 9–10) is somewhat similar to the *all-instrumental* scale (Table 9–8) in that both deal with instrumental activity across a variety of task situations. It is not at all surprising, then, that the two scales yielded results which were significant to roughly the same degree.

TABLE 9–11
Changes by People for Seven Summary Scales*

General Activity	−	+
ID	30	5
CL	11	22

$\chi^2 = 17.36$
$p < .001$

Instrumental Activity	−	+
ID	27	7
CL	2	31

$\chi^2 = 33.87$
$p < .001$

Expressive Activity	−	+
ID	23	11
CL	10	23

$\chi^2 = 8.02$
$p < .01$

Neighborhood	−	+
ID	24	8
CL	14	18

$\chi^2 = 5.26$
$p < .05$

Family	−	+
ID	27	8
CL	13	19

$\chi^2 = 7.79$
$p < .01$

Factory	−	+
ID	30	4
CL	4	26

$\chi^2 = 32.74$
$p < .001$

School	−	+
ID	24	10
CL	6	27

$\chi^2 = 16.63$
$p < .001$

* A plus indicates change in the together (collectivistic) direction.

Sex Differences. When the data in Table 9–11 (change by people) were broken down by sex, no significant differences were found. The experiment worked equally well for males and females.

Attitude Change (Before versus Follow-Up)

All of our 68 subjects were invited to return approximately one week after the final session was run. Fifty-six of them did and were administered the original questionnaire a third time. Since the experiment itself had run for two weeks, the interval between second and third administrations ranged from one to three weeks, the average lapse being close to 14 days. For these 56 subjects, we computed another whole set of statistics based this time on differences between the "before" and "follow-up" questionnaires. The object, of course, was to see what would happen to the attitude changes induced in the experiment after subjects had returned to their normal routines. To facilitate comparison with the before-after findings, the before-follow-up data are presented in exactly the same fashion.

Changes by Item. Out of 83 items on the questionnaire (seven again having been excluded because of extreme means), 79 showed an ID-CL mean change difference in the predicted direction. This yields a chi-square of 66.0 which is not only highly significant but slightly better than what we found for the before-after data where 77 out of 83 items worked as expected.

Changes by Area, Type of Activity, and Level of Abstraction. We start once again, by presenting mean changes, differences, and *t* ratios for each of the three types of activity within each of the four different areas. The results are shown in Table 9–12 below.

TABLE 9–12
Mean Changes and *t* Ratios for Types of Activity, by Area
(Before versus Follow-up)

Area	Type of Activity	Mean Change		d	t	p
		ID	CL			
Neighborhood ...	general	−2.21	0.11	2.32	1.53	ns
	instrumental	−2.89	0.96	3.85	3.85	.001
	expressive	−3.00	−0.57	2.43	1.32	ns
Family	general	−6.93	−2.14	4.79	2.15	.05
	instrumental	−5.64	0.46	6.10	2.74	.01
	expressive	−2.32	−1.32	1.00	0.51	ns
Factory	general	−5.39	2.86	8.25	2.92	.01
	instrumental	−5.68	10.96	16.64	5.78	.001
	expressive	−1.39	1.00	2.39	1.10	ns
School	general	−1.25	0.57	1.82	1.31	ns
	instrumental	−2.86	2.64	5.50	2.74	.01
	expressive	−1.93	1.96	3.89	2.78	.01

All of the ID-CL differences (column three) are again positive, indicating change in the expected direction. Seven of the 12 *t* ratios are significant at the .05 level or beyond, compared to nine out of 12 in the before-after tests. Once more the instrumental activity scales showed the greatest change except in the school area, although the *t* for the instrumental activity here is practically identical with the *t* for expressive activity, which was not the case previously.

There is one important difference between Table 9–12 and its before-after equivalent (Table 9–7) which may not be obvious at first glance. While the mean changes for the ID's are as large or larger than those we found in the before-after data, the mean changes for the CL's are in most cases considerably smaller. It appears that the ID's were unaffected by the lapse of time between second and third administrations of the questionnaire, retaining as they did roughly all the change induced at the time of the experiment. The CL's, although showing about as much change as the ID's right after the experiment, had regressed noticeably by the time the follow-up questionnaire was administered two weeks later. More will be said about this shortly.

In Table 9–13 we present summary data for each of the three types of activity. As before, the scores were computed by summing across the four different areas involved.

TABLE 9–13
Mean Changes and *t* Ratios for Type of Activity Scales
(Before versus Follow-up)

Type of Activity	Mean Change		d	t	p
	ID	CL			
General	−15.79	1.39	17.18	3.22	.01
Instrumental	−17.07	15.04	32.11	6.27	.001
Expressive	−8.64	1.07	9.71	2.05	.05

The same picture emerges here that we found in comparing scores from the first and second administrations of the questionnaire. Two weeks after the experiment, the instrumental items continued to show the most change with general second and expressive third. All had suffered some loss, however, due mainly to regression on the part of the CL's.

Data for the four area scales, computed by summing the three types of activity within each area, are given in Table 9–14. Three of the four *t* ratios (neighborhood, family, and factory) show signs of considerable attrition, while the fourth (school) has actually improved slightly. With this latter change, the findings approximate our original prediction, namely that factory would change the most, family the least, with school and neighborhood falling somewhere in between. As before, however, there is very little difference between the two low similarity areas, neighborhood and family.

Coming back to vertical generalization once again, we present data for our final three scales measuring different levels of abstraction (see

TABLE 9–14
Mean Changes and *t* Ratios for Area Scales
(Before versus Follow-up)

| Area | Mean Change | | *d* | *t* | *p* |
	ID	CL			
Neighborhood	−8.11	0.50	8.61	2.64	.05
Family	−14.89	−3.00	11.89	2.57	.05
Factory	−12.46	14.82	27.28	4.99	.001
School	−6.04	5.18	11.22	3.72	.001

Table 9–15). The pattern here is somewhat different from what we have seen thus far. The CL's, instead of regressing sharply, actually improved slightly, with the result that the middle scale (doing) which had shown nothing in the before-after analysis (see Table 9–10) easily reached significance at the .05 level.

TABLE 9–15
Mean Changes and *t* Ratios for Abstract Scales
(Before versus Follow-up)

| Scale | Mean Change | | *d* | *t* | *p* |
	ID	CL			
Working	−4.75	7.14	11.89	5.86	.001
Doing	−1.21	2.82	4.03	2.44	.05
Being	−2.96	1.32	4.28	2.47	.05

Changes by People. Having looked at the relevant mean changes, we turn to an analysis of the data in terms of the number of subjects who changed in the predicted direction. Chi-squares for each of the seven summary tables (three types of activity and four areas) are given in Table 9–16, where a plus indicates a change in the together direction and a minus a change in the alone direction.

According to Table 9–16, three of our summary scales (expressive activity, neighborhood, and family) are no longer significant, due to regression on the part of the CL's. The *ordering* of the chi-squares, however, is exactly what we had predicted. Among the type of activity scales, instrumental underwent the greatest change and expressive the least. Among the four area scales, factory did the best, family the worst, with school and neighborhood falling in between.

The relative superiority of the ID's over the CL's in retaining their new attitudes during the interim between experiment and follow-up is both quite striking and consistent, no matter which way the analysis is

TABLE 9–16
Changes by People for Seven Summary Scales
(Before versus Follow-up)

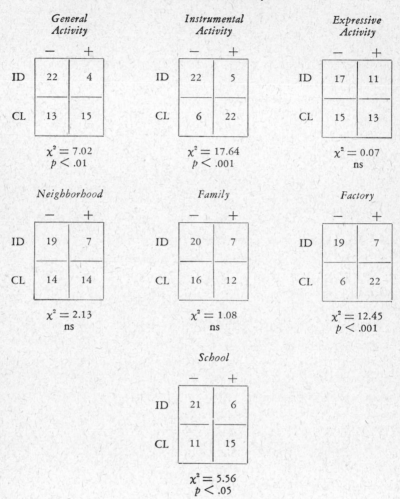

General Activity	−	+
ID	22	4
CL	13	15

$$x^2 = 7.02$$
$$p < .01$$

Instrumental Activity	−	+
ID	22	5
CL	6	22

$$x^2 = 17.64$$
$$p < .001$$

Expressive Activity	−	+
ID	17	11
CL	15	13

$$x^2 = 0.07$$
$$ns$$

Neighborhood	−	+
ID	19	7
CL	14	14

$$x^2 = 2.13$$
$$ns$$

Family	−	+
ID	20	7
CL	16	12

$$x^2 = 1.08$$
$$ns$$

Factory	−	+
ID	19	7
CL	6	22

$$x^2 = 12.45$$
$$p < .001$$

School	−	+
ID	21	6
CL	11	15

$$x^2 = 5.56$$
$$p < .05$$

done. The most likely explanation for this difference involves the fact that, during the experiment itself, the ID's experienced greater learning than did the CL's (see Table 9–4). It was not at all obvious to subjects that the ID tasks (especially brainstorming and the Bales prediction) could be done better alone than together. We knew they could but the subjects had to learn for themselves by experimenting on their own (i.e., trying each task both ways before doing it for pay). The three CL tasks (memory, tower, and crossword), on the other hand, lent themselves more obviously to a co-operative arrangement and thus evoked considerably less experimenting on the part of subjects assigned to that condition.

According to the before-after tests, ID's and CL's changed their attitudes to approximately the same extent, ID's having a very slight advantage. This suggests that the simple act of performing a task successfully (either alone or together) is enough to produce some attitude generalization to other areas and levels of abstraction. This is apparently the case regardless of how much learning actually takes place. In terms of our follow-up data, however, it appears that attitude change based simply on "participation," with minimal learning, is short-lived. Subjects in the CL condition performed most of their tasks as a group, both in the practice trials and the trials for pay. In doing so, they learned very little. They were, however, consistently rewarded for this behavior, which probably had the effect of making more salient to them the virtues of working together as a group. As a result, they showed considerable attitude change just after the experiment (before versus after). Two weeks later, when the experience was no longer as salient to them, they regressed to their original attitudes, particularly in those areas (neighborhood and family) furthest removed from the experiment itself. For the ID's, on the other hand, the laboratory experience was still highly salient two weeks after the experiment had been run, precisely because of the early learning involved.

This is, of course, a post hoc explanation and cannot be verified without further experimentation. A general finding of this type would have many implications for attitude change as a whole as well as our own theory in particular.[11]

To facilitate comparisons of the two sets of data (before-after and before-follow-up), a summary table is shown below (Table 9–17) giving t ratios for each of the 22 tests conducted. It is of interest to note that two of the four t ratios for *instrumental activity* within an area actually increased in the follow-up study, as did the t for our abstract

---

[11] There are two alternative explanations for the fact that the ID's retained their new attitudes longer than the CL's. First it is possible that the before-after changes for the 56 subjects who came back for the follow-up were different from the 12 who did not come back. To check on this possibility, we computed the before-after changes for just those 56 subjects who were in our follow-up sample. The results were almost identical to those already reported for the whole group of 68. The same scales produced significant differences and the two groups (ID's and CL's) changed approximately the same amount.

A second possibility is that the differences in retention were due to a tendency for all subjects to become more individualistic as a result of experiences outside of the laboratory. If all students in the university were (for some unknown reason) becoming more individualistic, this would have had the effect of pushing our ID's even more in the individualistic direction while neutralizing the collectivistic attitudes of our CL's. Without a control group, we have no way of checking on this possibility.

TABLE 9–17

t Ratios for All Scales Comparing Before-After with Before-Follow-up

Scale	t Ratio for Difference between ID and CL Changes	
	Before-After	Before–Follow-up
Neighborhood-general	2.93†	1.53
Neighborhood-instrumental	3.70‡	3.85‡
Neighborhood-expressive	2.55*	1.32
Family-general	2.71†	2.15*
Family-instrumental	4.14‡	2.74†
Family-expressive	1.08	0.51
Factory-general	5.35‡	2.92†
Factory-instrumental	8.53‡	5.78‡
Factory-expressive	0.60	1.10
School-general	1.83	1.31
School-instrumental	2.13*	2.74†
School-expressive	3.53‡	2.78†
All general	6.74‡	3.22†
All instrumental	7.99‡	6.27‡
All expressive	3.25†	2.05*
All neighborhood	4.38‡	2.64*
All family	4.28‡	2.57*
All factory	7.80‡	4.99‡
All school	3.44†	3.72‡
Working	5.61‡	5.86‡
Doing	1.09	2.44*
Being	3.89‡	2.47*

* $p < .05.$
† $p < .01.$
‡ $p < .001.$

working scale. On the other hand, all four *t* ratios for general activity and three out of four for expressive activity decreased. This suggests that similarity of task content may be responsible for both the original strength and the persistence of generalization from one situation to another.

DISCUSSION

In designing this final experiment, it was our desire to incorporate all of the major elements of our theory in a single study and to extend our understanding of the generalizing process. The results indicate that we were successful in producing significant differences in behavior, situationally specific orientations, and attitude change. By themselves, the early findings on behavior and specific orientations are of little interest. They can very easily be explained in terms of common sense. They are of importance primarily in that they represent the most basic responses to the task environment, reponses which can and do get generalized far beyond the immediate confines of the laboratory setting.

Without the overwhelmingly significant differences observed at this basic, specific level, it is unlikely that lateral and vertical generalization would have carried as far as they did.

While we have learned something more about the workings of lateral generalization, many questions remain unanswered. There would seem to be little doubt that similarity is important in accounting for which attitudes will be affected by the generalizing process. Our efforts to extend the analysis to attitudes dealing with different types of activity within each of the four areas met with considerable success in this regard. There is still some doubt however, as to the role of familiarity in lateral generalization. Our attempt to test for the relative importance of similarity and familiarity was severely limited by the arbitrary nature of the way in which we classified areas as more or less similar and familiar. Future studies would do well to provide a precise, empirical measure of each. With respect to familiarity, for example, subjects could be asked to indicate after each item on the questionnaire how familiar they are with the content of the statement, or better yet, how certain they are about their response to it.

In pre-testing for this experiment, we came across something of considerable interest to theory building in this area. In our first session subjects were paid at the flat rate of five dollars for the afternoon's work, regardless of how well or poorly they did. No standard was given indicating what constituted a successful performance. They were simply told to perform each task as well as they possibly could. Interestingly enough, we found considerable reluctance on the part of the subjects (females in this case) to engage in trial-and-error behavior, although they were given the same opportunity to do so as those in the actual experiment. This was most surprising with respect to one of the construction tasks which they insisted on doing alone even though common sense dictated that it could be done more efficiently as a group. When asked about this "irrational" behavior afterwards, subjects reported that they were having more fun doing it that way. It appears that with no standard of success and no *external* incentive for performance, subjects were actually making their choices according to their "intrinsic preferences," rather than a more universalistic criterion of efficiency.

This implies that in those situations where no external rewards are at stake (e.g., money), people will be guided in their behavioral choices primarily by the preferences, beliefs, and values which they bring to the situation. Without the external incentive, they may not be willing to try something which conflicts with these previously determined orientations. For this reason, they will be relatively impervious to change. Our theory assumes that people will be sensitive to rewards inherent in the situation. Task behavior must have *instrumental* reward value before it can lead to attitude change. Where the individual is guided primarily by the preferences, beliefs, and values which he brings to the situation, rather than a concern with achieving those rewards which are contingent upon successful performance of the task, there is no reason to expect him to change his attitudes. The more interested he is in achieving task rewards, the more likely it is that he will engage in behavior which is instrumental to task success. The more his behavior is guided by the exigencies of the situation itself, the more likely it is that attitude change will take place.

Several other features of the experiment are worth noting at this time. It is of interest to point out that revising the order of items on the questionnaire (with the ones least likely to change coming first) had no noticeable effect on the results. The possibility had suggested itself that when the most "obvious" scales come first, the respondent tends to develop a set which gets generalized to the other less obvious scales further on in the questionnaire. The fact that some of the scales in the middle of our questionnaire (e.g., factory) changed far more than those appearing at the beginning (neighborhood and family) leads us to believe that this is not an important consideration.

In response to another criticism, we went out of our way in this experiment to disassociate the attitude questionnaire from the experiment proper. The questionnaire was introduced, in all three administrations, as part of someone else's research, unrelated to the experiment at hand. Comparing the results of this study to those which came out of the last individualism-collectivism study, where no attempt at disassociation was made, we are again led to believe that the modification was of no consequence.

Certainly one of the most significant features of this present study was the finding that attitude changes induced during the experiment itself persisted (with some loss) up to three weeks later. In the before-after analysis, 18 out of 22 t tests reached the .05 level of significance while in the follow-up 17 of the 22 were still significant at that level, though many of the actual t's were smaller. Those scales with the smaller t's to begin with suffered more attrition than those which showed highly significant change immediately after the experiment. There was little shifting with respect to the rank order of change from scale to scale; if anything, however, the order of success more closely resembled our predictions in the follow-up than it did earlier.

On the basis of a theory which links experience to attitudes, we would expect changes induced in one isolated setting to "wear off" rather quickly in the face of subsequent and potentially conflicting experiences. In general, the more often the original experience is repeated, the more enduring should be its consequences. Given the isolated nature of our laboratory setting, it is of some interest that the attitude changes evoked there were still in evidence some two weeks later.

CONCLUSIONS

There are a number of reasons for feeling good about this final experiment. For one thing, our methodological changes (e.g., switching the order of items on the questionnaire) proved to have no adverse effect on the results. More importantly, most of the changes induced at the time of the experiment were still in effect more than two weeks later. This suggests that the changes induced represent something more than a specific, temporary reaction to the experimental situation. Perhaps the most significant contribution of this final study was to clarify some of the principles involved in the process of generalization. Predictions made on the basis of similarity, familiarity, and specificity received substantial support from the data, indicating that attitude generalization proceeds, not randomly, but according to a definite pattern.

In this final study we attempted the most complete and detailed test of our theory so far. The overwhelming majority of the findings, from behavior through situationally specific orientations all the way to abstract beliefs, values, and preferences, confirmed the predictions made on the basis of our theory. There can be no doubt, in the laboratory at least, that task experience operates as an important determinant of an individual's system of attitudes. Whether or not these findings will be supported by studies conducted outside the laboratory is another matter. The whole question of generality is discussed at some length in the next chapter. An attempt is also made there to indicate some of the research strategies that might be appropriate for testing the theory in other settings.

EXHIBIT G

NEIGHBORHOOD—GENERAL*

1. I would rather live in a neighborhood in which people did things together than one in which everybody went his own way. (+)

---

* Throughout the questionnaire, a (+) indicates that the item was weighted in the collectivistic direction, a (—) that it was weighted in the individualistic direction.

2. People should spend more time alone and less time with their neighbors. (—)
3. I would prefer a closely knit neighborhood in which members co-operated in many different ways to one in which individuals did things pretty much on their own. (+)
4. I would rather live in a neighborhood in which everybody left everyone else alone than in one in which people were always doing things together. (—)
5. People living in the same neighborhood should do things together rather than leaving each person to act independently of the others. (+)

NEIGHBORHOOD—INSTRUMENTAL

1. I would rather live in a neighborhood in which problems get solved primarily through the efforts of individuals working independently of one another than one in which most problems were approached through co-operative action. (—)
2. Neighborhood problems are best solved when each person does what he can on his own rather than everybody trying to work together on the same problem. (—)
3. The best way to solve neighborhood problems is for everybody to work together as a team rather than having each individual try to do what he can by himself. (+)

NEIGHBORHOOD—EXPRESSIVE

1. People should spend more of their leisure time by themselves and less time with their neighbors. (—)
2. I would prefer to live in a neighborhood in which people spent a good deal of their free time with each other rather than one in which everybody went his own way. (+)
3. Recreational activities are apt to be more enjoyable in the company of neighbors than they are alone. (+)
4. The best neighborhoods to live in are those where people spend most of their leisure time by themselves rather than in neighborhood activities. (—)
5. Neighborhoods in which everybody is expected to spend his leisure time alone are preferable to those in which people are expected to do things together. (—)
6. Neighbors should try to get to know each other through joint leisure-time activities rather than leaving everyone to go his own way. (+)

FAMILY—GENERAL

1. Family members should be encouraged to engage in more joint family activities and fewer independent pursuits. (+)
2. I would prefer a closely knit family in which members co-operated in many different ways to one in which individuals did things pretty much on their own. (+)
3. Family members should spend more time together and less time alone. (+)
4. I would prefer to be in a family in which independent activity was emphasized over group activity. (—)

5. Family members should feel free to pursue their own independent activities even if this means that the family rarely does anything as a whole. (—)
6. The most desirable kind of family life is that in which individual members are encouraged to do things by themselves rather than in conjunction with the other members of the family. (—)

FAMILY—INSTRUMENTAL

1. Family chores can be accomplished most efficiently by having each person work by himself rather than having everyone work together as a team. (—)
2. I prefer the kind of family in which household tasks get solved primarily through the efforts of individuals working independently of one another rather than one in which most tasks are approached through co-operative action. (—)
3. Whenever possible, family members should work on household chores together rather than leaving it up to each individual to do something on his own. (+)
4. In working on jobs around the house, a joint effort involving the whole family is usually more effective than a number of individual efforts carried out independently of each other. (+)
5. Family tasks are best solved when each person does what he can on his own instead of having everyone work together on the same problem at the same time. (—)
6. The families that are most effective in achieving desired goals are those in which individuals co-operate closely with each other instead of each one contributing something on his own. (+)

FAMILY—EXPRESSIVE

1. I would rather be part of a family in which everyone participated jointly in leisure-time activities than one in which each person went his own way. (+)
2. Families should spend as much of their free time together as possible rather than each person doing something on his own. (+)
3. People should spend more of their leisure time by themselves and less time with other family members. (—)
4. The best families are those in which individuals spend most of their free time in independent pursuits rather than in activities involving the family as a whole. (—)
5. I would like to belong to a family in which everyone felt free to engage in recreational activities independently of the others and little emphasis was placed on doing things together. (—)
6. Family members should be encouraged to spend more of their leisure time together and less of it off by themselves. (+)

FACTORY—GENERAL

1. I would rather work in a factory where people did many things together than one in which everybody went his own way. (+)
2. I would prefer a closely knit factory group in which members co-operated in many different ways to one in which individuals did things pretty much on their own. (+)

3. People who work in factories should try to keep their own activities as separate as possible from those of other workers. (—)
4. The factory worker who participates in extensive group activities with his fellow workers will usually be happier than the worker who keeps pretty much to himself. (+)
5. Factory workers should be encouraged to do things on their own rather than in conjunction with other people in the shop. (—)
6. In general, it would be better if factory workers spent more time alone and less time together. (—)

FACTORY—INSTRUMENTAL

1. In general, factory jobs are best accomplished by organizing workers into teams rather than having each person do his job independently of the others. (+)
2. In allocating factory work, it is usually more efficient to give each person a task and let him work alone rather than assigning a group of people to work on the same task together. (—)
3. In factory jobs it is best if workers are assigned to work on tasks co-operatively rather than having each person work on a task by himself. (+)
4. As far as possible, factories should be organized so that employees work independently of one another rather than co-operatively as members of a work group. (—)
5. If I were to work in a factory, I would rather be part of a work team than do something entirely on my own. (+)
6. If I were to take a factory job, I would rather be assigned a task I could do by myself than one which involved co-operating closely with other workers. (—)

FACTORY—EXPRESSIVE

1. People who work in the same plant should get together with each other in their leisure time as much as possible instead of leaving everyone to do things on his own. (+)
2. I would rather work in a factory where everyone went his own way after work than one in which people were expected to spend time doing things together. (—)
3. Workers should try to spend most of their leisure time doing things on their own rather than in the company of their fellow workers. (—)
4. Factory workers should be encouraged to get together in their spare time instead of doing things independently of each other. (+)
5. It would be desirable to have factory workers spend more of their leisure time with each other and less of it in independent pursuits. (+)

SCHOOL—GENERAL

1. In general, students should try to do things in conjunction with other students rather than pursuing activities completely on their own. (+)
2. Students should spend more time alone and less time with each other. (—)
3. The kind of student life I prefer is the independent life where contacts with other students are kept to a minimum. (—)

4. I would rather be part of a student body in which members co-operated in many different ways than one in which individuals did things pretty much on their own. (+)
5. Students should get together with their fellow students as often as possible instead of leaving each individual to go his own way. (+)

SCHOOL—INSTRUMENTAL

1. In the long run, students tend to learn more if they study together than if they study alone. (+)
2. I would rather discuss my school work with friends and classmates than trying to do it all by myself. (+)
3. When there is homework to be done, it is a lot more enjoyable to get together with some other people in the course than trying to do it completely on your own. (+)
4. In learning course materials, it is more efficient to study by yourself than to work together with other students. (—)
5. A student is better off doing his homework on his own without help from anyone else. (—)
6. Homework should be done independently rather than in groups. (—)

SCHOOL—EXPRESSIVE

1. Students should be encouraged to spend more of their leisure time in independent activities and less of it in formal or informal group affairs. (—)
2. Students will enjoy themselves more in their leisure time if they spend their time together than if they go off on their own. (+)
3. In general, I would rather spend my free time at school by myself than together with my fellow students. (—)
4. Ideally, students should spend most of their leisure time doing things together rather than going off by themselves. (+)
5. Students should be as independent as possible in the exercise of leisure time and minimize their participation in group affairs. (—)

BEING

1. For the most part, I would rather be by myself than with other people. (—)
2. People should spend more time alone and less time with others. (—)
3. In the ideal life, people would spend most of their time together rather than off by themselves. (+)
4. The greatest satisfactions in life are more apt to come from being with other people than from being alone. (+)
5. There are more pleasures to be gained from being by yourself than from being with other people. (—)
6. Life is more enjoyable when spent in the presence of others than when spent by oneself. (+)

WORKING

1. Ordinarily I would rather work with others than work alone. (+)
2. Given the choice, I would rather take on a task where I could work alone than one where I would have to work in a group with other people. (—)

3. People tend to work more efficiently when they are alone than when they are part of a group. (—)
4. Generally speaking, it has been found that people working together in groups are more productive than individuals working alone. (+)
5. People should be encouraged to work alone rather than co-operating as members of a single group. (—)
6. Given the choice, people should work together rather than independently of one another. (+)

DOING

1. In general, I would rather do things by myself than with other people. (—)
2. In most cases, I would rather do something as part of a group than do it by myself. (+)
3. People should do more things alone and fewer things with others. (—)
4. Whenever possible, people should do things as part of a group rather than doing them alone. (+)
5. In general, it is more rewarding to do things with others than to do them on your own. (+)
6. It is more desirable for people to plan their activities individually than in conjunction with others. (—)

CHAPTER 10

Conclusion

SEVEN STUDIES have now been reported. Each constitutes a separate chapter in a research narrative that began with a classroom experiment in Wisconsin and ended three years later in a small-groups laboratory at Cornell. In moving from one study to the next we have added propositions to our theory, made changes in our methodology, and reported a good many statistically significant findings. In view of the many innovations and facts presented along the way, it is possible that we have succeeded in obscuring the basic path along which our efforts have been directed. It is with this in mind that we have decided to begin this final chapter with a brief review of experimental results in terms of the progress made and the reasons behind it. The remainder of the chapter is taken up with an appraisal of the results in terms of their *generality* and a discussion of appropriate strategy for future research in this area.

REVIEW AND ANALYSIS OF EXPERIMENTAL RESULTS

In five of the seven studies reported, some version of either individualism-collectivism or equalitarianism-authoritarianism was taken as the major dependent variable. It is these five studies in particular that give us the clearest picture of how our theory has evolved. The other two (theism and achievement) are of interest here primarily in that they provide important evidence with respect to the generality of our theory across a variety of attitude dimensions. While each contributes something to our confidence in the assumptions we have made, neither adds substantially to the propositional content of the theory.

The five studies referred to yielded results ranging all the way from those of a borderline nature to those of unequivocal significance. As one might expect, the least significant results came in the beginning, the most significant ones later on.

Our first experiment (Wisconsin) was more complex than any of the others in that it was designed to test the effects of four different situational variables (task, incentive, size, and homogeneity) on two different attitude dimensions (individualism and equalitarianism). Yet it was simpler than any of the studies that followed in that no attempt was made to distinguish different areas or levels of lateral and vertical generalization. Only one scale was used for each dimension and all items were phrased in a highly abstract manner.

This was the only field experiment in the series. While the results at the behavioral level were quite marked, there were no attitude changes significant at the .01 level, and very few that made it as far as the .05 level. This is a far cry from our best laboratory studies where p values of .01 and .001 were quite common. The difference would appear to lie in (1) the content of the attitude questionnaires, and (2) the amount of control exerted by the experimenter. The only scales used at Wisconsin were designed to measure individualism and equalitarianism in the abstract. We know from later studies, of course, that it is the most abstract scales that are the hardest to change.

More importantly, the situation (a college classroom) did not lend itself to the same kind of control which the experimenter was free to impose in the laboratory. For one thing, subjects were not asked to go through any formal "trial-and-error" sequence, in which the task was approached first one way, then another, etc. What experimenting they did was informal and relatively unstructured. It was, moreover, only partially related to the issues raised in the individualism and equalitarianism questionnaires. This is quite unlike our other studies where the task experience was deliberately designed to parallel the content of the questionnaires (or vice versa). In most of the laboratory experiments the contrast between "alone" and "together" was very salient on *both* the task and attitude levels. This very likely intensified the impact of one on the other. In the Wisconsin experiment, subjects were never told to try the task first alone and then together; they were not even given the opportunity to do so if they wished; in fact, no mention was ever made of the alone-together distinction other than in the questionnaire. Although the subjects themselves discussed the problem of co-operation and its implications for success and failure, the experimenters never structured the problem for them the way they did for subjects in the laboratory experiments. Although we cannot be sure, we suspect that this was the major reason why the Wisconsin findings fell so far short of the others.

There are other factors that might be mentioned. There is, for example, the duration of the experiment, more specifically the fact that subjects met for only 50 minutes a week for 13 successive weeks. Although most of the laboratory experiments lasted only four hours, the total experience was concentrated in a single afternoon or evening. We now have reason to believe that four hours in one setting constitutes a more intense, salient, and memorable experience than 13 hours spread over a period of three months. It is quite possible that in the Wisconsin experiment those 13 hours got lost in the shuffle of competing events and for this reason lacked the salience required to produce significant attitude change.

We should also consider the fact that three different instructors participated in the Wisconsin experiment. Despite our best efforts to hold this feature of the situation constant, it is evident from our tape recordings that instructors varied widely in how much they talked, what they talked about, how much help they provided and so on. Any one of these differences could have contaminated the results.

Our second experiment (Chapter 4) was different from the first in many ways. Two of these differences stand out above the rest. In the first place, it was conducted in the laboratory with paid volunteers, and secondly, it introduced the concept of lateral generalization.

The importance of the laboratory has already been alluded to in our discussion of what went wrong with the Wisconsin experiment. In a word, the laboratory means control. In this second study, it meant control over the process by which subjects go about learning that with a given task certain modes of organization have greater instrumental reward value than others. Subjects were not only told which strategies to try (alone and together), but in which order to try them. So as to leave no room for error, the experimenter manipulated the performance scores in such a way as to guarantee that each subject would *always* do better when performing the task one way or the other. Actually, the same task was used for both the ID's (those we hoped to make more individualistic) and the CL's (those we tried to make more collectivistic). The only real difference was in the rewards, hence the importance of control.

The second major innovation in this second experiment involved the attitude questionnaire. An attempt was made to measure a variety of task areas, ranging all the way from doing homework in college to worshipping in church. Little was done on vertical generalization other than including many of the items from the Wisconsin individualism questionnaire.

It appears (from where we stand now) that we spent too much time working on our task controls and not enough working on the reliability of our new attitude scales. We were equally delinquent, moreover, in failing to standardize the conditions under which our before and after measures were administered. Both failings contributed heavily to the excessive amount of variation in our before-after change scores. This very likely contributed to the fact that only a few of the scales (4 out of 13) showed changes which were statistically significant.

In the third experiment (Chapter 5), an attempt was made to improve the reliability of our questionnaire by (1) writing items in bipolar form in order to increase internal consistency, and (2) administering the scales right before and right after the experiment in order to increase the test-retest reliability. The major change, of course, was in the dimension studied. In moving from individualism-collectivism to equalitarianism-authoritarianism, we hoped to learn something about the generality of our theory. At the task level there were few innovations beyond the fact that even more control was introduced through the use of an accomplice, a change that was dictated by the shift from an alone versus together strategy to one in which subjects performed alternately with and without a leader.

At the attitudinal level we gave operational expression to a more sophisticated conception of vertical generalization by writing items at three different levels of abstraction (discussion groups, groups in general, and equality in general), rather than the one level used in both previous studies. A variety of relatively specific items were also included for the purpose of testing lateral generalization. Surprisingly enough, it was the vertical items that worked best. As a matter of fact, the changes on discussion groups and groups in general (both significant at the .001 level) were the first unequivocally significant changes that we found. While this development was encouraging, to say the least, we remained frustrated by the interesting but inconclusive findings at the specific (lateral) level (politics was the only one out of four areas to show significant change). Although we did not know it at the time, a clean sweep of all task areas was to come only after a major innovation at the task level.

The next experiment (Chapter 6) was probably our most complete success. In the attitude questionnaire we included items dealing with small work groups, groups in general, way of life (these three to measure vertical generalization), family, and fraternity (the last two to measure lateral generalization). Four of the five scales yielded changes significant at the .001 level, the fifth (fraternity) reaching the .01 level. On the three vertical scales, the ordering of changes was just as predicted, with small work groups (the least-abstract scale) changing the most, groups in general second most, and way of life the least (but still at the .001 level).

There could be no doubt now that we were on the right track. In a period of less than four hours and without a single verbal reference to family, fraternity, way of life, or any of the other areas measured, we succeeded in changing a wide variety of attitudes ranging from specific beliefs about the most effective way to organize a work group to abstract values concerning the relationship between the individual and society. This evidence was taken to mean that task experience is capable of exerting a very powerful influence on all sorts of beliefs, values, and preferences which, to the casual observer, appear to be only remotely related to the task itself.

Although it is impossible to say with certainty just why this experiment was so much more successful than those which preceded it, there is little doubt in our own minds that the critical difference lay in the number of tasks used. In the two previous laboratory experiments, subjects worked on the same problem (Bales prediction task) over and over again. In this study, they were exposed to four different tasks, all of which lent themselves to the same organizational strategy (i.e., working alone or working together). Even though the total amount of time spent was no greater than previously, it is quite understandable that being rewarded for the same behavior in a *variety* of tasks should make it easier for a subject to generalize beyond the confines of the experiment itself.

In the next two experiments (theism and achievement) we made an attempt to learn more about the generality of our thesis across attitude dimensions. While both studies yielded findings which should be of considerable interest to the student of attitudes, neither produced results of unequivocal significance. The religion study in particular left much to be desired. While it is true that the two treatment groups (cooperative and competitive) differed significantly ($p < .01$) in the way their religious beliefs changed, we find it difficult to draw any definite conclusions in view of the fact that (1) the Wisconsin experiment produced results which ran in exactly the opposite direction and (2) the changes were significant only for the males. More studies are needed here before we can be certain of what is really happening.

While the theism results were in keeping with our general interest in the relationship between task experience and attitudes, they could not be explained in terms of the specific propositions employed in previous studies, namely those dealing with reinforcement and generalization. The same was true for most of the results in the achievement study.

With the exception of the effort-luck changes which were predicted directly from the theory, the results were explained in terms of the effect of task success on self-confidence. As in the religion study, no attempt was made to distinguish different areas or levels of lateral and vertical generalization. All items were written at a very abstract level, the idea being to cover a variety of achievement-related themes rather than any one dimension in depth.

The achievement study was more of a hypothesis-seeking endeavor than any of the others and should be judged in this light. Although relatively few significant findings emerged, enough happened to indicate that the experience of failing or succeeding at a task is causally related to a variety of beliefs and values involving the achievement theme.

In our final experiment, we returned to the main body of our theory as this had developed over the first four studies. With the very convincing results of Chapter 6 (the last ID-CL study) behind us, we felt that the time had come to relax our controls somewhat and see if we could produce comparable changes in a less contrived setting. The major innovation involved giving subjects the freedom to choose which way they wanted to perform each task, instead of having the experimenter lead them through a formalized sequence in which they first worked independently, then as a group, etc. Because we also made many changes in the attitude questionnaire, it is difficult to say whether the observed changes are any more or less significant than those found in the previous ID-CL study. In view of the fact that 18 of the 22 (before-after) scale changes were significant at the .05 level or better, however, we feel little hesitation in concluding that, if relaxing controls had any effect, it was of minor consequence.

This is important because it suggests that our previous results were not dependent on the very rigid controls employed at that time. Specifically, it indicates that a formalized "trial-and-error" sequence in which one organizational strategy is systematically contrasted with another is unnecessary for producing significant attitude change. In this light, it will be recalled that the CL subjects in this final experiment rarely voted to work on any of the tasks independently, being convinced from the start that the tasks could be performed more effectively in a group.

At first glance, this appears to be inconsistent with the results of both the Wisconsin study and the pre-test groups in Chapter 6 where subjects did everything one way, but where they underwent very little attitude change. The answer lies, we believe, in the fact that subjects in our final experiment were told that they could work the other way (i.e., alone) if they wanted to. Prior to each task, they were presented with the choice between working together versus alone. The fact that they almost always chose to work together should not be allowed to obscure the equally important fact that they were constantly reminded that there was another alternative, namely working alone. Even when they were working together they were implicitly comparing the chosen strategy with the rejected one. This presumably had the effect of structuring their thinking in terms of the distinction between doing things together and doing them alone, the same distinction which was made over and over again in the before and after questionnaires.

It may be, then, that a one-sided (no contrast) task experience is sufficient to produce attitude change, so long as the subject is aware that a specific alternative (though inferior) strategy exists. In the laboratory it is a simple matter to structure the situation so that subjects are aware of such an alternative. In the natural setting it is unlikely that the individual's cognitions would ever be structured this clearly. This difference between laboratory and field has important implications for the generality of our theory and will be discussed in that context later in this chapter.

It remains to comment on the questionnaire employed in our final experiment. An attempt was made to extend the idea of lateral generalization further than in previous studies by breaking each area (family, factory, etc.) down into three types of task activity (general, instrumental, and expressive). In most cases, instrumental items showed the greatest change, expressive items the least, with general items falling somewhere in between. This had been predicted on the grounds that the tasks used in the laboratory put a premium on instrumental problem-solving behavior. We had also predicted that the factory scale would change the most, family the least, with neighborhood and school in the middle. This was not entirely the case in the before-after data, although, strangely enough, it proved to be quite accurate for the follow-up data. A prediction had also been made for the relative amounts of change on the three vertical generalization scales (working, doing, and being). Here, too, we did better on the follow-up data, even though the prediction was never fully borne out in either case.

The important point to be made is that the theory does enable us to predict with considerable success the *ordering* of changes across areas, types of activity, and levels of abstraction. The 22 scales included in our questionnaire varied widely in the amount and significance of change observed; this variation was far from being random. We found that we could explain most of it with our three generalization principles, namely *similarity* and *familiarity* in the case of lateral generalization and *specificity* in the case of vertical generalization. While there may very well be other principles involved, these three appear to be of major importance in accounting for the observed pattern of attitude generalization. A great deal remains to be done, however, in clarifying the meaning of each, both conceptually and operationally. In any future extension of the theory, we expect developments in this area to play a critical role.

THE PROBLEM OF GENERALITY

While the results of our seven experiments lend considerable support to our theory, it should be obvious that the evidence presented is of a very limited character. While our theory seems to make meaningful most of the findings reported here, we have no way of knowing at present how appropriate or useful it would be in accounting for what happens in other settings. This is a question of generality. It is the most critical question that can be asked of any theory. To how many different situations does the theory apply? How many different facts will it explain? Under what conditions does it hold?

It has been suggested that there are three major types of generality which any adequate theory (in the behavioral sciences) should demonstrate.[1] A theory should first demonstrate *generality over people* or subjects. If not, it should at least specify to what population of subjects it does apply. Most psychological theories are developed on either college sophomores or hooded rats, although the intent of most researchers is clearly to make discoveries which will apply to people in general.

Secondly, a theory should show *generality across operations* or measures. Findings which are obtained with a single measure are often generalized without specifying the types of measures to which the theory applies. It cannot be guaranteed that results obtained with one measure will also be obtained when other measures are used. Such generality across operations must be demonstrated rather than assumed.

Finally, a theory should demonstrate *generality across conditions,* where the term "conditions" is used residually to refer to any aspect of the study situation other than people or operations. Many theories, especially those in psychology, are developed under highly controlled conditions, although such conditions are frequently left unspecified when the theory is being presented. If the theory is to have any significant explanatory power, it should hold outside of the exact conditions under which the original findings were obtained.

---

[1] W. A. Scott and M. Wertheimer, *Introduction to Psychological Research* (New York: John Wiley & Sons, Inc., 1962), pp. 49–64.

To a considerable extent, the previous chapters of this book may be seen as part of a continuing attempt to demonstrate the generality of our theory. The success or failure of this attempt can best be appraised in terms of the three criteria presented above.

1. Generality across People

It is with respect to sampling generality that our research probably suffers the most. As with so many other ideas developed in the laboratory, we have relied almost exclusively on college students for subjects. Although in our summer school studies subjects ranged in age from 16 to 45, the majority of those used in all seven experiments were freshmen and sophomores. We have no evidence that our theory is valid for younger children or adults, nor can we be sure that it applies to that part of the national population with IQ's under 120. Just as important, we have yet to demonstrate the relevance of our theory for people from cultures other than our own.

With respect to sex differences, we found no significant differences between males and females in amount of attitude change with the single exception of the religion study where the males changed more than the females. While it is reassuring to know that, in the main, our theory applies equally well to males and females, the fact remains that the vast majority of our males and females were drawn from a very narrow segment of the total population to which we would like to generalize.

2. Generality across Operations

In thinking about generality across measures, a number of things come to mind. First, the type of measuring device employed (e.g., projective, interview, questionnaire, etc.); secondly, the attitude dimension involved; thirdly, the response format; finally, the form of each individual item (variation, for example, in mode, polarity, and specificity).

Measuring Device. With respect to the type of measuring device used, it is unfortunate that we were unable to experiment with something other than the standard Likert-type scale. Given the abstractness and complexity of the dimensions we were measuring, it would have been quite awkward to develop a projective instrument or interview schedule which would discriminate among subjects and pick up changes over time. As a result we have no real evidence as to the construct validity of our scales. Whether or not we measured what we set out to measure cannot be said. It is nevertheless clear from the internal consistencies and test-retest reliabilities of most of our scales that the questions we did ask were meaningful to our subjects. It is true, however, that we have yet to demonstrate the generality of our theory across different kinds of measuring devices.[2]

Attitude Dimensions. With respect to generality across attitude dimensions, we are in a position to say that the theory has shown considerable predictive power in a number of cases dealing with quite different beliefs, values, and preferences. Some of the studies (e.g., Chapters 5 and 8) were deliberately conceived with the thought in mind of finding out how general the theory actually was in terms of attitude dimensions. The themes chosen for analysis had all received prior attention in the sociological and anthropological literature and were broad enough to satisfy our personal criterion that they be applicable to all cultures at all points in time. In the seven experiments reported, we succeeded in changing attitudes dealing with individualism-collectivism, equalitarianism-authoritarianism, religion, and achievement (the latter including effort-luck and control-acceptance). It seems evident that our theory has implications for a number of different attitude dimensions. There are presumably still other themes, as yet untested, to which our theory might apply.

Response Format. Of lesser concern in establishing generality across measures is the fact that the same type of response format was used in all of our studies. In most cases we employed a nine-point scale anchored at either end by the terms "Strongly Agree" and "Strongly Disagree." The Wisconsin experiment was different in two minor respects: (1) only six response categories were used, and (2) each category was given a label (Strongly Agree, Agree, Slightly Agree, Slightly Disagree, etc.). There were so many other variables more important than response format that we never found time to deal with it in any systematic way. It is possible, however, that the number of response categories used could have had a significant effect on the results obtained. In a four-hour laboratory experiment, for example, a format consisting of but five categories might not be sensitive enough to pick up the changes that we obtained with our nine-point scales. In a study extending over a whole year, on the other hand, a five-point scale might be quite appropriate. This is clearly an area which is pertinent to the generality of the theory but which has yet to be explored in any systematic fashion.

Item Form and Content. In evaluating the generality of our theory across items, it should be noted that most of them were written in a

---

[2] For a validation method that could be used in a case like this see D. T. Campbell and D. W. Fiske, "Convergent and Discriminant Validity by the Multitrait-Multimethod Matrix," *Psychological Bulletin,* Vol. 56 (1959), pp. 81–105.

bipolar fashion (i.e., contrasting one end of the continuum with the other). This is a limiting factor. It will be recalled, however, that in the first two studies (Chapters 3 and 4) simple, noncontrast items were used with a modest degree of success. While we cannot be certain that putting the items in bipolar form had any independent effect on our results, we suspect that this procedure at least helped to improve the internal consistency of our attitude scales.

Again, with respect to item content, we have consistent evidence to the effect that the *mode* (cognitive, cathectic, or evaluative) in which an item is written makes no difference as far as the amount of change is concerned. Finally, it is significant that we obtained positive results with items of many different degrees of abstractness. While there is considerable variation in the amount of change found, this is to some degree predictable within the theory itself (e.g., in terms of specificity).

There is one further consideration that should be mentioned in the context of our discussion of generality across operations. It has been pointed out that the administration of a questionnaire prior to the experiment may affect whether or not the treatment has the desired results.[3] In some cases the pre-test has been shown to interact positively with the treatment, in other cases negatively. In our own series of experiments, it is possible that the "before" questionnaire alerted or sensitized subjects to the treatment theme (alone versus together, with versus without a leader, etc.) and thus made the treatment a much more salient affair than it might have been otherwise. Presumably, the more salient the experience, the greater the attitude change.

It is equally possible, however, that the "before" questionnaire served to dampen the effect of the treatment by giving subjects an opportunity to think about and clarify their attitudes before the experiment began. The more fixed a person is in his original beliefs, values, and preferences, the less changing he is likely to do.

There can be little doubt that the "before" questionnaire had some effect on the results of the experiment. Without further studies, however, we have no way of knowing what that effect was. To find out, it will be necessary to try something like the Solomon Four-Group design in which tests are made separately for treatment and pre-testing effects as well as the interaction between the two.[4] Until such tests are made, we cannot be sure whether our theory has any predictive power beyond

---

[3] Donald T. Campbell, "Factors Relevant to the Validity of Experiments in Social Settings," *Psychological Bulletin,* Vol. 54 (1957), pp. 297–312.

[4] R. W. Solomon, "An Extension of Control Group Design," *Psychological Bulletin,* Vol. 46 (1949), pp. 137–50.

those situations in which subjects are questioned about their attitudes prior to being exposed to a certain kind of task experience.

3. Generality across Conditions

The relevant question here is the extent to which our theory can be generalized to conditions other than those specific to the findings reported. With this in mind, we shall briefly consider the nature of the task, the incentive system, duration of the experiment, the role of choice, the use of contrast in the experimental design, and the demand characteristics of the laboratory situation.

Nature of the Task. Over the course of our seven experiments, we used more than a dozen different tasks. It is clear, in this respect, that our results are not restricted to a single task or set of tasks. Although we have used many different tasks (manual and intellectual, difficult and easy, group and individual), it remains questionable to what degree these tasks are representative of the broader population of tasks found in less contrived settings. Only in some abstract sense can our game-like problems be said to resemble the kinds of tasks with which men are confronted in their day-to-day routines. It is these more serious tasks of everyday life that we are most interested in. Until we have had the opportunity to study tasks of this sort directly, we must reserve judgment with respect to the generality of our theory.

Incentives. In some of our experiments, subjects were paid according to task performance; in others they received a flat rate (e.g., $5.00 for the evening). The results were equally good in both cases. On the basis of this limited data, we would conclude that task experience has an impact on attitudes whether the performance incentive is extrinsic (paid according to how well you do) or intrinsic (the feeling of accomplishment you get from performing a task well, regardless of the external rewards involved). Although the *type* of incentive makes no difference, the *degree* to which a person is rewarded is very likely a critical factor in the change process.

Time. There are two questions involving time that have implications for the generality of our theory. First, is our theory tied to any specific time (reinforcement) schedule and, secondly, over what time span are the changes effective? With respect to the first question, it should be recalled that the Wisconsin experiment convened once a week for 13 consecutive weeks, the first ID-CL experiment two hours a day every other day for one week, and the rest of the experiments for four hours in a single afternoon or evening. From this it seems evident that our theory is not restricted to any specific time arrangement, although it is our impression that the longer the time period and the fewer the interruptions, the better will be the results.

With regard to the second question, it will be recalled that in two different experiments (Chapters 7 and 9) we administered the attitude questionnaire three times: right before the experiment, just afterwards, and one to four weeks later. In both studies, we found that on the third administration subjects regressed somewhat to the attitudes they held prior to the experiment. It is important to note, however, that the regression was not complete; in both cases significant changes were still observable.

Choice.   In all but one of our laboratory experiments, subjects had virtually no choice in organizing themselves for work on the task. The arrangement in any specific case was dictated by the experimenter; subjects were told to spend 30 minutes working together, then another 30 minutes working independently, etc. This lack of choice poses certain problems for the generality of the theory since many if not most tasks in life allow for much more freedom than this. In this context, it is especially important that when we finally did get around to giving our subjects considerable choice (in the last experiment), our results turned out to be as good as any of those obtained previously. Although choice in this final experiment was limited to only two alternatives (alone versus together), the very significant findings which emerged would suggest that our theory is not tied to a completely controlled situation.

The Use of Contrast in the Experimental Design.   Contrast here refers to the fact that subjects were asked to (or given the opportunity to) perform each task two different ways (e.g., alone versus together). A very clear contrast was provided in four of our studies (Chapters 4, 5, 6, and 9); these are the studies that produced the best results. Where subjects spent all of their time using the same basic strategy (as in Chapters 3, 7, and 8), the attitude changes observed were of only moderate significance. In another case (pre-test for Chapter 6), a no-contrast design failed to produce any change at all.

While it is important to keep in mind that we did achieve a certain amount of change without contrast, it cannot be denied that the rather substantial difference between the two sets of findings has implications for the generality of our theory. Even though the results are not altogether comparable (involving as they did different attitude dimensions etc.), they at least suggest that the theory is most appropriate for those situations where the individual is free (or obliged) to engage in a certain amount of experimentation with the task before deciding what his strategy will be. The importance of trying something at least two different ways is that it helps to make salient the fact that some ways of doing things are *more* effective than others, that some modes of behavior are *preferable* to others, and that some approaches to the task are *more appropriate* than others. Without some form of contrast, it is less likely that the individual will develop sharply defined comparative judgments of a cognitive, cathectic, and evaluative sort.

One of the reasons we were able to achieve significant changes in the laboratory is that we were in a position to structure both the task experience and the attitude questionnaire in the same way. In many of the experiments, subjects were asked to try each task first one way, then the next; in the questionnaire they were asked to respond to a series of bipolar items in which one approach was always contrasted with the other. If the alone-together contrast was used at the task level, the same distinction was drawn in the questionnaire. Cognitively, the total situation was defined in terms of a single variable. This obviously had the effect of facilitating the "transfer" of what was learned and felt at the task level to what was asked for in the questionnaire.

It is often tempting to think that, if we were this successful in producing attitude change with only four *hours* at our disposal, the changes would be infinitely more significant in the natural setting (e.g., a factory) where before and after measures could be administered four or more years apart. The implication here is that time is the most important consideration. Our discussion above, however, suggests that the structure imposed by the experimenter may play an equally critical role. By virtue of the rigorous control which it makes possible, the laboratory may more than make up for the fact that it is short-lived. It would be naïve to assume that our laboratory results, because of the time handicap under which they were obtained, necessarily represent an underestimate of what we are likely to find out in the "real" world.

Demand Characteristics of the Laboratory Situation. Orne has recently reminded us that in any experiment subjects will make an attempt to figure out what the experimenter is trying to prove and in doing so will seize upon any and all cues they can find in the laboratory environment (e.g., the composition and size of the group, the presence of a mirror, the materials administered, even the expression on the experimenter's face).[5] The assumption is that once the subject has decided what the experimenter is really looking for, he will behave in such a

---

[5] Martin T. Orne, "On the Social Psychology of the Psychological Experiment, with Particular Reference to Demand Characteristics and their Implications," *American Psychologist*, Vol. 17 (1962), pp. 776–83.

way as to give the experimenter what he wants. If enough subjects are doing the same thing, the experimenter may come up with some rather impressive results, which unfortunately reflect little more than the subjects' perception of the purpose of the experiment.

The question of "demand characteristics" is of concern to us here because of its implications for the generality of our theory. It is possible, although we believe quite unlikely, that we were able to obtain significant results only because our subjects figured out what we were trying to do and decided to help us by changing their attitudes in the predicted direction. If this were true, we would be left with a theory which could only be generalized to other laboratory settings where subjects figured out what they were supposed to be doing and acted accordingly.

Taking the series of experiments as a whole, there are good reasons for concluding that our subjects did not deliberately change their attitudes in order to make our predictions come true. In the first place, it is quite clear that very few subjects ever came close to figuring out the true purpose of the experiment. Some attempt was made in every study to find out what the subjects perceived our motives to be. In two cases (Chapters 5 and 6) we took great pains to ask each individual (verbally) what he thought we were looking for. In a third study (Chapter 7) we asked subjects to write down (1) what they thought the real purpose of the experiment was, (2) whether we were looking for anything other than what we told them in the beginning, and (3) if so, what they thought we had expected to find. In all of this questioning, only a few subjects ever indicated that they were aware of our interest in changing their attitudes. Whether they came to this conclusion *prior* to being questioned is not known.

While a few subjects suggested that we might be interested in exploring interpersonal relations, leadership, or the effect of attitudes on behavior, most of them simply repeated what they had been told by the experimenter at the beginning of the experiment. This is understandable in view of the fact that the explanations given at the beginning of each experiment were highly plausible and in keeping with the design of the study, the measures employed, and the experimenter's subsequent instructions. In most cases, the explanation given was couched in terms of our interest in finding out more about the relationship between task, incentive system, group size, etc. on the one hand, and productivity or problem-solving strategy on the other. For all but a few of our subjects this explanation was accepted as a valid one.

Subjects' remarks following the experiment make it clear that the attitude questionnaires were perceived as only peripherally related to the main body of the experiment. This was partly due to our own efforts to minimize the importance of the questionnaires. In the early studies we introduced the after questionnaire by saying that we thought it might "help us to understand some of the things that took place in the experiment," a statement which was presumably as meaningless to them as it was to us. In the last three studies, we went one step further and introduced both *before* and *after* questionnaires as part of someone else's research, completely unrelated to the experiment at hand. In one study (Chapter 7) we had someone else actually administer the questionnaires. Since we never isolated this particular variable (manner in which the questionnaires were introduced), we have no way of knowing how important it is. Our guess (based on a comparison of Chapter 6 where only a modest attempt was made to disassociate the questionnaire from the experiment and Chapter 9 where it was introduced as part of someone else's research) is that it makes little difference which way it is done.

It is our belief that all but a few subjects accepted the formal rationale given prior to the experiment and, thus, did not actively seek out cues which would support an alternative explanation. In this definition of the situation, the questionnaires (which ordinarily took about 15 minutes each) were assigned little significance. They were seen as but slightly related to our main concern with the determinants of productivity.

If we can assume that, with few exceptions, subjects did not perceive the true purpose of the experiment, it follows that the results represent something more than responses to the "demand characteristics" of the situation. There is another kind of evidence that lends support to the same conclusion. When asked if their attitudes had changed in any way as a result of what happened in the experiment, subjects for the most part insisted that they had not. On those parts of the questionnaire most closely related to the experimental situation (e.g., small work groups), there were some subjects who said that they had changed slightly. No individual, however, ever admitted to having changed (even slightly) on the more abstract scales (e.g., way of life). In fact they found it hard to understand why we expected them to do so.

This evidence is relevant here because it suggests once again that the findings reported cannot be explained in terms of the subjects' desire to help the experimenter. If subjects changed their attitudes in order to please the experimenter, we would expect them to show some awareness of the fact that their attitudes had changed (especially when asked by the experimenter himself). Even though the specific item changes were in most cases very slight, the cumulative effect should have been salient to anyone who was deliberately trying to change his responses. The fact that the vast majority of subjects revealed no awareness of having changed cannot be squared with the notion that subjects changed their attitudes to please the experimenter, unless it is contended that the whole process was unconscious. It might be argued that subjects unconsciously "perceived" what the experimenter wanted and proceeded, again without awareness, to change their attitudes accordingly. There is, of course, no evidence for this point of view. It is, moreover, far removed from what Orne had in mind in his analysis of the highly rational process by which subjects go about integrating cues and inducing hypotheses with respect to the experimenter's intentions.

The fact that subjects revealed so little awareness of having changed is more easily explained in terms of the fact that most of the *item* changes were very small. The average item change for any given scale was rarely over one step to the right or left on a response form consisting of nine positions. The use of a nine-point scale, moreover, made it very difficult for subjects to remember how they answered a given item the first time around. In view of both the modest nature of most item changes and the difficulty involved in recalling one's original responses, it is little wonder that subjects were unaware of most of the changes that took place.

Our own conclusion is that the vast majority of subjects never came close to guessing that it was our primary or even our secondary purpose to change their attitudes. For this reason, they were in no position to give the experimenter what he wanted, even if they were so motivated. The fact that they changed their attitudes is due less to the "demand characteristics" of the situation than to the treatments designed for this purpose by the experimenter. In short, we rule out the possibility that the subjects' desire to please the experimenter had any significant effect on our findings.[6]

---

[6] The preceding discussion should not be taken to suggest that we are claiming "attitude change without awareness" for our subjects. Awareness of the hypotheses of the experimenter and awareness about whether one has changed or not are only two possible types of awareness which might be of relevance in experiments such as ours. Of more importance, in our view, are two other cognitive factors: (1) awareness of the meaning of the experience (i.e., "people do not work as well in groups as they do alone"), and (2) awareness of the relationship (or similarity) between the task experience and the attitude questionnaire. Although we did not question our subjects with regard to the latter two factors, we believe that these *are* important factors in determining the degree of attitude change.

The point of the discussion of the "demand characteristics" was not to imply that our theory was "noncognitive" but rather to show that our results were more than a function of the subjects' desire to please the experimenter.

A STRATEGY FOR FUTURE RESEARCH

Despite our repeated caveats about assuming generality before it has been demonstrated, we are convinced that the theory we have developed on the basis of experiments done in the laboratory has meaning for situations common to the everyday world. Just how general the theory is, under how many different conditions it will hold, and how many different facts it is capable of explaining cannot be determined, however, until we have had the opportunity of following up the research reported here. While there are many directions in which we might move, it is clear that the first step should be to examine with considerable care the relationship between job experience and attitudes.

A. Jobs and Attitudes

If our theory is capable of explaining anything at all outside the laboratory, it should be of special relevance to the study of how occupational experience affects one's system of beliefs, values, and preferences. An occupation can best be thought of as a system of tasks, in the same way that the problems making up one of our experimental treatments can be considered a system of tasks. In any task or set of tasks, whether inside or outside of the laboratory, some forms of behavior will have greater instrumental reward value than others. As such, they will be repeated more often than any of the others. In turn, they will become the object of situationally (occupationally) specific beliefs, preferences, and values in which they are seen as effective, enjoyable, and morally desirable. Eventually, orientations specific to the given occupation will be generalized laterally to other equally specific task situations and vertically to more inclusive categories of human experience.

To study the relationship between job experience and attitudes, we first need a measure of each. Developing attitude scales to cover a wide variety of attitude dimensions is a time-consuming operation but one that we know can be done. Many such scales are already available (including our own) and need only be altered for use with a non-college population. The major stumbling block to the systematic study of job experience as a source of beliefs, values, and preferences is the lack of a suitable instrument or series of instruments for measuring differences in job experience. It is not enough simply to give each job or occupation a name. Without at least an ordinal scale on which many different jobs can be placed simultaneously, it is impossible to gain any *systematic* understanding of the relationship between job experience and attitudes. The only scales we have at present are those which order occupations in terms of status or prestige. While status is one of the dimensions we expect to be important in the relationship between job experience and attitudes, it is certainly not the only one.

We also need scales which will enable us to order jobs according to situational characteristics of the sort referred to in our laboratory experiments, e.g., the degree of conjunctivity (interdependence) involved, the frequency with which decisions are required, the amount of planning called for, opportunities for advancement, the nature of the incentive system, the degree to which activities are determined by others, size and homogeneity of work group, etc. It is task characteristics of this sort that determine what kinds of behavior will have the greatest instrumental reward value and, thus, what kinds of attitudes will be induced. Just how we should go about measuring these characteristics (e.g., what kind of items would be most suitable) is not altogether clear at this point. Nor is it clear that the best person to tell us about the task situation is the job occupant himself. It is he, of course, who will be filling out the *attitude* questionnaire, raising the possibility that his attitudes will lead him to perceive the situation in a biased way. Unless the items are very objective in content, this could easily produce a spurious correlation between attributes of the job and attitudes of the job holder. One partial solution (beyond making the items as objective as possible) would be to have a supervisor fill out the job questionnaire; another would be to sample a number of different occupants of the same job and use the mean of their individual scores. The feasibility of these and other solutions can only be ascertained through pre-testing in the field.

Looking at the study as a whole, the most appropriate strategy would seem to call for developing a fixed set of dimensions (scales) in terms of which *any* given job could be described. Each job so described would have a series or *profile* of scores indicating a relative position on each of the several dimensions involved. A survey of college professors, for example, might reveal a rather low mean score on task interdependence, a high mean score on amount of planning called for, a low mean score on degree to which activities are determined by others, a high score on opportunities for achievement, and so on. A sample of assembly-line workers might be expected to yield a profile just the opposite of this. Plumbers, physicians, stenographers, executives, miners, and librarians will all have different profiles, each representing a unique distribution of task attributes. In this way each job can be broken down into its constituent elements, the elements which are most likely to have some bearing on attitudes. It is these elements that we are most interested in. Once the job is converted into a profile of scores, the title it goes by in everyday language becomes of minor importance. With a large number of jobs described in terms of the same basic dimensions, it will be possible to explore a wide variety of job-attitude relationships, only some of which can be predicted directly from our present theory.

Our first objective will be to find out what dimensions of job experience are associated with what kinds of attitudes. This involves computing two sets of scale scores (one for job characteristics and another for attitudes) and then correlating one with the other. In this form the data do not lend themselves readily to analysis in terms of cause and effect. A significant correlation between one of the job dimensions and one of the attitude dimensions could be explained in either of two ways: (1) the attitudes were developed in response to the job (as indicated by our theory), or (2) the job was chosen because of its attractiveness in the light of attitudes that were there to begin with.

In some instances the direction of influence is fairly clear, although there is reason to be cautious even here. The clearest case for job experience as the *independent* variable can be made when the individual has little or no choice in which job he takes. A significant correlation between job and attitudes here would seem to indicate that the attitudes changed to "fit" the job, since the assignment was made irrespective of the original attitudes. It could still be possible, however, that the individual redefined the job somewhat to fit his beliefs, values, and preferences. Since we are dealing here with a sample of individuals, moreover, we must consider the possibility that all those whose attitudes were "incompatible" with the job quit, leaving only those whose attitudes were more in keeping with the nature of the job. Either of these developments could produce a significant correlation between job and attitude even though no attitude change of the sort predicted by our theory took place.

There is no getting around the fact that, having left the laboratory, we are going to be hard put to demonstrate that job experience is responsible for attitude formation. There are nevertheless a number of things that we can do. In the first place, we can draw a sample of college seniors who are planning to get a job right after graduation, administer our attitude questionnaire, then wait for a year or two and administer it again along with the questionnaire which asks them about their jobs. The analysis would involve getting a measure of how much they changed on each attitude dimension and then correlating this with the various scores on the job questionnaire. We would expect to find a number of significant correlations between attributes of the job and change in attitudes.

Another strategy would involve getting permission in some organization to administer the questionnaire to all new employees prior to their being assigned to a specific job, waiting a year and then giving the same questionnaire again along with the job questionnaire. Change scores would then be correlated with scores measuring attributes of the job itself.

There is a third strategy which would be somewhat more difficult to implement. This would involve finding an organization which was about to introduce (but had not yet announced) a major innovation which would entail significant changes in job content for a large number of employees. Before and after measures could then be taken on both attitudes and job characteristics, the prediction being that the two sets of changes would be systematically related. Although these three strategies represent the major alternatives available to us at this point, there are presumably others that will suggest themselves to us once we get out into the field.

Although there are many problems inherent in each of these strategies, there is one problem in particular that should be noted. With both the first and second strategies there remains the possibility that attitude change in the direction predicted by our theory could be explained in terms of *socialization*. It might be argued, for example, that when an individual takes a new job he undergoes a certain amount of persuasion or socialization at the hands of his new colleagues. They may "teach" him to be more individualistic or collectivistic, more equalitarian or authoritarian. This, of course, is not what we are looking for. We are not interested in attitude change which is brought about through verbal communication. We are interested in only that change which can be attributed to the task experience itself. In assessing whatever changes are found in terms of their implication for the theory, it is essential that some way be found to keep the two sources (task experience and persuasion) separate. There would appear to be no simple solution that is applicable in all situations.

B. Elements of Change in Contemporary Society

Once armed with a set of reliable questionnaires and a variety of research designs which enable us to make inferences about causality, we shall be in a position to give systematic study to the relationship between job experience and attitudes. Beyond this, however, it should prove feasible to adapt our tools to the exploration of a somewhat broader category of phenomena, i.e., the cultural implications of massive changes at the technological and social structural levels. While there are many things happening today that promise to have important consequences for the beliefs and values we live by, two developments in particular stand out above the rest. We refer to (1) the pervasive growth of complex organizations and (2) the introduction of automation into white-collar occupations.

(1) Complex Organizations. It can hardly be denied that the growth of large-scale complex organizations represents a major re-structuring of our task environment. It is considerably less clear what the consequences of this have been and will be for our system of cultural beliefs and values. A number of commentators, most notably William H. Whyte in his *Organization Man*,[7] have pointed to the progressive bureaucratization of work as a major factor in the emergence of a group-centered, organization-dominated set of attitudes which threatens to undermine our traditional concern with individual freedom, initiative, and responsibility. Despite the eloquence and frequency with which the argument has been made, we lack the evidence indicating that (1) such a change in attitudes is actually taking place and (2) that the reputed change has its roots in the rise of bureaucratic organizations. The argument is nevertheless a highly plausible one and can easily be rephrased in terms of our own theory.

The day-to-day task experiences of the manager in a large corporation differ quite radically from those common to the small, independent businessman. Among other things, the former is part of a complex set of role relationships in which he is constantly reminded of the fact that the way he performs his own job may have serious consequences for the ability of many others to perform theirs and in turn for the functioning of the organization as a whole. If the organization is to maximize its effectiveness, it must find some way of synchronizing the activities of its many members. Co-ordination implies constraint. If the individual is to succeed in this kind of setting, he must learn to accommodate his own actions to the needs and demands of the many others with whom he works. While some sort of interpersonal adjustment is required in any situation where two or more people are involved, the large, complex organization maximizes task interdependence and in turn the instru-mental reward value of co-operative, "team" activity.

---

[7] William H. Whyte, Jr., *The Organization Man* (Garden City, N.Y.: Doubleday & Co., Inc., 1957). For a conflicting view, see Leonard R. Sayles, *Individualism and Big Business* (New York: McGraw-Hill, 1963).

To the extent that a man is rewarded for putting the organization's goals first, harmonizing his own efforts with those of his colleagues, and making himself personally attractive to the people around him, he will develop situationally specific orientations in which co-operation, harmony, teamwork, etc. are seen as instrumental to success, intrinsically pleasureable, and morally desirable. From his job, such orientations can be expected to spill over to his family, community, and even society as a whole. This, it will be recalled, is precisely the sort of thing we found in the laboratory.

We may not find it in the field, however, because there are features of the task situation which have the very opposite effect. It may be, for example, that we have exaggerated the importance of interdependence and constraint and overlooked the possibility that in a very large organization many individuals have the feeling that what they do or fail to do is immaterial as far as other members of the organization are concerned. It should not be difficult, using the questionnaires described earlier, to find out just how much interdependence there is in a bureaucratic setting compared to nonbureaucratic task situations. Assuming we find that complex organizations score high on task interdependence and that this is causally related to attitude change in the collectivisitic direction, it would be reasonable to conclude that the spread of bureaucracy to more and more areas of life will lead, other things being equal, to a redefinition of the individual's role in society.

(2) Automation. In terms of long-run consequences, perhaps the most significant development here is the gradual introduction of electronic data-processing equipment into organizations at the white-collar level. Although only a few empirical studies have been reported thus far, it is already clear that the change-over to computers has important consequences for the work environment.

For one thing, it leads to a general tightening up or *routinization* of the task structure. In a longitudinal study of a large electric power company, it was found that the change-over to electronic data processing "increased markedly the level of formalization within the organization. Work was further rationalized. Rules and regulations were substituted for individual decision-making. . . . Variations in work pace and process were further restricted. Deadlines became more important, standards of performance higher and more rigidly enforced."[8] Although we have no findings bearing directly on the issue, we would be

---

[8] Floyd C. Mann, "Psychological and Organizational Impacts," in John T. Dunlop (ed.), *Automation and Technological Change* (Englewood Cliffs, N.J.: Prentice-Hall, Inc., 1962), p. 58.

surprised if these changes in task structure did not lead in turn to systematic changes in attitudes.

The attitudes most likely to be affected are those dealing in some way with the activity-passivity theme. The more routine, programmed, and mechanical a job becomes, the less likely it is that the occupant of the job will be rewarded for making some attempt to exert personal control over his task environment. He will be better off instead if he learns to accept his environment, adjust to it, and take things as they come. Given sufficient time, he will develop a set of beliefs, values, and preferences which reflect this particular matrix of rewards and punishments. In his attitudes he will make much of the virtue of "not expecting too much out of life and being content with what comes your way." He will speak of the need to accommodate oneself to an environment which is seen as relatively fixed and unchangeable. He will deny that the individual has either the capacity or the obligation to shape his environment to meet his own personal needs. He will speak of these things specifically as they apply to his immediate job environment and then abstractly as they relate to life in general.

With the increasing rationalization of the work situation, the responsibility for decision making tends to become more and more *centralized*. As the number of processes brought under automatic control expands, the co-ordination of individual activities takes on greater and greater instrumental reward value. This should show up eventually in a change of beliefs, values, and preferences dealing with the theme of equalitarianism-authoritarianism (see Chapter 5 for a laboratory experiment involving this same dimension). Individuals who are rewarded for subordinating their activities to the authority of some central figure or agency can be expected to move in the direction of endorsing strong, centralized leadership as a good thing not only at work but in general.

There is one other job-attitude relationship that should be mentioned. A summary of the results of several studies focusing on the impact of automation on white-collar work reveals that the introduction of high-speed, data-processing machines has a marked effect on the distribution of opportunities for *promotion*. The effect is essentially a leveling one in that "there are substantially fewer jobs at both higher and lower skill levels."[9] For the individual worker, this "reduction in the number of higher classes means less opportunity for progression."[10] Whether or not there are opportunities for advancement has implications for attitudes dealing with effort and achievement. In one of our laboratory

[9] *Ibid.*, p. 63.
[10] *Ibid.*

experiments we found degree of success to be causally related to change in those attitudes concerning the relative importance of luck and effort in getting ahead in life. On the basis of that evidence, there is reason to believe that a sharp reduction in opportunities for advancement would lead to an increased emphasis on luck as the major determinant of success or failure. Luck, we know, is already an important part of the lower-class conception of things. It is significant that here we are talking about office workers, members of the middle class. We should not be surprised at this possible convergence, however, in view of the finding that "work in the plant and the office are becoming more alike with increasing automation."[11]

The changes we have speculated upon thus far are limited to those people whose jobs have been or will be affected directly by the introduction of electronic data-processing equipment. There are other changes attendant upon the spread of automation which promise to be much more universal. We refer to the impact of automation on our general conception of the relationship between man and nature. By virtue of the many spectacular things it makes possible, automation will help to convince those of us who still need convincing that man is capable of mastering his natural environment. This needn't be explained in terms of reinforcement and generalization. It is simply a direct inference from what we see going on around us. It is, of course, no less important for that reason.

C. Industrialization and Cultural Change

Beyond those changes taking place in our own society, there lies the infinite array of problems connected with the spread of industrial technology to other areas of the world. Given the very radical restructuring of the task environment which industrialization involves, the study of cultural changes in the "developing" countries would appear to be a highly appropriate setting to test our theory. While there are many methodological problems unique to cross-cultural research, there is no reason why the same basic strategy, using one questionnaire to measure attributes of the task situation and another to measure attitudes, could not be employed.

The impact of industrialization on any given individual will obviously vary with that individual's location in the industrial process. Whether he becomes more or less collectivistic, for example, will depend on the kind of job he is assigned. Some may respond to the stimulus of in-

---

[11] *Ibid.*, p. 64.

dustrialization by becoming more individualistic, others by becoming more collectivistic. The same is true of other themes we have dealt with, e.g., equalitarianism. With respect to still other themes, however, it is possible that industrialization will affect everyone in pretty much the same way, regardless of differences in occupational role.

We have in mind those beliefs and values central to the distinction between Gemeinschaft and Gesellschaft. In a very broad sense, for example, an industrial task system conditions its members to treat each other *universalistically*, i.e., in accordance with general rules covering all occupants of a given position rather than in terms of personal ties, loyalties and obligations.[12] While this seems more than obvious, it remains true that the Japanese have found a way of making the industrial system work even while maintaining many of the particularistic elements traditional to that culture.[13] We may not be too far afield, however, in assuming that the long-run effect of industrialization is to undermine the role of particularistic factors in favor of more formal, universalistic standards. The effect will be felt first and most strongly in the work setting; only later will it spill over to areas outside the plant.

Achievement-ascription is another theme of similar generality which is likely to undergo change as a result of industrialization regardless of differences in specific task setting.[14] It is difficult if not impossible to operate an industrial system when priority in the treatment of individuals is given to a consideration of who they are rather than what they can do. The problem is especially acute when a high level of skill is involved.

Evaluations made on the grounds of membership in a given family or ethnic group rather than on the basis of past or potential performance are incompatible with the efficient use of an industrial technology. The conditioning of choice behavior along lines favoring achievement over ascription should have an impact on a wide variety of beliefs, values, and preferences ranging from those specific to the job environment to those dealing with relations in the family, community, nation, and life in general.

These are but two of the many themes that are certain to undergo significant change with the coming of industrialization. Just as likely to be affected are beliefs and values concerning time orientation (future

---

[12] Talcott Parsons and Edward A. Shils (eds.), *Toward a General Theory of Action* (Cambridge, Mass.: Harvard University Press, 1954), pp. 81–82.

[13] See James G. Abegglen, *The Japanese Factory* (Glencoe, Ill.: Free Press, 1958), pp. 11–25.

[14] For a definition of the concept in attitudinal terms, see Parsons and Shils, *op. cit.*, pp. 82–83.

versus present), fatalism (control versus acceptance), achievement (effort versus luck), and mastery over nature (man versus his environment). Just how much change will be involved in each case depends on the content of the culture prior to the introduction of industrial methods. It would be naïve to assume that each piece of equipment imported carries with it a whole new set of attitudes which will be eagerly accepted by those hired to work on it. Cultural beliefs and values which have their roots in past experience can be expected to interact with the new technology at every point along the way. While there seems to be no doubt that the spread of industrialism to all corners of the globe will have a homogenizing effect on world culture,[15] there would appear to be little chance that cultural differences will ever become completely blurred.

---

[15] For a discussion of what is likely to happen along these lines in the next 25–75 years, see Alex Inkeles' comments in "Evolution and Man's Progress," *Daedalus*, Vol. 90 (1961), pp. 528–33.

Index

This book has been set in 12 point and 10 point Garamond Intertype, leaded 1 point. Chapter numbers are in 14 point Garamont italic caps and chapter titles in 24 point Garamont italic c.&l.c. The size of the type page is 27 by 45½ picas.